Intellectual Property Rights and ASEAN Development in the Digital Age

The trade-investment-service-intellectual property (IP) nexus remains at the heart of economic development and the main features of which are global value chains (GVCs) and digitalisation. The protection of intellectual property rights (IPR) has become a critical issue not only for advanced economies but also for emerging markets. This edited volume contributes to the debates on IPR protection and economic development from the perspective of Association of Southeast Asian Nations (ASEAN) member states. The book provides insights into the mechanism and evidence on how effective IPR protection will increase economic and social welfare via promoting innovation activities and providing incentives to diffuse knowledge and transfer technologies.

Written by economists and lawyers from the region, these experts share their latest findings and thoughts on how countries in Southeast Asia have been progressively improving IPR protection and increasing the interoperability of different IPR regimes through regional cooperation to facilitate business operations in the context of digital transformation.

Lurong Chen is Senior Economist at the Economic Research Institute for ASEAN and East Asia (ERIA). He obtained his PhD in International Economics from the Graduate Institute of International and Development Studies, Geneva. His research interests include international trade and development, digital economy, and Asian regionalism. He advises governments, international organizations, and the private sector on development issues related to digitalization and regional integration.

Fukunari Kimura is Chief Economist at the Economic Research Institute for ASEAN and East Asia (ERIA) and Professor at the Faculty of Economics, Keio University. He obtained his PhD in economics from the University of Wisconsin-Madison, USA. His research interests include international trade and development, economic growth, applied microeconomics, and Japanese and Asian economies. Dr Kimura was President of the Japan Society of International Economics (2010–2012) and Dean of the Graduate School of Economics, Keio University (2015–2017). He advises governments and international organizations on trade policy and development issues.

Routledge-ERIA Studies in Development Economics

Social Protection Goals in East Asia
Strategies and Methods to Generate Fiscal Space
Edited by Mukul G. Asher, Fauziah Zen and Astrid Dita

World Trade Evolution
Growth, Productivity and Employment
Edited by Lili Yan Ing and Miaojie Yu

Emerging Global Trade Governance
Mega Free Trade Agreements and Implications for ASEAN
Edited by Lurong Chen, Shujiro Urata, Junji Nakagawa and Masahito Ambashi

East Asian Integration
Goods, Services and Investment
Edited by Lili Yan Ing, Martin Richardson and Shujiro Urata

Developing the Digital Economy in ASEAN
Edited by Lurong Chen and Fukunari Kimura

The Effects of Globalisation on Firm and Labour Performance
Edited by Chin Hee Hahn, Dionisius Narjoko, Ha Thi Thanh Doan and Shujiro Urata

Financial Inclusion in Asia and Beyond
Measurement, Development Gaps, and Economic Consequences
Edited by Tony Cavoli and Rashesh Shrestha

Globalisation and its Economic Consequences
Looking at APEC economies
Edited by Shujiro Urata and Ha Thi Thanh Doan

Intellectual Property Rights and ASEAN Development in the Digital Age
Edited by Lurong Chen and Fukunari Kimura

For more information about this series, please visit: www.routledge.com/Routledge-ERIA-Studies-in-Development-Economics/book-series/ERIA

Intellectual Property Rights and ASEAN Development in the Digital Age

Edited by Lurong Chen and
Fukunari Kimura

Routledge
Taylor & Francis Group
LONDON AND NEW YORK

ERIA
Economic Research Institute
for ASEAN and East Asia

First published 2022
by Routledge
2 Park Square, Milton Park, Abingdon, Oxon OX14 4RN

and by Routledge
605 Third Avenue, New York, NY 10158

Routledge is an imprint of the Taylor & Francis Group, an informa business

British Library Cataloguing-in-Publication Data
A catalogue record for this book is available from the British Library

Library of Congress Cataloging-in-Publication Data
Names: Chen, Lurong, editor. | Kimura, Fukunari, editor.
Title: Intellectual property rights and ASEAN development in the digital age / edited by Lurong Chen and Fukunari Kimura.
Description: Abingdon, Oxon ; New York, NY : Routledge, 2022. | Series: Routledge-ERIA studies in development economics | Includes bibliographical references and index.
Identifiers: LCCN 2021025358
Subjects: LCSH: Technological innovations--Economic aspects--Southeast Asia. | Intellectual property--Southeast Asia. | Intellectual capital--Southeast Asia. | Economic development--Southeast Asia.
Classification: LCC HC441.Z9 T455 2022 | DDC 338/.0640959--dc23
LC record available at https://lccn.loc.gov/2021025358

ISBN: 978-0-367-70709-5 (hbk)
ISBN: 978-0-367-70907-5 (pbk)
ISBN: 978-1-003-14765-7 (ebk)

DOI: 10.4324/9781003147657

Typeset in Galliard
by SPi Technologies India Pvt Ltd (Straive)

Contents

Figures

Tables

Contributors

Keon-Hyung Ahn is Assistant Professor at the Department of International Commerce, Department of International Trade, Kyonggi University, Republic of Korea. He obtained a PhD in Business Administration from the Graduate School of SungKyunKwan University, Republic of Korea.

Lurong Chen is Senior Economist at the Economic Research Institute for ASEAN and East Asia. He obtained his PhD in International Economics from the Graduate Institute in Geneva, Switzerland.

Wenting Cheng is Grand Challenge Research Fellow at the College of Law, Australian National University (ANU). She received her Doctor of Law degree from ANU, Australia.

Christopher E. Cruz is the University Legal Counsel of De La Salle University (DLSU), Director of the DLSU Intellectual Property Office, and Manager of the DLSU Innovation and Technology Office. He received his Doctorate in Philosophy from the DLSU, Manila.

Hang Thu Dinh is Deputy Director of the Department for General Economic Issues and Integration Studies, Central Institute for Economic Management. She holds a Master of International Business from the Graduate School of International Studies, Ajou University, Republic of Korea.

Hanira binti Hanafi is Senior Lecturer at the Department of Administrative Studies and Politics, Faculty of Economics and Administration, University Malaya, Malaysia. She received her Doctor of Philosophy in Islamic Finance from the University of Durham, United Kingdom.

Chawana Huangsuntornchai is a Data Privacy Counsel at Central Group, Thailand. He was formerly a researcher at the Thailand Development Research Institute.

Fukunari Kimura is Chief Economist at the Economic Research Institute for ASEAN and East Asia and Professor at the Faculty of Economics, Keio University, Japan. He obtained his PhD in Economics from the University of Wisconsin-Madison, United States of America.

Jakkrit Kuanpoth is currently an advisor to the Thailand Development Research Institute, Thailand. He was formerly Associate Professor at the Faculty of Law, University of Wollongong, Australia. He holds a PhD from the University of Aberdeen, United Kingdom.

Kung-Chung Liu is Lee Kong Chian Professor of Law (Practice) at the Singapore Management University. He is the founder of the Applied Research Centre for Intellectual Assets and the Law in Asia (ARCIALA). He obtained his Doctor of Law degree from the Ludwig Maximilian Universität, Germany.

Nurhidayah binti Abdullah is Senior Lecturer at the Department of Administrative Studies and Politics, Faculty of Economics and Administration, University Malaya, Malaysia. She received a PhD degree from the University of Sydney, Australia.

Liliana Lizarazo-Rodríguez is Research Professor at the Brussels School of Governance (Vrije Universiteit Brussel VUB, Belgium) and Assistant Professor at the University of Antwerp, Belgium. She holds a PhD in Law from the University of Ghent, Belgium.

Duong Anh Nguyen is Director of the Department for General Economic Issues and Integration Studies, Central Institute for Economic Management. He holds a Master of Economics from the Australian National University, Australia.

Peter Immanuel D. Tenido is Project Director of the De La Salle University Innovation and Technology Office and a member of the Leaders in Innovation Fellowship of the Royal Academy of Engineering. He received a Master of Business and Science degree from Rutgers, the State University of New Jersey, United States.

Kenbert Alan I. Ting is an Intellectual Property Consultant. He has a degree in Electronics and Communications Engineering from the De La Salle University and a Master of Business Administration from the University of Bradford, United States.

Thanh Tri Vo is Senior Economic Expert of the Central Institute for Economic Management of Viet Nam and the Chair of the Vietnamese Committee for Pacific Economic Cooperation Council. He is also the President of the Institute for Brand and Competitiveness Strategy. He obtained a PhD in Economics degree from the Australian National University, Australia.

Poppy S. Winanti is Senior Lecturer at the Department of International Relations, Faculty of Social and Political Sciences, Universitas Gadjah Mada, Indonesia. She received her PhD in Politics from the University of Glasgow, United Kingdom.

Acknowledgements

Intellectual property (IP) issues and intellectual property rights (IPR) protection are closely related to ASEAN development in the digital era. This volume consists of the outputs of ERIA's research project on 'IPR Protection for Asian Development: Opportunities and Challenges from GVCs and Digital Economy', where economists and lawyers share their latest findings and thoughts on how Southeast Asian countries have been progressively improving IP regimes in the context of digital transformation.

Above all, we are indebted to all contributors for their unwavering enthusiasm and involvement from the initial research project and subsequent dialogues to complete this book.

We express the depth of our gratitude to Professor Hidetoshi Nishimura, President of ERIA, and Koji Hachiyama, Chief Operating Officer of ERIA. Their encouragement and strong support were critical to the success of the project.

We are profoundly grateful for the invaluable advice and generous help from our colleague, Shujiro Urata, throughout the compilation of this book. The comments and suggestions from anonymous referees during the review stage of manuscript preparation were likewise extremely helpful.

Thanks to Maria Priscila P. del Rosario, Stefan Alois Wesiak, Fany Trianingsih, and Rachmadea Aisyah, who proofread and commented on the manuscript. Our thanks also go to Yuanita Suhud, Meilawati, and Cindy Aulia Agustine for their excellent research assistance.

We also gratefully acknowledge the support in various forms from Taizo Hara, Koshi Yamada, Izuru Kobayashi, Shigeki Kamiyama, and Takeo Tsukuda.

Lurong Chen and Fukunari Kimura

Introduction

Lurong Chen and Fukunari Kimura

The importance of intellectual property (IP) and intellectual property rights (IPR) protection has become increasingly prominent. Global value chains (GVCs) and digitalisation are the main features of the 21st-century economy (Chen and Kimura 2019). As the global economy is increasingly organised within the GVCs, the trade–investment–services–IP nexus remains at the heart of international relations (Baldwin 2011, 2016). International IPR protection has become a critical issue not only for advanced economies but also for emerging markets.

The Association of Southeast Asian Nations (ASEAN) has been one of the main destinations of global outsourcing activities. With digitalisation, the world economy is transforming from product-based to information-based. The traditional source of comparative advantage, such as the abundance of natural resources and cheap labour, may not be sufficient to maintain the region's attractiveness in the digital era. This is especially when new technologies, such as artificial intelligence, robotics and machine learning, and new profit models based on servicification, will give new connotations to manufacturing and lead to new GVC patterns. An additional institutional effort is needed to consolidate ASEAN's role in GVCs via promoting foreign investment, technology transfer, and offshoring to the region. Improving domestic IP regime and international cooperation in IPR protection to protect intangible properties shall be part of the institutional effort's main content.

ASEAN is seeking new development opportunities from GVC restructuring driven by digitalisation and Industry 4.0. An efficient IPR protection system can deeply impact economic and social welfare through its effects on price, demand elasticity, market efficiency, and, most importantly, the long-term innovation potential. The studies in this book add value to the growing literature on IPR protection and ASEAN development by taking the perspective of developing countries and focusing on the new challenges they are facing in the digital economy, where innovation becomes more disruptive and there are calls on decision makers to change their mindset to make the countries more competitive.

This book contributes to the debate on IPR protection and economic development from ASEAN member states' perspective. It provides insights into the mechanism and evidence on how effective IPR protection will

DOI: 10.4324/9781003147657-1

increase economic and social welfare via promoting innovation activities and providing incentives to diffuse knowledge and transfer technologies. The investigations on the link between IPR protection and economic growth are mainly from the aspect of (i) the participation in the GVCs, and (ii) the adoption to the digital economy. Within the GVCs, the competitive edge and division of value-added mainly depends on the capacity to innovate than on the advantage on labour cost, access to raw materials, or ease of obtaining capital. From developing countries' perspective, improvement in IPR protection could help attract foreign investment, facilitate technology discussion, and thus accelerate economic catch-up. Moreover, the vitality of IPR is further highlighted in the digital economy as the digital revolution delivers an unprecedented set of tools to bolster growth and productivity and improve world welfare. The facility of data and knowledge movement calls for additional effort in protecting IP to endorse technology transfer and innovation dynamics.

Combining legal and economic analyses, economists and lawyers from the region share their thoughts on how ASEAN countries have been progressively improving IPR protection and increasing the interoperability across national IPR regimes through regional cooperation to facilitate business operations in the context of digital transformation. The book identifies related weaknesses, threats, and challenges in ASEAN and introduces lessons and experiences from other countries and regions. In addition to this introductory chapter, the book consists of nine chapters. Chapter 1 introduces the analytical framework and provides an overview. Chapters 2–7 offer country insights from six ASEAN countries – Singapore, Indonesia, Thailand, Malaysia, the Philippines, and Viet Nam, respectively. The last two chapters offer supplementary insights on the issues. Chapter 8 introduces the Republic of Korea's (henceforth Korea) experience in accelerating technological progress via IPR protection. Finally, Chapter 9 provides an interregional comparative analysis discussing the role of regional collaboration on IPR protection to promote innovation and technology transfer.

The findings and arguments here reflect the region's latest understanding, attitudes, and opinions related to IPR protection and economic development. Policy recommendations are from three aspects: (i) protecting IPR to support growth and development; (ii) corporation global standards and domestic reforms on IPR protection; and (iii) participating in global rule-settings on IPR protection.

Chapter synopses

Chapter 1 by Lurong Chen and Fukunari Kimura, 'IPR Protection and Global Value Chains in the Digital Era: With Policy Implications for ASEAN Development', analyses the significance of IPR protection to Asia's economic growth and discusses its prosperity based on the framework of the trade–investment–services–IP nexus proposed by Baldwin (2011). Depending on how technological progress can drive down trade costs and enable a finer division of labour, one can categorise economic globalisation into three stages, from the first to the third unbundling. With the second unbundling of globalisation driven by the information revolution, GVCs have been the main trend of international economic relations. Increasingly, ownership and rights of IP use are separated following fragmented production, and IP transfer accompanies offshoring activities. Granting a foreign user the right to use IP via licensing, for example, serves as an additional channel of technology transfer and international trade and foreign direct investment. The digital revolution opens a new chapter of globalisation to the third unbundling by delivering new tools for further bolstering the GVCs from manufacturing activities to services. With this new trend is the intensifying international flows of data and information and, therefore, cross-border IP exchanges. For many developing countries, IPR protection shall be integral to efforts that facilitate technology adoption and stimulate incremental innovations.

The chapter examines ASEAN's multi-layered efforts on enhancing IPR protection. These efforts include the Agreement on Trade-Related Aspects of Intellectual Property Rights (TRIPS) and other multilateral IP treaties administered by the World Intellectual Property Organization. Also included are regional trade agreements, such as the Comprehensive and Progressive Agreement for Trans-Pacific Partnership (CPTPP), the Regional Comprehensive Economic Partnership (RCEP), and bilateral free trade agreements (FTAs). The chapter sheds light on how the region could improve adherence to international agreement(s) containing robust IPR standards to gain access to, or secure an established presence in, the GVCs. For ASEAN, implementing the RCEP and the CPTPP is at the top of the agenda, which calls for domestic adjustments and regulatory reform. The IP laws and regulations must meet the TRIPS Agreement requirements and always aim for higher-level standards. It will be crucial to increase public awareness of IP in general and its associated rights in particular. Moreover, ASEAN member states are recommended to participate in global IPR rule-making, and the related IPR disciplines must be binding and practically enforceable.

Chapter 2, titled 'IPR Protection for Asian Development: Opportunities and Challenges from the Global Value Chains and the Digital Economy – Singapore', was written by Kung Chung Liu and Wenting Cheng. As a high-income open market, Singapore has seen services playing a vital role in the economy. The new goal of development is to build a creative and innovative Smart Nation. To promote its national innovation ecosystem, Singapore introduced the ten-year IP Hub Masterplan aimed at 'developing Singapore as a Global IP Hub in Asia'.[1] Meanwhile, Singapore is very active in FTA negotiations. Many FTAs have provided the impetus to amend its domestic laws. The Singaporean government took a positive attitude and showed its willingness to accept high-level IP standards, especially from the agreements with the United States (US) and the European Union (EU). This helps Singapore create the most robust IP regime in the region. The benefit of an effective IP protection system has started to take shape. For instance, most of the world's leading medical technology firms have either located their regional headquarters or conducted manufacturing and R&D in Singapore.

Empirically, Singapore's IPR protection system has proved to be effective in boosting the country's global competitiveness and supporting its moving up in the GVCs. Other ASEAN member states could learn from Singapore's experience in IPR protection to support economic growth and transition by (i) establishing a strategy suitable for the industrial structure and the current position in the GVCs, (ii) aligning statutory laws with international rules and standards, and (iii) holding a clear and pragmatic vision in international trade negotiations balancing the local capability and the interests in the long-term competitiveness.

In Chapter 3, 'The Challenges of Digital Economy and Copyright Protection in Indonesia', Poppy S. Winanti investigates how digital transformation affects the economic and legal rationale of IPR protection in Indonesia, particularly on copyright issues. Indonesia has included the creative economy as a new pillar in its national development plan. The creative economy covers sectors that are IP intensive and copyright based. However, only a few industries have copyright protection in effect, showing the country's limited response to new challenges for copyright protection. Indonesia has stayed on the Priority Watch List of the US Trade Representative Special 301 Report since 2010 due to the country's inadequate and ineffective IPR regime (USTR 2020).

Winanti argues that the lack of public awareness of copyright is primarily part of Indonesia's historical and cultural barriers when the country tries to strengthen its IPR protection system. The development of the creative economy in Indonesia calls for mindset changes in policymaking. IPR protection shall aim to maximise the value, not the restriction, of IP use. Accordingly, policy design should weigh more on IP's effect in facilitating innovation and new technology diffusion.

Chapter 4 by Jakkrit Kuanpoth and Chawana Huangsuntornchai, 'Intellectual Property and Digital Technology in Thailand: Opportunities and Challenges', analyses the factors and criteria adopted by the Thai IP regime to protect the copyright of digital works from the legal perspective. It then extends the discussion to socio-economic issues related to digital transformation in Thailand. With a strategic focus on innovation, Thailand 4.0, the country's masterplan for development, sees improving IP protection as a booster of economic growth, particularly when the government is promoting foreign investment in the Internet of Things and artificial intelligence sectors in Thailand.

Generally speaking, Thailand has made substantial progress in legislation in electronic transactions, personal data protection, and cybersecurity. Despite so, the country still needs more effort to improve digital-related legislation further. The authors suggest the country keeps an eye trained on the EU and the US and learns from their experience in regulating the IP of digital products, such as virtual reality, social media, e-commerce, and online services. A big challenge in making IPR protection effective in supporting

Thailand 4.0 is to balance the legal and socio-economic concerns on IP and digital technology.

Chapter 5, 'Copyright Protection in Malaysia: Development and Challenges of the Digital Economy', was prepared by Nurhidayah binti Abdullah and Hanira binti Hanafi. In the context of the country's national strategy to be a high-income nation by harnessing Industry 4.0 and promoting the creative economy, the chapter systematically introduces Malaysia's IP regime and recent progress on the reforms of the domestic legal system to accommodate the related international standards, especially those committed in the CPTPP. On improving IPR protection in Malaysia, there are still various problems, such as the lack of awareness, the cumbersome procedure of IP registration, and financial constraints faced by small and medium-sized enterprises. Some of them are also part of the barriers the country has encountered in ratifying the CPTPP.

It is still challenging for Malaysia to balance domestic and international laws and the CPTPP. Moreover, the authors suggest that (i) IPR protection needs to be complemented by an increased social awareness through social media, (ii) the development of the talent pool to help promote IP compliance and registration, and (iii) coordination between government agencies to strengthen IP enforcement.

In Chapter 6, 'Assessing IPR Protection in the Semiconductor and Electronics Industry in the Philippines: Challenges and Opportunities in the Global Value Chains', Christopher E. Cruz, Kenbert Alan I. Ting, and Peter Immanuel D. Tenido chose the Philippine semiconductor and electronics industry as a case to study how IPR protection can effectively affect the sector's competitiveness in the world market. In the Philippines, although there already exists a relatively complete legal framework on IPR protection, the implementation and enforcement of IP laws and regulations are problematic. The survey on Philippine companies also reveals that low IP awareness and lack of strategic IP management seem to be ubiquitous in the semiconductor and electronics sector.

This led to a vicious circle: since the Philippine semiconductor and electronics companies stay at the lower end of the value chain, they do not see IPR protection as their primary concern. Because of that lack of attention, foreign investors are reluctant to outsource higher value-added, more IP-intense stages of production to the Philippines, making it difficult for the country to move up the value chains. Cruz, Ting, and Tenido then proposed policy efforts from three aspects: (i) increasing IP awareness in the industry, (ii) promoting local innovation, and (iii) improving IP legislation and enforcement.

Chapter 7, 'Enforcing IPR to Leverage Viet Nam's Benefits from the GVCs and the Digital Economy', by Duong Anh Nguyen, Thanh Tri Vo, and Hang Thu Dinh examine Viet Nam's IP regime with a focus on the country's IP policy and its implications for economic development in the context of the GVCs, digitalisation, and regional integration. Viet Nam's current IPR protection is not sufficient to expedite technology transfer from foreign investors and support the changing trade structure to increase the share of technology. Thus, the government has adopted various measures to improve the level of IPR protection, including the implementation of a series of five-year national programs. The participation in the high-quality FTAs, such as the CPTPP and the EU–Viet Nam FTA, and the implementation of the commitments under these agreements are inducing Viet Nam's further reforms on its IP regime. It is evident in the country's trade expansion and the changing trade structure towards a higher share of technology.

To make IPR protection work on increasing investors' confidence in, and facilitating technology transfer between, foreign firms and domestic counterparts, Viet Nam needs to further improve the effectiveness of its enforcement mechanism. In this regard, the authors recommend that the country continue reforming its IP regime concerning international best practices in enforcing IP regulations, especially to include small and medium-sized enterprises in the process.

In Chapter 8, 'Korea's Intellectual Property Protection Strategy and Its Implications for ASEAN', Keon-Hyung Ahn shares Korea's experience in developing an effective national IP system and protecting IPR to secure activities with economic value and potentials for fast growth. This will be particularly meaningful for ASEAN countries since Korea is the first nation to transit from a former aid recipient to an aid donor (as a member of the OECD Development Assistance Committee) since the 1950s.

Ahn's study shows that the Korean government has put in continuous effort to enhance IPR protection to realise its vision of leading Industry 4.0 with IP. For this, the government has amended some major IP-related laws and made changes to the judicial system over IP disputes. Signing FTAs with advanced economies, such as the EU and the US, and implementing the IP-related provisions in the agreement could provide additional fuel to improve the local IP regime. This experience is similar to that of Singapore.

As the digital age development calls for a better environment to create, use, and protect IP, many countries seek to establish an optimal administrative structure for IP. ASEAN must not lag behind. One policy priority is to fill the gap between statutory levels and enforced levels of IP protection. Commitment for a higher level of IPR protection with leading trade partners will help push forward domestic reforms. Finally, regarding the ASEAN–Korea cooperation in IPR protection, geographical indication seems to be one of the issues requiring particular attention.

From a comparative perspective, Chapter 9 discusses the experience in Latin America, the other regional economy mainly composed of developing countries, to enrich our understanding of the role of an IP regulatory framework in stimulating innovation and technology transfer. The chapter is titled 'A Patent Regulatory Framework in ASEAN in the Light of New-Generation FTAs: A Comparative Analysis with the Andean Community and the Pacific Alliance', and is prepared by Liliana Lizarazo-Rodríguez. The chapter, combining statistical and comparative legal assessments, compares paths of enhancing IPR protection, particularly those related to patent protection, undertaken by the ASEAN with the Andean Community and the Pacific Alliance. The chapter further explores whether these countries' FTAs with the EU and the US can be a valid option to foster innovation and technology transfer.

Lizarazo-Rodríguez's study shows that, for most developing countries, a strong institutional patent protection alone is not sufficient to enable local innovation and technology transfer. Such phenomena exist not only in Asia but also in Latin America. The governments' adoption of a context-sensitive approach with a balance between stringent IPR protection and economic and institutional upgrading in investment in education, research, and infrastructure seems to be necessary to support ASEAN development. Additionally, a region-wide IPR protection mechanism tends to benefit all ASEAN member states. Accommodating international norms with regional and national rules will be crucial. In this regard, ASEAN should learn from the related IPR clauses in new-generation FTAs.

Note

1 The masterplan was first published in 2013 and got updated in 2017.

Bibliography

Baldwin, R.E. (2016), *The Great Convergence: Information Technology and the New Globalization*. Cambridge, MA: Belknap.

Baldwin, R.E. (2011), '21st Century Regionalism: Filling the Gap between 21st Century Trade and 20th Century Trade Rules', *WTO ERSD Working Paper*, ERSD-2011-08.

Chen and Kimura (2019), Chen, L. and F. Kimura (2019), 'Introduction', in L. Chen and F. Kimura (eds.), *Developing the Digital Economy in ASEAN*. New York: Routledge, pp. 3–13.

USTR (2020), *2020 Special 301 Report*. Washington, DC: USTR.

1 IPR protection and global value chains in the digital era

With policy implications for ASEAN development

Lurong Chen and Fukunari Kimura

1.1 Introduction

Intellectual property (IP), the intangible property of the human intellect, and intellectual property rights (IPR),[1] a reward to creators and inventors for their innovative achievements, have been crucial in economic growth, innovation, and competitiveness. With digitalisation, international flows of goods and services tend to be more IP-intensive than ever before. Accordingly, policy effort to enhance IPR protection is critical when promoting research and development (R&D) and innovation, and sustaining society's long-term development.

For long, it has been widely debated how IPR laws and the related international agreement(s), particularly in the case of patents, could fairly balance IP owners' interests and that of IP users, and reconcile social judgements with economic efficiency. For instance, the normal way for IP owners to get a reward for their creation is to gain temporary monopoly market power for a given period. Economically, this is at the cost of reducing consumer surplus, discouraging follow-on innovations, and losing a dynamic competition (Falvey et al. 2006, Lee and Fukunaga 2013, Aghion et al. 2002, Correa 2007). On the one side, without sufficient IPR protection measures, the introduction of imitation products could make the original IP owners lose their market shares or, to an extreme, even crowding them out totally. On the other side, proper IPR protection should facilitate the knowledge spillover among inventors and expedite the sharing of off-patent intelligence. Too harsh terms tend to increase the cost of using the related technologies and discourage following R&D. Internationally, the very restrictive IPR regime would have side effects on hindering technology diffusion and slowing down the pace of technological progress.

Globally, an efficient IPR protection system can stimulate economic growth as part of the incentive mechanism that encourages local innovation and facilitates technology transfer. International trade has evolved trade in goods and, increasingly, cross-border exchanges of value-added generated by innovation, creativity, and branding (WTO 2015). For that reason, IP issues have become an integral part of the multilateral trading system, particularly when the global economy is increasingly organised within the global value

DOI: 10.4324/9781003147657-2

chains (GVCs). Improving international cooperation in IPR protection has been a common issue for all countries. But countries' interests and appeals on IPR protection vary greatly, depending on their development stage and position in the GVCs. Generally speaking, developed countries aim to stimulate their innovative activities and support their technological advance by enhancing IPR protection. Developing countries, especially middle-income ones, see IPR protection as a key to improving the local market's capacity to host large foreign direct investment (FDI) inflows that would come with the country's deeper involvement in the GVCs and, meanwhile, facilitating the domestic adoption of foreign technology (OECD 2016). Many empirical studies have shown evidence of the positive relationship between IPR protection and FDI, such as Lee and Park (2013), Awokuse and Yin (2010), Branstetter et al. (2007), OECD (2003), Mayer and Pfister (2001), and Maskus (1998).

Asian economies are already highly interdependent with each other via the GVCs, and ASEAN is an essential link to it. Production sharing, which first occurs in manufacturing and later increasingly extends to services, has proved to be an effective growth-driving mechanism of the regional economy (Kimura and Ando 2005, Obashi and Kimura 2017, Kimura and Chen 2018). Economically, digitalisation enables a finer division of labour and leads to extensive and intensive expansion of the GVCs. Development in information and communication technology has further facilitated information dissemination, making it easier than ever for data and knowledge to flow and be accessible and shared online (Chen 2019). The associated IP has been part of production sharing in the region, augmented to capital, goods, and services.

The idea is to have the IPR protection system incentivise innovative activities, considering the necessary compensation to the consequent social cost and balancing the short-term loss in competition with long-term gains in innovation. As production dispersion internationalises the need to coordinate production stages, the trade–investment–services–IP nexus stays at the heart of the 21st-century trade (Baldwin 2011, 2016). For Asia, this provides a useful policy framework to improve ASEAN's adherence to international agreement(s) containing robust IPR standards to help businesses gain access to, or secure an established presence in, the GVCs, which needs domestic and international efforts on IPR protection to be more integral to efforts that facilitate technology adoption and stimulate innovations.

1.2 IP in the trade–investment–services nexus of the world economy

For over two centuries since Adam Smith and David Ricardo first revealed potential welfare gains from international trade and cooperation, it has been widely accepted that trade is not zero-sum. Instead, through international division of labour, technology-rich economies will find a competitive advantage and specialise in technology-intensive activities. In contrast, technology-scared economies will participate in the world trading system by exporting labour-intensive products. Since the Industrial Revolution, technological progress has made the geographic dispersion of production and consumption – the so-called first unbundling of globalisation – feasible (Baldwin 2011, 2016). In the context of North–South trade and economic cooperation, both sides tend to benefit from the combination of advanced technology in the North with the low-cost labour in the South (Chin and Grossman 1998). In this way, a higher degree of economic specialisation leads to higher welfare gains globally though the income gap between the North and the South expanded under the first unbundling regime.

1.2.1 The significance of IPR in GVCs

In the second half of the 20th century, the information revolution drove the world economy to the next stage of globalisation, the so-called second unbundling in Baldwin (2011), which manifested itself by widening the spectrum of goods and services in international trade. This also explains the phenomena of international fragmentation and offshoring of the production process, which first occurred in the vertical dimension and later extended to its horizontal aspects (Jones and Kierzkowski 1990, 2001). The finer division of labour tightens the North–South, North–North, and South–South economic ties, leading to the world economy's new pattern featuring the intensive network of international trade and investment.

International fragmented production has effectively lowered the threshold for global production sharing, creating new opportunities for developing countries to achieve progressive development. The IP system is integral to efforts promoting international technology transfer and follow-on innovation (UNECE 2004). For instance, when development is constrained with capital and technology at the early stage, the participating country could first specialise in labour-intensive and low value-added activities of GVCs. Developing countries will then be able to improve labour skills and productivity by absorbing know-how from outsourcers and gradually building up export capacity and competitiveness. On that basis, the economy could move towards more capital- or technology-intensive and higher value-added stages (Chen 2008). For advanced economies with a better endowment of human capital, participating in GVCs allows them to outsource non-core business abroad and allocate more resources in R&D activities. As a result, the GVCs made the world economy more integrated than ever before. Instead of labelling products 'made in China', 'made in India', or made elsewhere, producers should more appropriately label these products 'made by the world'. This is because the final products are made up of intermediate goods, either tangible (parts and components) or intangible (design and services).

Reduced communication costs accelerated the movement of ideas across national borders, making it feasible to separate IP ownership and right of use. The owner and the IP user could share the value-added generated by the IP by taking various roles in the GVCs. Internationally, the significance of IPR protection is to consolidate innovators' monopolistic power in the existing market(s) and help explore new market(s). Granting foreign users the right of IP use via licensing, for example, serves as an additional channel of technology transfer along with international trade and FDI. For countries that join GVCs for economic take-off and growth, having an effective local IP regime with a commitment to international agreements shall be part of their policy package to encourage inflows of foreign investment and offshoring activities (Chen et al. 2018).

More and more common is IP transfer accompanying offshoring activities. On one side, the IP owner is motivated to share the related know-how with external business partners and authorises them to use specific techniques and processes to ensure that the outsourced supply meets the required quality. Meanwhile, international cooperation on IPR protection is needed to facilitate business transactions across countries and to promote trade by reducing the expense of activities designed to inhibit local imitation. When the original producer injects IP as part of the intangible assets into the outsourcing suppliers, the related IPR needs to be appropriately valued and entered into the businesses' balance sheets and be protected like any private properties. Therefore, the effectiveness of IPR protection should be seen as a key measure of the host country's overall investment environment.

On the other side, most receivers of outsourcing activities are still catching up with technology. A policy focus is to create the incentive structure to facilitate knowledge generation and technology diffusion, which often come with foreign investment. Enhancing IPR protection can effectively improve the investment environment and be seen as part of the new entry requirements to get involved in the GVCs.

Both technology-rich and technology-scared countries could gain from GVC participation – sourced from the combination of international capital and know-how in some countries and abandoned production factors, such as land and cheap labour, in others. Setting international rules and regulations on IPR protection tends to help such a combination and benefits all. This has motivated countries from both sides to enter the negotiation.

Nevertheless, IPR protection is one of the most controversial issues in international trade negotiations. In most cases, the IP-exporting countries prefer to have more 'protective' IP provisions, that is, prolonging the patent validity period. That could generate more revenue from authorising the use of the related IP and winning more time and resources for further R&D to create more IPs. The IP-importing countries will negotiate for the terms that give them more space for possible technology substitution and incremental innovation. From the economic point of view, a loose IPR regime can lower product price, generate more consumer surplus, and lead to higher global welfare in the short run. However, in the long term, due to insufficient producer surplus, inadequate IP protection could cause innovators to lose their incentives investing in R&D or become too cautious when exporting products or outsourcing tasks to foreign countries. Similarly, the regime that overprotects IPR can cause short-term welfare loss and hinder worldwide technological progress.

The digital revolution delivers a new set of tools to bolster the GVCs. Digitalisation tends to shorten the time needed for technology diffusion as it further facilitates the international flow of data and information. Meanwhile, it also helps shift more value-added links from manufacturing activities to services (via the so-called 'servicification'), and increase the share of services in international trade. It tends to intensify the cross-border exchange of IP and, therefore, increase the prominence of IPR protection to endorsing cross-border technology transfer and innovation in GVCs. For that reason, the IP issue has been an integral part of policy considerations on how to facilitate international trade in knowledge and creativity. A well-functioning IP protection system could help knowledge spillover amongst inventors and expedite intelligence sharing. On the contrary, a poorly designed system could have the opposite effect. It may be akin to non-tariff barriers or technical barriers to trade that protect the domestic market against foreign competition by discriminating foreign IP, or providing an umbrella for domestic IPR erosion.

IP's increasing importance in the world economy is evident in the growth of IP filing activities worldwide (Figure 1.1). By the end of 2019, around 15 million patents were in force globally. There were 3.2 million patent applications and 1.5 million patent grants worldwide in 2019, 74% and 84% higher than those of 2009, respectively. Of all applications filed, 65% were received by IP offices in Asia. China had surpassed the United States (US) as the top filer of international patent applications (WIPO 2020a). Since 2010, the total

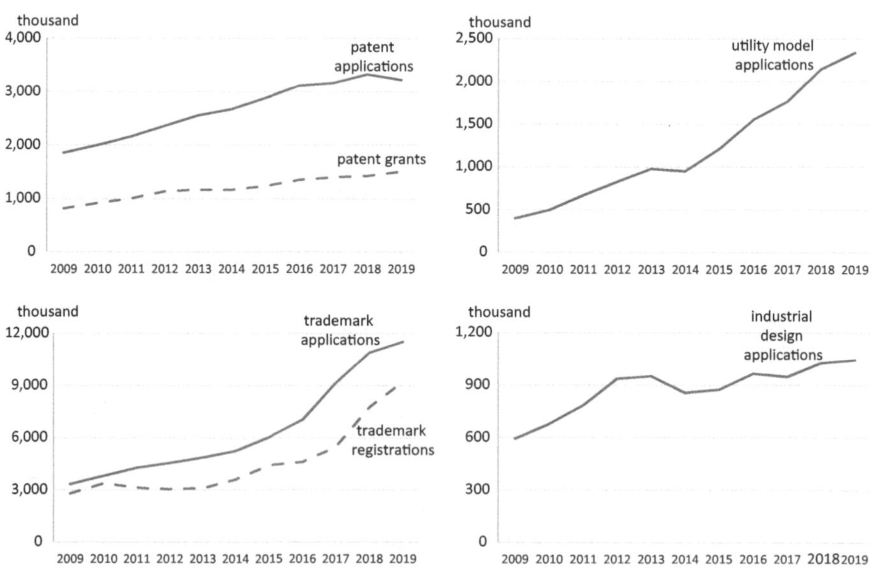

Figure 1.1 Worldwide IP Filing Activities, 2009–2019.

number of utility model applications worldwide has skyrocketed, increasing nearly five times. During that period, the number of trademark applications and registrations also saw consecutive growth. Trademarks had 11.5 million applications and 9.2 million registrations in 2019, nearly 3.5 times ten years earlier. In comparison, the total number of industrial design applications increased rapidly by more than 50% from 2009 to 2012. It kept growing but slowed down afterwards.

1.2.2 The international standard for IPR protection

The Agreement on Trade-Related Aspects of Intellectual Property Rights (TRIPS) serves as the most relevant multilateral IP treaty to international trade. It was designed to ensure that both producers and consumers benefit from IP protection, while such protection subsequently contributes to technology transfers and innovation. Since its signing in 1994, the TRIPS Agreement has been the most important multilateral instrument dedicated to establishing some minimum international standards of IPR protection.

Legally, the TRIPS Agreement recognises the significance of links between IP and trade. It is binding on all World Trade Organization (WTO) members, aiming to narrow the gaps in the way these rights are protected and enforced around the world and to bring them under common international rules (WTO 2015). Instead of pushing for IP law harmonisation across countries, it practically tries to set up a baseline standard for international trade-related IPR regulation. TRIPS respects countries' legal systems. It allows each country to determine the best way to implement its disciplines while encouraging member states to undertake a deeper level of commitment to IPR regulation to the extent that such agreements do not violate the TRIPS provisions. This multilateral agreement requires universally enforceable national treatment and most-favoured-nation treatment. The violation may result in dispute settlement proceedings before the WTO's panels or its appellate body.

By default, the WTO membership requires the ratification of the TRIPS Agreement, which mandates compliance with the Berne Convention.[2] Despite this, TRIPS grants least-developed countries an extended transition period. Part of the agreement's objectives is to promote 'technological innovation and the transfer and dissemination of technology'.[3] This is in line with developing countries' interests in having technology transfer as part of the bargain in which they have agreed to protect intellectual property rights (WTO, n.d.). For ASEAN, the TRIPS Agreement has undoubtedly served, and will still serve, as the IPR protection system's benchmark. Moreover, the agreement also has inbuilt safeguards and flexibilities that allow latecomers to adopt measures necessary to pursue public interest objectives within the multilateral legal framework. With this, Cambodia, the Lao PDR, and Myanmar can further enjoy an extended transition that the TRIPS Agreement provides for least-developed countries to create a viable technological base.

As the global forum for IP policy, services, information, and cooperation, the World Intellectual Property Organization (WIPO) has administered 26 treaties by the end of 2020, including 15 on national IP protection, six on global protection system, and four on classification. In response to the rising popularity of digital electronic publishing and digital products, WIPO concluded the WIPO Copyright Treaty (WCT)[4] and WIPO Performances and Phonograms Treaty (WPPT),[5] the so-called 'Internet treaties', to deal with copyright protection in cyberspace. The WCT and the WPPT entered into force in 2002. They clarify that the existing rights, that is, those required by the Berne Convention and the Rome Convention, shall continue to apply in the digital environment. Both of them try to balance interests between IP owners and the public and give member states the flexibility to grant exceptions for the non-profit use of IPs in the public interest. They require countries to provide adequate legal protection and effective remedies against the circumvention of technological measures used by rights holders. They also prohibit the deliberate alteration or deletion of information which accompanies any protected material, and which identifies the work, its creators, performer, or owner, and the terms and conditions for its use (WIPO 2003).

The fast pace of digital transformation and the rapid expansion of GVCs call for higher IP standards, coupled with effective enforcement mechanisms to support the knowledge economy. In comparison, the pace of multilateral rule setting on international IPR protection lagged behind technological progress and market changes.[6] Alternatively, bilateral or regional rule setting has flourished and has complemented the multilateral approach to establishing global IP norms. The IP issue has been compulsory in free trade agreements. Most advanced economies, such as the US, the European Union, and Japan, promote higher global standards on IPR protection.

It is worth noting that their interests in establishing global governance on IPR protection mirror their domestic IP regimes. Take the US, for example. The country is one of the biggest net suppliers of IP-laden goods and services, foreign domestic investment, and licensing contracts worldwide. The US economy's competitive edge depends mainly on its capacity to innovate, especially in the high-margin, knowledge-intensive businesses. According to the Bureau of Economic Analysis of the US Department of Commerce, the top five IP-intensive sectors[7] have jointly employed nearly 30% of manufacturing workers. They account for almost half of the gross output of American manufacturing industries. Accordingly, the enforcement of IPR protection results in monumental gains for the US economy, including millions of new job opportunities and a sustained push for rapid-pace innovation.

Domestically, the US has one of the world's most-developed and strictest IP regimes; internationally, the country is the main driving force pushing for robust global IPR protection. Since the late 1990s, the US had carried out extensive bilateral negotiations that frequently resulted in trade and investment agreements to promote 'high-standard' rules and regulations in global governance, especially in IP and related issues. The US has consistently promoted IPR enforcement at the international level, predominantly in bilateral and plurilateral rule settings.[8]

1.3 IPR protection in ASEAN

Regional production sharing in the second unbundling is a notable feature of ASEAN and East Asian economies. Since the 1980s when the regional economy broke away from its original 'flying-geese' formation of sequential industrialisation, the East Asian business network has turned into a multi-layered network intertwined by intensive intra-regional trade and investment (Chen and Intal 2017). The development of an intensive regional production-sharing network is considered as a core characteristic of the 'Asian approach' of growth and integration. Participating in GVCs has increased interdependence and enhanced the economic ties among Asian countries and between the regions and the world (Chen and De Lombaerde 2019). The region has emerged as the world's most important production base ('Factory Asia'), of which ASEAN member states are an integral part.

In many ASEAN member states, IPR protection is still a weak point of development. However, they have increasingly paid attention to IP issues and continuously made progress on strengthening the protection. As Table 1.1 reveals, among the seven ASEAN member states with available data published by the US Chamber of Commerce (2020), only Singapore and Malaysia passed the 50% benchmark of the well-being of IPR protection.

Based on the development stage, the ten ASEAN member states belong to three income categories: two are high income, two are upper-middle income, and six are lower-middle-income countries (Table 1.2). According to WIPO (2020b), all ASEAN member states are net payers of IP, based on available data.[9] The IP payment as a share of international trade value ranged from 0.5% in Brunei Darussalam to 2.9% in Singapore. Singapore and Malaysia are the only two countries that received foreign IP payments. As the Global Innovation Indicator (GII) scores reveal, Singapore is the only ASEAN member state whose innovation capacity ranked in the first decile.[10] It is followed by Malaysia, which was in the third decile. Relatively, the country's rank in innovation outputs[11] is higher than that in innovation inputs.[12]

Table 1.3 shows a large portion of non-resident filing of IP applications in ASEAN member states. The non-resident shares of patent applications ranged from 73% in Indonesia to 95% in Brunei Darussalam, while the world average was around 30% in 2019. Similarly, the share of non-resident filings of trademark and industrial design applications was also much higher than that of the world average. According to WIPO (2020a), Singapore and Indonesia saw the largest increase in patent applications between 2018 and 2019. While the rise in non-resident applications mainly drove the strong growth in Singapore, there was an increasing ratio of resident applications for utility models in Indonesia.[13] Overall, non-resident-filed patent applications still tripled as much as resident-filed applications.

Table 1.1 ASEAN Score of US Chamber IP Index, 2020

Category	*(full score)*	*Country*						
		Brunei Darussalam	*Indonesia*	*Malaysia*	*Philippines*	*Singapore*	*Thailand*	*Viet Nam*
Overall	50	20.56	15.12	25.62	19.97	42.21	16.98	18.31
1. Patents, Related Rights, and Limitations	9	5.5	3	3.75	4.25	8.75	2.72	3
2. Copyrights, Related Rights, and Limitations	7	1.53	2.77	4.53	1.78	6.49	2.28	1.28
3. Trademarks, Related Rights, and Limitations	4	2	1.75	2.25	2.25	3	2	2.25
4. Design Rights, Related Rights, and Limitations	2	1.1	0.9	1.5	0.85	1.35	0.9	1.1
5. Trade Secrets and the Protection of Confidential Information	3	0.25	0.5	1.25	0.5	1.75	0.5	1.25
6. Commercialisation of IP Assets	6	4.33	0.25	3.92	2.17	5.5	1.67	1.58
7. Enforcement	7	1.85	1.2	2.92	1.67	5.12	2.66	1.85
8: Systemic Efficiency	5	1	2.75	3.5	3.5	4.25	3.25	2.5
9: Membership and Ratification of International Treaties	7	3	2	2	3	6	1	3.5

Notes: The figures underlined show the scores greater than or equal to 50% of the full score of the respective category of measure.

Source: US Chamber of Commerce (2020).

Table 1.2 ASEAN GII Score

Country	*Income Level*	*GII Rank 2020*			*IP Payment (% of trade)*	*IP Receipt (% of trade)*
		Overall	*Input*	*Output*		
Brunei Darussalam	high	71	39	113	0.5	..
Cambodia	lower middle	110	117	101	..	..
Indonesia	lower middle	85	91	76	0.9	0
Lao PDR	lower middle	113	127	95	..	..
Malaysia	upper middle	33	34	36	0.8	0.1
Myanmar	lower middle	129	129	120	0.7	0
Philippines	lower middle	50	70	41	0.7	0
Singapore	high	8	1	15	2.9	1.5
Thailand	upper middle	44	48	44	1.6	0
Viet Nam	lower middle	42	62	38	..	..

GII = Global Innovation Indicator.

Source: WIPO (2020a, 2020b).

Table 1.3 ASEAN IP Filing, 2019

	Patent		*Trademark*		*Industrial Design*	
	Total applications	*Non-resident share, %*	*Total applications*	*Non-resident share, %*	*Total applications*	*Non-resident share, %*
Brunei Darussalam	141	95.0	4,727	94.4	116	100.0
Cambodia			13,862	78.5		
Indonesia	11,481	73.1	85,837	52.5	2,668	32.6
Malaysia	7,551	85.8	46,707	51.9	1,904	69.9
Philippines	4,380	88.6	62,672	45.6	1,735	36.0
Singapore	14,136	87.8	53,288	79.1	4,769	91.8
Thailand	8,172	90.0	66,411	51.3	5,293	33.1
Viet Nam	7,520	90.4	112,388	33.7	4,387	49.5
World	3,224,200	30.8	15,153,700	15.7	1,360,900	16.4

Source: WIPO (2020a).

The higher rate of non-resident IP filings mirrors high economic interdependence within ASEAN and between ASEAN and the rest of the world. Meanwhile, it also exposes the limitation of the local innovation capacity and the importance of foreign knowledge in supporting local economic growth. Increasing non-resident IP applications could result in more international technology transfer to the region, either complementing or substituting for FDI. In this regard, ASEAN shall see strengthening IPR protection as a policy priority to motivate foreign firms to transact more advanced products and processes and increase domestic innovation capacity in the host countries.

In addition to the TRIPS membership, all ASEAN member states, except Myanmar, were already the contracting parties to the Berne Convention, Paris Convention, Madrid Protocol, and Patent Cooperation Treaty.[14] The countries adopted the related standards of global protection into their domestic IP protection system. Table 1.4 summarises the participation of ASEAN member states in WIPO-administered treaties until the end of 2020.

For Asia, a very influential agreement is the Comprehensive and Progressive Agreement for Trans-Pacific Partnership (CPTPP). The predecessor of

Table 1.4 The Participation of ASEAN Member States in WIPO-Administered Treaties

IP Protection	*BN*	*KH*	*ID*	*LA*	*MY*	*MM*	*PH*	*SG*	*TH*	*VN*
Beijing Treaty on Audiovisual Performances		Y	Y							
Berne Convention[a],[b]	Y	Y	Y	Y	Y		Y	Y	Y	Y
Brussels/Satellites Convention								Y		
Madrid Agreement										
Marrakesh Treaty		Y	Y				Y	Y	Y	
Nairobi Treaty			Y							
Paris Convention[a],[b]	Y	Y	Y	Y	Y		Y	Y	Y	Y
Patent Law Treaty (PLT)										
Phonograms Convention							Y			Y
Rome Convention[b]		Y					Y			Y
Singapore Treaty on the Law of Trademarks (STLT)[a],[b]								Y		
Trademark Law Treaty (TLT)			Y							
Washington Treaty										
WIPO Copyright Treaty (WCT)[a],[b]	Y		Y		Y		Y	Y		
WIPO Performances and Phonograms Treaty (WPPT)[a],[b]	Y		Y		Y		Y	Y		
Budapest Treaty[a],[b]	Y						Y	Y		
Hague Agreement[b]	Y	Y						Y		Y
Lisbon Agreement		Y		Y						
Madrid Agreement (Marks)										Y
Madrid Protocol[a],[b]	Y	Y	Y	Y	Y		Y	Y	Y	Y
Patent Cooperation Treaty (PCT)[a],[b]	Y	Y	Y	Y	Y		Y	Y	Y	Y

a Required by the Comprehensive and Progressive Agreement for Trans-Pacific Partnership (CPTPP) agreement

b Required by the Regional Comprehensive Economic Partnership (RCEP) agreement, BN = Brunei Darussalam, KH = Cambodia, ID = Indonesia, LA = Lao PDR, MM = Malaysia, MM = Myanmar, PH = Philippines, SG = Singapore, TH = Thailand, VN = Viet Nam.

Source: www.WIPO.int.

CPTPP is the Trans-Pacific Partnership (TPP), established under the US leadership. After the US withdrew from the TPP, the CPTPP agreement was finally signed and entered into effect in 2018. Four ASEAN member states – Brunei Darussalam, Malaysia, Singapore, and Viet Nam – are among the signatories.[15]

The CPTPP is built upon TRIPS and several related treaties, such as the Patent Cooperation Treaty (PCT), the WCT, and the WPPT. The CPTPP's IP chapter (Chapter 18, 'Intellectual Property')[16] has a longer text than other chapters in the agreement. It consists of 11 sections, 83 articles, and six annexes. The chapter 'retains' some important aspects of the TPP's IP chapter[17] and 'provides a clear and unambiguous requirement that border officials in all contracting parties have the right to take ex officio action against suspected infringing goods' (US Chamber of Commerce 2020, p. 85). Additionally, Chapter 9 on 'Investment' and Chapter 29 on 'Exceptions and General Provisions' also address some IP issues. With these, the CPTPP comprehensively covers a wide range of topics related to rules and regulations on IPR protection. It contributes to establishing a transparent and predictable standard to protect and enforce IP rights in Asia-Pacific (Global Affairs 2020). To a great extent, Chapter 18 of the CPTPP agreement inherited the multilateral-set requirements on IPR protection. Each party needs to affirm its commitment to the Declaration on TRIPS and Public Health and accept the 2005 Protocol Amendment of the TRIPS Agreement. Additionally, member states are asked to ratify or accede to a series of WIPO-administered treaties, including the PCT, the Paris Convention, the Berne Convention, the Madrid Protocol,[18] the Budapest Treaty, the Singapore Treaty, the WCT, and the WPPT, as well as the International Convention for the Protection of New Varieties of Plants.

Among many others, Kato (2018) sees CPTPP's Chapter 18 as a model IP chapter of 21st-century trade agreements. The chapter introduces the provisions that go beyond countries' commitments in multilateralism and surpass the level under TRIPS ('TRIPS-plus'), as well as the detailed obligations on how to enforce TRIPS-plus protection (Table 1.5). The more stringent regime is expected to incentivise multinational firms to introduce their products in Asian markets. The agreement's implementation tends to require more 'beyond-the-border' economic reforms than 'at-the-border' liberalisation.

In comparison, the Regional Comprehensive Economic Partnership (RCEP) signed in November 2020 covers all ASEAN member states. The RCEP also addresses a wide range of issues required to support the parties' engagement in the GVCs and is said to be 'modern', 'comprehensive', and 'mutually beneficial' for Asian countries. Chapter 11 of the agreement specifies the IP issue. Similar to those agreed in the CPTPP, RCEP's IP provisions were also built on the TRIPS Agreement and several existing WIPO-administered multilateral agreements. In addition to CPTPP requirements, all RCEP signatories must also commit to the Hague Agreement and the Rome Convention. Given the development gaps across countries, Annex 11A of the RCEP agreement provides country-specific schedules, and Annex 11B details technical assistance requests to smoothen the transition period.

Table 1.5 CPTPP Articles Containing TRIPS-Plus Provisions

Section	*Articles*
Section A: General Provisions	4,6,9
Section B: Cooperation	12–16
Section C: Trademarks	18–20,22–28
Section E: Geographical Indications	31–35
Section F: Patents and Undisclosed Test or Other Data	37–39, 42–51, 53
Section G: Industrial Designs	55
Section H: Copyright and Related Rights	63–67, 70
Section I: Enforcement	72–80
Section J: Internet Service Providers	81–82

CPTPP = Comprehensive and Progressive Agreement for Trans-Pacific Partnership.
Source: Kato (2018).

Both the CPTPP and the RCEP mention the potential challenge of the Internet and digitalisation to the enforcement of IPR protection. Chapter 11 of the RCEP agreement includes a specific article (Article 11.75) on 'Effective Action against Infringement in the Digital Environment'. In the CPTPP, the related content was part of 'General Obligations' under 'Enforcement'.[19] In both, the signatories are required to treat equally online violation of copyrights, trademarks, and the related rights with those offline acts of infringement.[20]

Relatively, the CPTPP's IP chapter provides more detailed requirements. Article 18.66 of the agreement emphasises that '[E]ach Party shall endeavour to achieve an appropriate balance in its copyright and related rights system … including those for the digital environment, giving due consideration to legitimate purposes …'. Additionally, Section J and Annex E of Chapter 18 specify the obligations of Internet service providers 'to facilitate the enforcement of copyright on the Internet and to avoid unwarranted market disruption in the online environment'.

In addition to the conclusion of the CPTPP and the RCEP, ASEAN countries have signed nearly 50 bilateral free trade agreements (FTAs) with other countries and regions since 2000, either as a group or individually (Table 1.6). Many of these agreements have addressed IP and IP-related issues. Thirty of them have a separate chapter on IPR, of which one-quarter are the South–South agreements.[21] It is worth noting that Singapore is the first ASEAN country that included an individual IPR chapter in its bilateral FTAs.[22] Fourteen out of its 19 FTAs (including the CPTPP and RCEP) contain a separate chapter addressing IP issues.

1.4 Policy implications

With economic digitalisation, the role of IP is increasingly prominent. IPR enforcement should be placed high on the agenda, and one policy component to support ASEAN's competitive edge should come from ASEAN's

Table 1.6 ASEAN FTAs With or Without a Separate IP Chapter

FTA	*Year of Signing*	*IP Chapter*	*Notes*
United Kingdom–Viet Nam	2020	Y	
United Kingdom–Singapore	2020	Y	
EU–Viet Nam	2019	Y	
EU–Singapore	2018	Y	
EFTA–Indonesia	2018	Y	
Chile–Indonesia	2017	N	Article 3.10 contains provisions on geographical indications.
EFTA–Philippines	2016	Y	Chapter 8 and Annex XVIII to the agreement cover protection of intellectual property rights, specifically reaffirming or incorporating WTO TRIPS Agreement.
ASEAN–China	2004, 2007, upgrade of 2015	Y	In the 2015 upgrade protocol, Article 7.11 (Areas of Economic and Technical Cooperation), the parties agree that subject to review by the agreement, they will abide by their commitments to the provisions of disciplines on IPR in the WTO Agreements.
Rep. of Korea–Viet Nam	2015	Y	
EAEU–Viet Nam	2015	Y	
Turkey–Singapore	2015	Y	
ASEAN–India	2009, 2014	N	Under Article 3, the Parties state that they shall commence consultations on each other's trade regimes, including on intellectual property rights rules and regulations.
Turkey–Malaysia	2014	N	Under Article 9.12 (Cooperation in Intellectual Property), the Parties agree to cooperate according to their own capabilities and subject to the laws, regulations and policies on matters relating to the practice, promotion, dissemination, management, protection and effective application of IPRs.
Singapore–Chinese Taipei	2013	Y	

(*Continued*)

Table 1.6 (Continued)

FTA	*Year of Signing*	*IP Chapter*	*Notes*
Chile–Thailand	2013	N	Chapter 11 on economic cooperation contains an article on geographical indications.
Malaysia–Australia	2012	Y	
Indonesia–Pakistan	2012	N	Article 9.8 contains provision on cooperation on IPR issues.
Chile–Viet Nam	2011	N	Article 3.10 requires that the Parties shall provide procedures for the registration of geographical indications.
India–Malaysia	2011	N	Article 4.8 (Cooperation and Capacity Building) contains provision on IP issues.
Costa Rica–Singapore	2010	Y	
Chile–Malaysia	2010	N	Chapter 3 contains specific disciplines agreed by the Parties on the recognition of geographical indications for some wines and spirits.
New Zealand–Malaysia	2009	Y	
ASEAN–Australia–New Zealand	2009	Y	
ASEAN–Korea, Rep. of	2006, 2008	N	Under the Framework Agreement they also agree to explore and undertake cooperation projects in a number of areas including intellectual property.
Japan–Viet Nam	2008	Y	
Peru–Singapore	2008	N	Under Article 2.17, the Parties affirm that their obligations in the TRIPS. Under Article 2.18, the Parties endeavour to consider the recognition of Geographical Indications after one year from the entry into force of the agreement.
China–Singapore	2008	N	
GCC–Singapore	2008	N	Chapter 6 (government procurement) contains provisions on IP issues.
ASEAN–Japan	2008	N	Annex 5 of the Agreement establishes a work programme and a Special Sub-Committee for cooperation on IP issues.

(*Continued*)

Table 1.6 (Continued)

FTA	*Year of Signing*	*IP Chapter*	*Notes*
Japan–Thailand	2007	Y	
Pakistan–Malaysia	2007	Y	
Japan–Indonesia	2007	Y	
Brunei Darussalam–Japan	2007	N	Article 97 contains provisions governing intellectual property.
Panama–Singapore	2006	N	Chapter 9 (Investment) contains provisions on IP issues.
Japan–Philippines	2006	Y	
Korea, Rep. of–Singapore	2005	Y	Chapter 17 specifically reaffirms or incorporates WTO TRIPS Agreement.
India–Singapore	2005	Y	
Thailand–New Zealand	2005	Y	
Japan–Malaysia	2005	Y	
Jordan–Singapore	2004	N	In Article 8.8 of chapter 8 (general provisions), the Parties affirm their commitments under the WTO TRIPS Agreement.
Thailand–Australia	2004	Y	
United States–Singapore	2003	Y	
Singapore–Australia	2003	Y	
India–Thailand	2003	N	Article 6 (Other Areas of Economic Cooperation) contains provisions on IP issues.
Japan–Singapore	2002	Y	
EFTA–Singapore	2002	Y	
New Zealand–Singapore	2000	Y	Chapter 12 specifically reaffirms or incorporates WTO TRIPS Agreement.

ASEAN = Association of Southeast Asian Nations, EAEU = Eurasian Economic Union, EFTA = European Free Trade Association, EU = European Union, GCC = Gulf Cooperation Council, WTO = World Trade Organization.

Source: Authors. Raw data from the ASEAN Secretariat, WTO Regional Trade Arrangement gateway, ADB Asia Regional Integration Center (ARIC) Database and country official websites.

further effort on improving IPR protection. ASEAN and its member states should treat IPR protection as part of the entry requirements for GVC participation. Countries without an effective IP regime would risk exclusion from the GVCs. Since many Asian countries are already middle- or high-income economies with increasing domestic innovation capacity, it is in their long-term economic interest to implement a high-standard IPR regulation to stimulate local innovation and protect their rights.

Region-wide, the ASEAN economic ministers had signed the ASEAN Framework Agreement on Intellectual Property Cooperation at the Fifth ASEAN Summit. The IP officials of ASEAN member states established in 1995 the Working Group on Intellectual Property Cooperation to promote all IPR-related programs and activities in the region. Although these achievements have laid down a solid institutional framework for regional collaboration, additional policy effort will be needed to improve the region's overall IPR protection standard, primarily to deal with new issues and situations concerning GVC expansion and digitalisation. After the conclusion of the CPTPP and the RCEP, on top of ASEAN member states' agenda is to implement the agreement(s) and conduct domestic adjustments or reform to meet their commitments. Such could result in a challenging process for those countries that have not yet established a mature legal system and still have relatively low public awareness of IP and IPR protection.

Above all, establishing and improving a robust IP regime must be part of the main content of a country's legal construction. Measures to strengthen IPR protection should be integral to efforts that aim to facilitate knowledge diffusion and technology adoption. The fundamental criterion to judge an IPR system's effectiveness is to see how well it could spur local creation and innovation. With this in mind, a country should sufficiently consider IP issues when setting its investment policy, competition policy, industrial policy, foreign policy, and education policy.

Ultimately, the public's consciousness and support in protecting IP will spell the difference. Without this, the effect of the governments' sanctioning of illegal IPR infringements could be limited. Therefore, a critical step is to increase public awareness of IP and its associated rights. In general, this will require more efforts on education and closer public–private partnerships.

Despite their shortcomings, the rules and regulations set by the TRIPS Agreement and IP treaties of the WIPO are still relevant in 21st-century economic governance. However, digitalisation and its consequent changes in GVCs are continuously introducing new elements related to IPR protection. The establishment of a local IP regime must at least meet the standards set by multilateral agreements. It should always aim for higher-level standards as far as they take full cognisance of the constraints stemming from domestic social tolerance and the cost of transition resulting from net economic loss due to reduced consumer surplus in the short term. Developing countries may welcome the new initiatives based on the 'shared' feature of the digital economy, such as setting up the mechanism to encourage more rights holders to donate or license patents either voluntarily or under mutually agreed terms and conditions. But it is worth noting that such a solution must work at equality and be voluntary as well. The innovator shall not be forced to transfer technology by any means.

Regulations on IPR protection set by international agreement(s) must be binding and practically enforceable. Ensuring both the transparency and the predictability of rule setting and implementation is essential, and the language used must be less ambiguous and easy to understand. A practical dispute settlement mechanism must also be established as this is a necessary condition to guarantee the agreement's terms to be complied with. Moreover, given the de facto strong economic interdependence within Factory Asia, region-wide cooperation in strengthening IPR protection and a country's domestic effort should complement each other and result in mutual stimulation.

In a nutshell, IP issues and innovation are closely linked. In many ASEAN member states, the limited supply of qualified human capital usually constrains invention and local innovation. The lack of human skill could also affect the effectiveness of IPR protection. In this regard, a country's education and training policies must support its innovation strategy and IPR policy. For the late-comer countries, such as Cambodia, the Lao PDR, and Myanmar, technical assistance programs as presented in the RCEP IP chapter's annex will be particularly helpful in capacity building. These then call for deeper regional cooperation in the social dimension.

Looking forward, digitalisation and GVCs have deeply changed the world economic landscape (Baldwin 2016, Chen and Kimura 2019). More disruptive changes are yet to come, for which ASEAN and its member states should always get themselves well prepared. New global IPR rules and regulations are still taking shape. ASEAN member states shall actively participate in global rule making and get their voice heard from the beginning. By doing so, they could negotiate for better conditions rather than later, in a relatively passive way, accepting those requirements that others before them had set. Suppose the market is not yet enthusiastic enough to do so proactively, ASEAN leaders shall consider pushing forward such process politically, as long as the protection of inventors' rights of definitive monopoly power does not sacrifice much dynamic competition in the market and countries' long-term innovation potential.

Notes

1 There are different types of intellectual property rights (IPR), including trademarks, geographical indications, industrial designs, copyright and related rights, patents, agricultural chemical products, and trade secrets. The discussion in this chapter uses IPR as the general concept, which covers all categories.

2 By the end of 2020, Myanmar is the only ASEAN member state that has not yet ratified the Berne Convention.

3 Article 7 ('Objectives') of the TRIPS Agreement states that the protection and enforcement of IPR should contribute to the promotion of technological innovation and the transfer and dissemination of technology, to the mutual advantage of producers and users of technological knowledge in a manner conducive to social and economic welfare, and to a balance of rights and obligations.

4 The WIPO Copyright Treaty (WCT) is a special agreement under the Berne Convention that deals with the protection of works and the rights of their authors in the digital environment.

5 The World Performances and Phonograms Treaty (WPPT) deals with the rights of performers and producers of phonograms, particularly in the digital environment.

6 In the World Trade Organization (WTO), there were protocol amendments on patents and public health to the TRIPS Agreement in 2003. In 2005, the WTO members approved to make those changes permanent. The amendment took effect on 23 January 2017.
7 The five sectors are petroleum and coal product manufacturing, transportation equipment manufacturing, medical equipment manufacturing, computer and electronic product manufacturing, and chemical manufacturing.
8 The new-generation free trade agreements (mega FTAs) continue to strengthen IPR, facilitate international technology transfer, and go beyond the standard of the WTO (Chen et al. 2018).
9 Data are not available for Cambodia, Lao PDR, Myanmar, and Viet Nam.
10 A total of 131 countries are in the reports of the World Intellectual Property Organization (WIPO).
11 The forces that pull ideas and technologies towards application, exploitation, and impact.
12 The forces that push knowledge creation, exploration, and investments.
13 In 2019, nearly one-quarter of patent applications in Indonesia were for utility models, of which 97% were filed by resident applicants.
14 Only five of them signed the Internet treaties of the World Intellectual Property Organization (WIPO).
15 The other seven CPTPP member states are Australia, Canada, Chile, Japan, Mexico, New Zealand, and Peru. The Trans-Pacific Partnership (TPP) can be traced back to the Trans-Pacific Strategic Economic Partnership, also known as the 'Pacific 4' (P-4), concluded between Brunei Darussalam, Chile, New Zealand, and Singapore in June 2005. After Washington formally joined the negotiating process in 2009, the US has been playing as the de facto leader of the initiative.
16 Other chapters, such as Chapters 9 and 29, and some bilateral agreements between individual parties also provide for related IP regulations.
17 It includes the key provisions of (i) the membership of international treaties, (ii) mechanisms for notification, (iii) design rights, (iv) copyright, (v) IP rights enforcement, (vi) trade secrets, and (vii) government use of licensed software.
18 The Protocol Relating to the Madrid Agreement Concerning the International Registration of Marks.
19 See paragraph 2, Section I, Article 18.71.
20 In RCEP, the corresponding enforcement procedures are set out in Articles 59 to 64 (on Civil Remedies) and Article 74 (Criminal Remedies) while in the CPTPP, they are defined in Article 18.75 (Provisional Measures) and Article 18.77 (Criminal Procedures and Penalties).
21 Free trade agreements or economic partnership agreements with WTO notification by 1 January 2021.
22 Singapore–New Zealand FTA in 2000.

Bibliography

Aghion, P., N. Bloom, R. Blundell, R. Griffith, and P. Howitt (2002), 'Competition and Innovation: An Inverted U Relationship', *NBER Working Paper* No. 9269, Cambridge, MA: NBER.

Awokuse, T.O. and H. Yin (2010), 'Intellectual Property Rights Protection and the Surge in FDI in China', *Journal of Comparative Economics*, 38(2), pp. 217–224.

Baldwin, R.E. (2011), '21st Century Regionalism: Filling the Gap between 21st Century Trade and 20th Century Trade Rules', *WTO ERSD Working Paper*, ERSD-2011-08.

Baldwin, R.E. (2016), *The Great Convergence: Information Technology and the New Globalization*. Cambridge, MA: Belknap.

Branstetter, L., R. Fisman, F. Foley, and K. Saggi (2007), 'Intellectual Property Rights, Imitation, and Foreign Direct Investment: Theory and Evidence', *NBER Working Paper* No. 13033, Cambridge, MA: NBER.

Chen, L. (2008), *Production Sharing and Regional Integration*. Geneva: Graduate Institute of International and Development Studies.

Chen, L. (2019), 'ASEAN in the Digital Era: Enabling Cross-border E-commerce', in L. Chen and F. Kimura (eds.), *Developing the Digital Economy in ASEAN*. Abingdon and New York, NY: Routledge, pp. 259–275.

Chen, L. and P. De Lombaerde (2019), 'ASEAN between Globalization and Regionalization', *Asia Pacific Business Review*, 25(5), pp. 729–750.

Chen, L. and P. Intal (2017), 'ASEAN Foreign Trade, Investment, and Integration in Comparative Perspective', in P. Intal and L. Chen (eds.), *ASEAN@50: ASEAN and Member States: Transformation and Integration*. Jakarta: ERIA, pp. 34–61.

Chen, L. and F. Kimura (2019), 'Introduction', in L. Chen and F. Kimura (eds.), *Developing the Digital Economy in ASEAN*. New York, NY: Routledge, pp. 3–13.

Chen, L., S. Urata, J. Nakagawa, and M. Ambashi (2018), 'Introduction: Mega FTAs in the 21st Century Global Trade Governance', in L. Chen, S. Urata, J. Nakagawa, and M. Ambashi (eds.), *Emerging Global Trade Governance: Mega Free Trade Agreements and Implications for ASEAN*. New York, NY: Routledge, pp. 1–11.

Chin, J.C. and G.M. Grossman (1998), 'Intellectual Property Rights and North–South Trade', *NBER Working Paper* No. 2769, Cambridge, MA: NBER.

Correa, C.M. (2007), 'Intellectual Property and Competition Law: Exploring Some Issues of Relevance to Developing Countries', *ICTSD Intellectual Property and Sustainable Development Series* No. 21. Geneva: ICTSD.

Falvey, R., N. Foster and O. Memedovic (2006), *The Role of Intellectual Property Rights in Technology Transfer and Economic Growth: Theory and Evidence*. Geneva: UNIDO.

Global Affairs (2020), 'Comprehensive and Progressive Agreement for Trans-Pacific Partnership (CPTPP)', www.international.gc.ca/trade-commerce/trade-agreements-accods-commerciaus/agr-acc/cptpp-ptpgp (accessed 16 November 2020).

Jones, R.W. and H. Kierzkowski (1990), 'The Role of Services in Production and International Trade: A Theoretical Framework', in R. Jones and A. Krueger (eds.), *The Political Economy of International Trade: Essays in Honor of Robert E. Baldwin*. Oxford: Basil Blackwell, pp. 32–48.

Jones, R.W. and H. Kierzkowski (2001), 'Globalization and Consequences of International Fragmentation', in R. Dornbusch, G. Galvo, and M. Obsfeld (eds.), *Money, Capital Mobility and Trade*. Cambridge, MA: MIT Press, pp. 365–383.

Kato, A. (2018), 'Understanding the IP-Related Contents of the Trans-Pacific Partnership Agreement', in L. Chen, S. Urata, J. Nakagawa, and M. Ambashi (eds.), *Emerging Global Trade Governance: Mega Free Trade Agreements and Implications for ASEAN*. New York: Routledge, pp. 97–133.

Kimura, F. and M. Ando (2005), 'Two-Dimensional Fragmentation in East Asia: Conceptual Framework and Empirics', *International Review of Economics and Finance*, 14(3), pp. 317–348.

Kimura, F. and L. Chen (2018), 'Value Chain Connectivity in Indonesia: The Evolution of Unbundlings,' *Bulletin of Indonesian Economic Studies*, 54(2), pp. 165–192.

Lee, C. and Y. Fukunaga (2013), 'Competition Policy Challenges of Single Market and Production Base', *ERIA Discussion Paper* No. 2013–17, Jakarta: ERIA.

Lee, M. and D. Park (2013), 'Intellectual Property Rights, Quality of Institutions, and Foreign Direct Investment into Developing Asia', *ADB Economics Working Paper* No. 354, Mandaluyong: ADB.

Maskus, K.E. (1998), 'The International Regulation of Intellectual Property', *Review of World Economics*, 134(2), pp. 186–208.

Mayer, T. and E. Pfister (2001), 'Do Stronger Patent Rights Attract Foreign Direct Investment? Evidence from French Multinationals', *Location, Region et Development*, 13, pp. 99–122.

Obashi, A. and F. Kimura (2017), 'Deepening and Widening of Production Networks in ASEAN, *Asian Economic Papers*, 16(1), pp. 1–27.

OECD (2016), *Trade in Value Added*. Paris: OECD.

OECD (2003), *The Impact of Trade-Related Intellectual Property Rights on Trade and Foreign Direct Investment in Developing Countries*. Paris: OECD.

UNECE (2004), 'Report on Conference on Intellectual Property Exploitation in the Internet Era', www.unece.org/fileadmin/DAM/ie/Wp5/ipr/report0404wrs.pd (accessed 16 November 2020).

US Chamber of Commerce (2020), *Art of the Possible – US Chamber International IP Index*. Washington, DC: US Chamber of Commerce.

WIPO (2020a), *World Intellectual Property Indicators 2020*. Geneva: WIPO.

WIPO (2020b), *Global Innovation Index 2020*. Geneva: WIPO.

WTO (2015), *Understanding the WTO*. Geneva: WTO.

WIPO (2003), *The WIPO Internet Treaties*. Geneva: WIPO.

WTO (n.d.), 'Technology Transfer', www.wto.org/English/tratop_e/techtransfer_e.htm (accessed 7 December 2020).

2 IPR protection for Asian development

Opportunities and challenges from global value chains and the digital economy – Singapore

Kung Chung Liu and Wenting Cheng

2.1 Global value chain: the importance of intellectual property

Value chains refer to the full range of activities that firms undertake to bring a product or a service from its conception to its end use by final consumers (De and Miroudot, 2013). Global value chains (GVCs) emerged in the mid-1980s when firms in many industries focused on core competencies and outsourced other activities across national boundaries. Baldwin (2013) identified two reasons for the rise of GVCs: (i) the information and communications technology revolution made it possible to coordinate complexity at a distance, and (ii) the vast wage differences between developed and developing nations made the separation of labour profitable. Economically, the GVCs represent the process of ever-finer specialisation and geographic fragmentation of production. Within each GVC is always an incentive by the GVC's organiser, often a multinational corporation, to move its labour-intensive portions to a place with lower wages. This partially explains why the world's manufacturing sites first moved to Japan and the Republic of Korea (henceforth, Korea) in the 1960s, and to Taiwan, Singapore, Hong Kong, and then to China and Southeast Asian countries in the last four decades.

Recent economic studies concerning the GVCs have focused on value distribution. After studying 560 GVCs from 1995 to 2008, Timmer et al. (2014) found that the GVCs provide a similar pattern of value addition. The distribution of value-added by each location along the GVC timeline presents a U-shaped curve, which some scholars refer to as the 'smiling curve' (Shin et al. 2012; Li et al. 2010; Wang and Jia 2010; Chen 2004) (Figure 2.1). The curve reveals that the greatest value is captured by upstream (research and development [R&D]) and downstream (marketing) firms, and the lowest value is captured by the assembly firms located in the middle of GVCs (Shin et al. 2012). Multinational corporations (MNCs) have control over the two ends of the curve; they possess product planning capabilities and market access advantages, and protect them with intellectual property rights (IPR). The MNCs also control manufacturing through contractual agreements

DOI: 10.4324/9781003147657-3

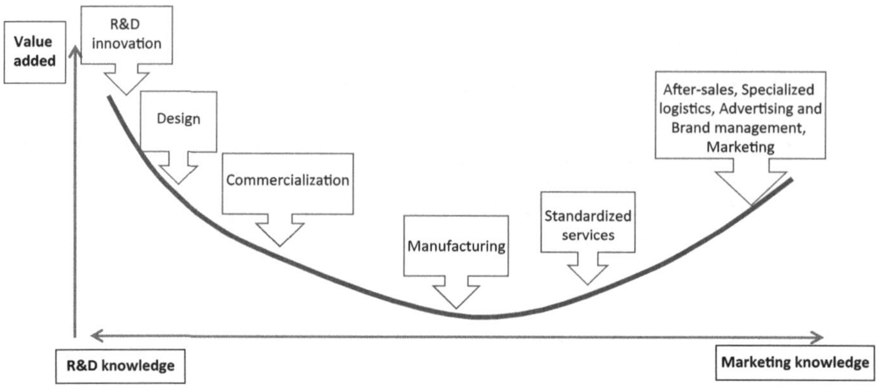

Figure 2.1 The Smiling Curve of Value Creation.

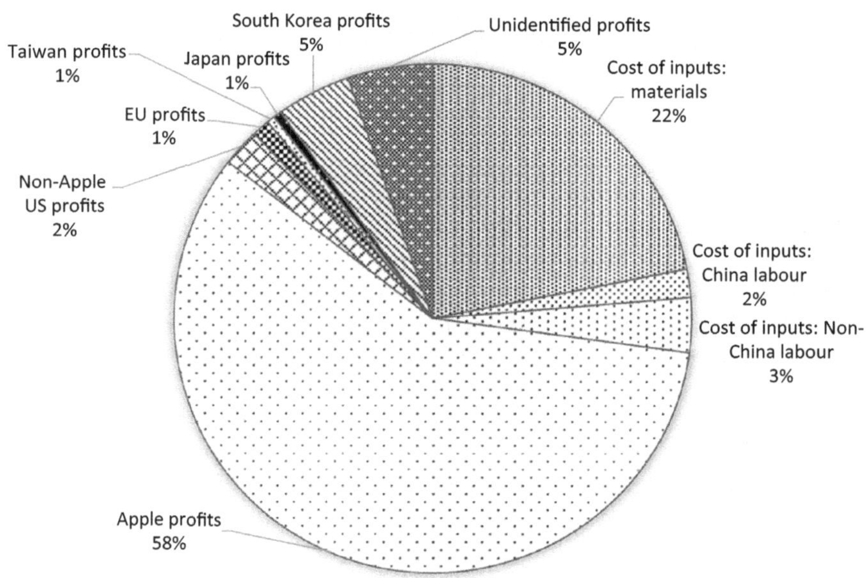

Figure 2.2 Distribution of Value for iPhone, 2010.

with original equipment manufacturers, so they have the final say in the distribution of value derived from the GVCs (Chen 2004). A general trend is that the smile is getting deeper as Timmer et al. (2014) had found that value-added shares of low-skilled workers in emerging economies have been declining from 1995 to 2008.[1]

A typical example of the smiling curve is Apple. According to the empirical study by Kraemer, Linden, and Dedrick (2011), Chinese labour assembles Apple products. Still, it accounts only for 1.8% of the total value for iPhone (Figure 2.2) and 2% of the total value for iPad (Figure 2.3). Most profits go to product development and branding (Apple's profit accounts for 58.5%

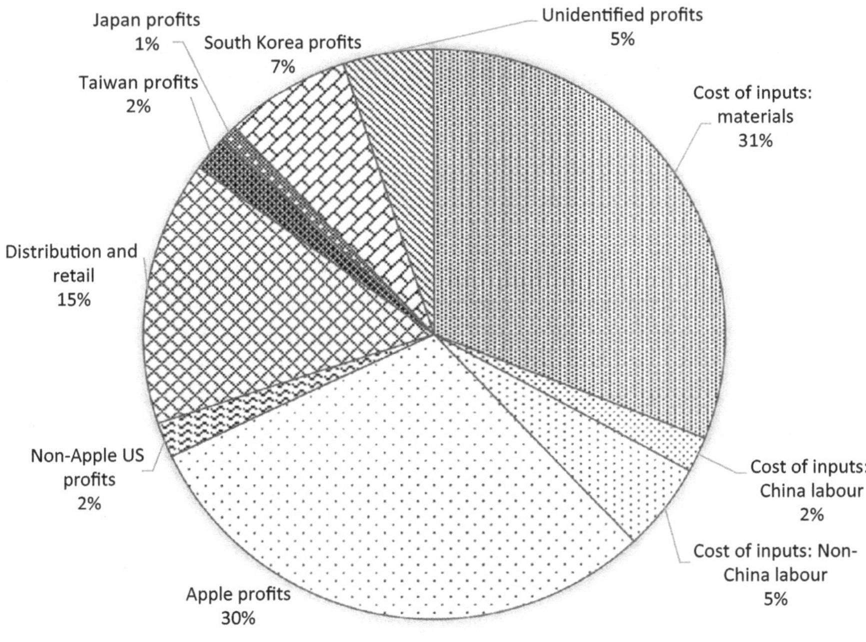

Figure 2.3 Distribution of Value for iPad, 2010.

and 30%, respectively). Kraemer et al. (2011) further clarified that 'it is a common misconception that China, where the iPad is assembled, receives a large share of money paid for electronics goods. That is not true of any name-brand products from the US' (Kraemer et al. 2011, p. 5). Although the study's finding is overwhelming, one should be careful about generalising a conclusion that also applies to other GVCs. For instance, Dedrick, Kraemer, and Linden (2010) compared the value distribution, particularly the profits from innovation, in the GVCs of iPad and personal computers (Lenovo and HP), and found that the gross margins for Apple from iPad are higher than those earned by HP and Lenovo from personal computers. Relatively, either HP PC's or Lenovo PC's smiling curve is less deep than that of Apple.

As Mudambi (2008) suggested, multinational corporations (MNCs) can control the GVCs by concentrating on R&D and marketing while outsourcing low value-added assembly and processing to firms in emerging economies. However, economic literature stops here and does not ask how such a 'control' can be happening, namely, who regulates the GVCs, particularly who defines the rules as how much each party located at the GVCs can gain? And how? We, therefore, turn to the literature of regulation.[2] Traditionally, states assume the role of regulators. However, private actors, particularly the MNCs, play an essential role in regulatory capitalism, including the regulation of the GVCs, although sometimes the underpinning power relations behind the value distribution of the GVCs are not well spelled out.

After researching Chinese firms at the GVCs, Chen (2004) argued that in the GVCs the MNCs are the regulators while the Chinese original equipment manufacturers (OEMs) are the 'regulatees'. Being a supplier for the MNCs located at the bottom of the smiling curve leads to Chinese OEMs' dependence on their multinational partners in the GVCs (Morck et al. 2008).

The MNCs regulate their GVCs through IP laws. Therefore, the MNCs often have much stronger bargaining power as opposed to the manufacturers. The MNCs create a legal framework to protect all forms of intangibles and tangibles as property at all ends of the GVCs. The IP system confers exclusive rights to the IP owners. Any other person or company that desires to use these intangible resources must ask for authorisation from the owner through a licensing agreement. However, IP is a territorial right, as defining the proper scope and level of IP protection is a state's sovereign decision. If the MNCs' creations or brands cannot be protected in the country where they manufacture and/or sell the products, they cannot collect the profits of the GVCs. To prevent this from happening, the MNCs have been motivated to ratchet up IP protection standards globally. According to Sell (2011), the Agreement on Trade-Related Aspects of Intellectual Property Rights (TRIPS Agreement) resulted from powerful lobbying by US-based MNCs that wished to ratchet up international IP protection standards to protect their markets.

In sum, understanding who regulates the GVCs and how such regulation has been achieved through IPR is important for Asian governments to reflect on when trying to upgrade or improve their positions at the GVCs.

2.2 The Singapore economic model and their position in the GVC

2.2.1 In general

Singapore has been one of the world's important ports since the 19th century. Until today, shipping industry-related services are still an essential part of Singapore's economy. After the country's separation from Malaysia in 1965, it began to work on industrialisation. Since the 1980s, the young country has transformed itself from a labour-intensive economy into a highly skilled and technology-driven one. After experiencing its first economic recession in 1985 after independence, the Singaporean government redirected its economic development from manufacturing to services. In the new millennium, it is striving to become a creative and innovative Smart Nation. Among other efforts, Singapore launched in 2013 the IP Hub Masterplan and Update to the IP Hub Masterplan 2017. Figure 2.4 illustrates Singapore's economic development agenda.

Regarding economic structure, Singapore has developed its sophisticated service industries, such as financial, information technology, medical, electronics, aviation, and education services. From 1973 to 2013, Singapore's gross domestic product (GDP) increased by 37 times, from S$8,745 million to S$324,592 million (based on 2005 constant prices). The average annual growth rate during this period was 7.2%. According to the International

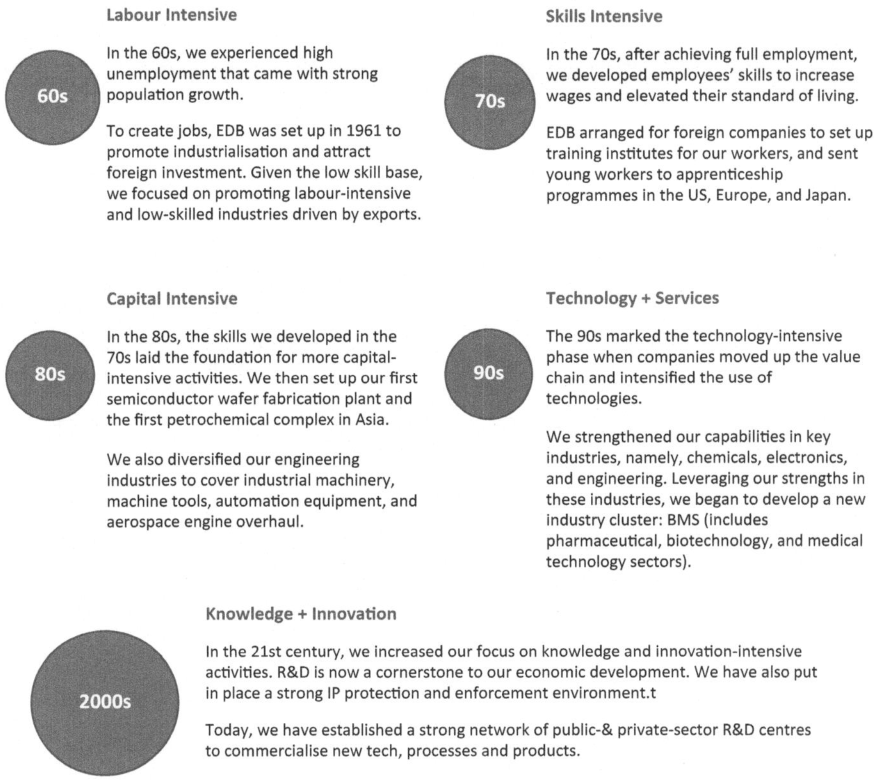

Figure 2.4 Singapore's Economic Transformation (1960s onward).

Monetary Fund, in 2017, the country's per capita GDP ranked third globally (Toh 2017).

According to the Ministry of Finance:

> Singapore's economic structure reflects the realities of a small country. It is diversified across manufacturing and services, but both are heavily exposed to global markets. As a city-state with a population of four million, businesses have far greater incentive to serve global markets than domestic consumption. Operating revenues, at 15% of GDP, are lower than in any developed economy. The vast majority of businesses and households enjoy effective tax rates that are the lowest in Asia.
>
> (WSJ Asia 2009)

One 2018 report by the ASEAN–Japan Centre on Singapore's role in the GVCs shows that the largest share of value addition in Singapore belongs to foreign trade. The share of foreign value-added in gross exports varies from industry to industry, with an all-industry average of 62% (Fujita 2018). Among ASEAN countries, Singapore's share of foreign value-added is 20% higher than the next largest economies, Malaysia and Viet Nam (Fujita 2018). Table 2.1 illustrates the breakdown of foreign value-added.[3]

Table 2.1 Structure of Value-Added Exports from Singapore, by Sector and by Industry, 2015

Sector and Industry	*Gross Exports, Billion US$*	*Domestic Value Added (DVA), Billion US$*	*Foreign Value Added (FVA), billion US$*	*Share of FVA in Total Gross Exports, %*
Total	**356.2**	**137.1**	**219.1**	**61.5**
Primary	**1.7**	**1.1**	**0.6**	**34.3**
Agriculture, hunting, forestry, and fishing	1.7	1.1	0.6	34.3
Secondary	**261.3**	**78.2**	**183.1**	**70.1**
Food, beverages, and tobacco	6.1	2.4	3.7	60.7
Textiles, clothing, and leather	2.8	0.9	1.9	67.2
Wood and wood products	0.7	0.3	0.4	56.7
Publishing, printing, and reproduction of recorded media	5.4	2.6	2.7	50.7
Coke, petroleum products, and nuclear fuel	43.8	4.4	39.4	89.9
Chemicals and chemical products	28	14.3	13.7	48.9
Rubber and plastic products	5.4	2.1	3.4	61.7
Non-metallic mineral products	1	0.4	0.6	56.8
Metal and metal products	13.8	4.8	9	65.4
Machinery and equipment	18.1	7.9	10.2	56.3
Electrical and electronic equipment	113.9	27.8	86.1	75.6
Precision instruments	13	6	7	54.1
Motor vehicles and other transport equipment	8.6	4.2	4.4	51.3
Other manufacturing	0.8	0.1	0.7	89.5
Tertiary	**93.1**	**57.7**	**35.4**	**38**
Electricity, gas, and water	0.1	0.1	0	17.8
Construction	2	1.2	0.8	39.9
Trade	12.3	8.3	4	32.8
Hotels and restaurants	5.5	4	1.5	27.1
Transport, storage, and communications	25.9	12.1	13.8	53.2

(*Continued*)

Table 2.1 (Continued)

Sector and Industry	*Gross Exports, Billion US$*	*Domestic Value Added (DVA), Billion US$*	*Foreign Value Added (FVA), billion US$*	*Share of FVA in Total Gross Exports, %*
Finance	9.9	7.2	2.7	27.7
Business activities	28.5	18.5	9.9	34.8
Education	1.7	1.4	0.3	19.5
Health and social services	1.2	0.8	0.4	31.9
Community, social, and personal service activities	5.1	3.4	1.7	33
Other services	0.9	0.7	0.2	22.7

Source: Fujita (2018).

A series of rankings have recognised the Singapore government's efforts to make the country more friendly to foreign businesses. In 2018, the Index of Economic Freedom of the Heritage Foundation (2018) ranked the country as the world's second most open economy. It is also the world's second most pro-business regime, according to the World Bank's *Doing Business* report, only next to New Zealand (World Bank 2018).

2.2.2 Digital economy

In the new millennium, Singapore has been striving to become a creative and innovative Smart Nation. The value of digitalisation is immense; Microsoft estimated that the digital economy will contribute an additional US$10 billion to Singapore's GDP by the end of 2021. The Committee on the Future Economy, formed to chart the next phase of Singapore's economic growth, has affirmed the importance for Singapore to take the lead in the global digital economy. Four key areas were identified for development: immersive media, artificial intelligence, cybersecurity, and the Internet of Things. On the enterprise front, firms in Singapore are also increasing their investments in digital assets to enhance their digital capabilities. Specifically, firms' gross capital expenditure on digital fixed assets rose at a compounded annual growth rate of 7.1% in 2013–2015, thereby resulting in a significant accumulation of digital fixed assets among firms over this period. In tandem with their digital assets investments, firms are also increasingly adopting digital tools in their day-to-day business activities. For instance, according to the Infocomm Media Development Authority, a higher share of enterprises uses e-payment systems and mobile services to do business.

For a city-state such as Singapore where everything is conveniently concentrated, and people enjoy shopping as part of their social life, the digital economy is slowly emerging.

2.3 IP system in Singapore

2.3.1 The importance of IP

Singapore has been a latecomer in the IP game. It did not accede to the Paris Convention and the Berne Convention until it reached significant economic development: 1994 (effective 1995) and 1998 (when it declared that it availed itself of the faculties provided for in Articles II and III of the Appendix for a developing country [Special Provisions Regarding Developing Countries] until 2004), respectively. According to the World Integrated Trade Solution, Singapore's GDP per capita in 1990–1994 was US$11,864; US$14,505; US$16,144; US$18,302; and US$21,578, respectively.[4] From around that time, the Singapore government realised the importance of IP: it could elevate its position from the bottom to the higher end of the GVCs. Thus, it endeavoured to raise its IP protection standards in its domestic laws to comply with the TRIPS standards. Singapore has made huge progress ever since. The main driver of this progress is, without doubt, the visionary Singapore government. Many international organisations have ranked Singapore as the best performer in IP protection. According to Fujita (2018):

> Singapore occupies both ends of the (smiling) curve, in other words, the highest value-added parts of production chains. The assembly and manufacturing parts of the GVC curve have the potential to be upgraded, given the level of technology and GVC participation of the largest export industry, electrical, and electronic equipment.

2.3.2 Singapore's role in specific GVCs

This conclusion can be further supported by looking at Singapore's role in specific GVCs. Take the growing medical technology market, for example. With its strategic location in Asia, Singapore has attracted over 60 multinational medical technology companies to undertake various activities from regional headquarters and manufacturing to R&D. The multinational companies have relied on the country's design and engineering capabilities, its base of automation suppliers, and high-quality assurance standards to manufacture high-value medical products. In addition to manufacturing, 50 regional headquarters from the world's leading medical technology firms are based in Singapore, from which they are implementing their 'Asia strategy' to expand into the region (EDB Singapore 2017, 2018). The pharmaceutical industry has been well known for its demands for a high level of IP protection.

Qualcomm, the world giant in the wireless telecommunications industry, has also located its patent holding in Singapore. Qualcomm has moved its Qualcomm CDMA Technologies non-US headquarters to Singapore. The tax incentives in Singapore are the primary reason for the move. During the third quarter of fiscal year 2018, Qualcomm entered into a new tax incentive agreement with Singapore that reduced the tax rate from March 2017 through March 2022, provided that the specified employment and investment criteria in Singapore are met (Qualcomm 2018).

In 2017, Qualcomm and TDK Corporation formed a joint venture, RF360 Holdings Singapore PTE. Ltd. The joint venture is 51% owned by Qualcomm Global Trading Pte. Ltd. (Qualcomm Global Trading), a Singapore corporation and wholly owned subsidiary of Qualcomm, and 49% by EPCOS AG, a German wholly owned subsidiary of TDK. The joint venture will enable Qualcomm's RF front-end (RFFE) business to deliver RFFE modules and RF filters into fully integrated systems for mobile devices, the Internet of Things, automotive applications, connected computing, and more. F360 Holdings will be a Singapore corporation and will have a global presence with R&D and manufacturing and/or sales locations in Europe and Asia, and its headquarters in Munich, Germany (Qualcomm 2017). Another similar story is MediaTek, a Taiwanese company specialising in chipset technology for smart TVs, voice assistant devices, Android tablets, feature phones, optical and Blu-ray DVD players, and mobile phones. The company is headquartered in Taiwan, with sales and research subsidiaries in Singapore, China, Hong Kong, India, United States, Japan, Korea, England, Finland, Sweden, France, Holland, and Dubai. According to its 2017 annual report, the Singapore government is the largest stakeholder of MediaTek. Also, the company established four affiliations in Singapore, with one holding MediaTek's IP rights (MediaTek 2017).

Clearly, an effective IP protection system is a prerequisite for multinational companies' headquarters in Singapore. Dyson, which is now relocating its global headquarters to Singapore, is another example (Jack 2018). Dyson has made it clear that the centre of gravity now lies in Asia, where it sees the biggest growth opportunities. It is a strategic plan for the smart allocation of resources along the GVC because only 2%–3% of the supply chain is in Europe, and that goes east and not west (BBC 2019).

2.3.3 IP authorities

The IP authorities in Singapore include the Ministry of Law and its Intellectual Property Office of Singapore, Attorney-General's Chambers, and specialised IP court and judges.

2.3.3.1 Ministry of law

The Ministry of Law has its Intellectual Property Policy Division in charge of IP policies and legislation (specifically patents, trademarks, copyright, registered designs, plant varieties, geographical indications, and trade secrets), and IP-related industrial policies. The Ministry of Law's policy position is to maintain an IP regime that is balanced, well-regarded internationally, fosters the growth of a vibrant IP services sector, and supports value creation (Ministry of Law 2018).

2.3.3.2 Intellectual Property Office of Singapore (IPOS)

IPOS is mainly responsible for implementing IP laws, including providing advice on IP laws, maintaining the IP registers, and engaging businesses on their IP needs (Ministry of Law 2018).

2.3.3.3 Attorney-General's Chambers

The Attorney-General's Chambers (AGC) is mainly responsible for IP enforcement. It performs this function by playing the role of public prosecutor in criminal cases concerning IP infringement. In addition to enforcement, the AGC is also responsible for international negotiations related to IP. For instance, AGC's International Affairs Division represents Singapore at bilateral and multilateral negotiations, and in international disputes (AGC 2018).

2.3.4 Judicial system: specialised IP court and judges

In addition to traditional civil litigation and criminal prosecution, alternative dispute resolution (ADR) and specialised IP court are two recent trends in Singapore's judicial system related to IP. The World Intellectual Property Organization (WIPO) Arbitration and Mediation Centre collaborates with the Ministry of Law in Singapore to promote the use of ADR in solving IP disputes in Singapore. Alternatively, the Ministry of Law designated the WIPO Centre as a mediation service provider in Singapore (National Archives of Singapore 2017). Based on such consensus, WIPO and the IPOS have developed (i) a mediation option for trademark and patent proceedings and (ii) an expert determination option for patent proceedings pending before IPOS. Both of them are voluntary and follow WIPO rules.[5]

In 2002, Singapore established a specialist IP court within the High Court with four designated IP judges. All IP cases are managed by a designated senior assistant registrar who conducts all pre-trial conferences and hears all summonses for directions applications. A designated assistant registrar is also assigned to each IP case to hear and decide on all interlocutory applications and conduct inquiries for post-trial assessment of damages and accounting of profits. Furthermore, Singapore revised its Constitution (Article 94[4]) in 2014 to allow the appointment of persons for a fixed period whom the Chief Justice considers having appropriate experience and qualifications to be associate judges of the Supreme Court. The Singapore International Commercial Court (SICC), a division of the High Court and part of the Supreme Court of Singapore, was set up in 2015. All appeals from the SICC will be heard by the Court of Appeal of Singapore. The Singapore High Court judges and international judges of the Supreme Court may be designated by the Chief Justice to hear cases in the SICC. The Chief Justice and judges of appeal may also hear cases in the SICC.

2.4 IPR standards under free trade agreements

According to Enterprise Singapore, Singapore has signed 25 free trade agreements (FTAs) by the end of 2020, the latest one being the Regional Comprehensive Economic Partnership (RCEP) signed in November 2020. Table 2.2 overviews the Singapore FTAs. Considering the scope of this chapter, we will not elaborate on each FTA but analyse the FTAs with Singapore's major trading partners,[6] namely, United States (US)–Singapore FTA, Japan–Singapore FTA, Korea–Singapore FTA, China–Singapore FTA, and the EU–Singapore FTA.

After TRIPS, IP negotiations have been conducted in IP fora, such as the World Trade Organization (WTO) and WIPO, and other multilateral fora, such as the Convention on Biological Diversity that deals with the intersection between IP and other access-related issues (access to medicines, access to knowledge, and access to seeds by farmers) (Helfer 2004). On the other hand, the US has also incorporated IP into its post-TRIPS FTA negotiations

Table 2.2 FTAs of which Singapore is a Party

FTAs as an ASEAN Member (6)

- ASEAN–Australia–New Zealand Free Trade Area
- ASEAN–China Free Trade Area
- ASEAN–India Free Trade Area
- ASEAN–Japan Comprehensive Economic Partnership
- ASEAN–Korea Free Trade Area
- ASEAN Free Trade Area

Other Regional Trade Agreements (4)

- EFTA–Singapore Free Trade Agreement
- GCC–Singapore Free Trade Agreement
- Comprehensive and Progressive Agreement for Trans-Pacific Partnership (CPTPP)
- Regional Comprehensive Economic Partnership (RCEP)

Bilateral FTAs (15)

- China–Singapore Free Trade Agreement
- EU–Singapore Free Trade Agreement
- India–Singapore Comprehensive Economic Cooperation Agreement
- Japan–Singapore Economic Partnership Agreement
- Korea–Singapore Free Trade Agreement
- New Zealand–Singapore Comprehensive Economic Partnership
- Panama–Singapore Free Trade Agreement
- Peru–Singapore Free Trade Agreement
- Singapore–Australia Free Trade Agreement
- Singapore–Costa Rica Free Trade Agreement
- Singapore–Jordan Free Trade Agreement
- Sri Lanka–Singapore Free Trade Agreement
- Turkey–Singapore Free Trade Agreement
- United Kingdom–Singapore Free Trade Agreement
- United States–Singapore Free Trade Agreement

Note: As of 28 February 2021

Source: www.enterprisesg.gov.sg/non-financial-assistance/for-singapore-companies/free-trade-agreements/ftas/overview#

and introduced various TRIPS-plus standards.[7] These two trends of the international IP negotiations in the post-TRIPS era provide two perspectives for the analysis in this section: flexibilities to TRIPS and TRIPS-plus standards in the selected Singapore FTAs.

2.4.1 US–Singapore FTA

After Singapore and the US signed a bilateral FTA in 2003, Singapore amended its domestic laws for compliance. According to the US Congress publication on the three-year assessment on the US–Singapore FTA:

> The FTA provided the impetus for the Singapore government to amend its laws to create one of the strongest IPR regimes in Asia. In July 2004, amendments to the Trademarks Act,[8] the Patents Act, the Layout Designs of Integrated Circuits Act, Registered Designs Act, a new Plant Varieties Protection Act, and a new Manufacture of Optical Discs Act came into effect. This was followed in 2005 by an amended Copyright Act[9] and Broadcasting Act. Singapore also has implemented or ratified various international conventions or treaties dealing with IPRs
>
> (Nanto 2008)

Singaporean officials took a positive attitude towards such an amendment. For instance, they indicated that strengthened IPR protection in Singapore has contributed to attracting foreign direct investment and attracting big pharmaceutical and telecommunication companies to invest and locate their research centre in Singapore (Nanto 2008).

In addition to a commitment to amend domestic legislation, Singapore also acceded to the following multilateral IP treaties following its FTA commitments (date of accession indicated in bracket) (Hsu 2015):

i. The International Convention for the Protection of New Varieties of Plants (30 July 2004)
ii. The WIPO Copyright Treaty (17 April 2005)
iii. The WIPO Performances and Phonograms Treaty (1996) (17 April 2005)
iv. The Hague Agreement Concerning the International Registration of Industrial Designs (17 April 2005)

The US–Singapore FTA is an example of how the US strategically shifts fora for international IP negotiations from the multilateral to the bilateral level (Sell 2011). This FTA includes what the US Trade Representative considers major advances for the US: IP protection (Chapter 16), environment, labour, transparency, and customs cooperation (Nanto 2008). IP is also clearly mentioned as a form of asset that has the characteristic of investment.[10]

Table 2.3 illustrates the significant differences between the US–Singapore FTA and TRIPS. These TRIPS-plus provisions have made Singapore one of the jurisdictions with the highest level of IP protection in the world.

Table 2.3 Comparison of IP Standards between US–Singapore FTA and TRIPS

Issues	*US–Singapore FTA*	*TRIPS*
Term for copyright protection	Life of author plus 70 years.	Life of author plus 50 years.
Technological protection measures	Adequate protection against acts of circumvention. Ban on circumvention devices. Civil liability in case of wilful infringement. Criminal liability in case of wilful infringement for commercial purposes. Non-profit libraries, archives, educational institutions, as well as acts related to reverse engineering, troubleshooting, protection of minors, computer or network security, and lawfully authorised government activities can be exempted.	No provision on this issue.
Liability of Internet service providers	Limited liability of Internet service providers on the condition that they block infringing content upon notification by the copyright holder.	No provision on this issue.
Patent term extension due to delays in examination	Extension is given for delays caused by the regulatory approval process. Also, an extension is given when a delay in the granting of the patent exceeds four years from the filing of the application.	20 years, no extension is provided.
Compulsory licences	Compulsory licences limited to national emergencies, as an anti-trust remedy, and for public non-commercial use.	More broadly permitted on the condition that before unauthorised use, the proposed user has made efforts to obtain authorisation from the rights holder on reasonable commercial terms and conditions and that such efforts have not been successful within a reasonable period. National emergency is a condition for waiving the above-mentioned requirement.

(*Continued*)

Table 2.3 (Continued)

Issues	*US–Singapore FTA*	*TRIPS*
Linkage between patent and drug marketing approval	Marketing approval of a generic drug is prohibited during the patent term unless authorised by the patent owner.	No provision on this issue.
Data exclusivity	Data exclusivity for five years. Also, where drug regulators rely on foreign marketing approvals, data exclusivity applies automatically at home.	No provision on this issue. Test data and other data are protected as undisclosed information under Art. 39.3 TRIPs.
Parallel imports of patented products	Patent holders may limit parallel imports of pharmaceutical products through licensing contracts.	None of its provisions, except those dealing with non-discrimination ('national treatment' and 'most-favoured-nation treatment'), can be used to address the issue of exhaustion of IPR in a WTO dispute.
Institutional flexibilities in IPR enforcement	Resource constraints cannot be invoked as an excuse for not complying with specific enforcement obligations.	TRIPS imposes no extra obligation for the distribution of resources as between enforcement of IPR and the enforcement of the law, in general.
Scope of border measures	Imported, exported, and transiting goods.	Imported goods.
Civil and administrative procedures	Obligation to fine infringers of copyright and trademark rights irrespective of the injury suffered by rights holders.	No such obligations.
Criminal procedures and remedies	Criminal procedures apply in case of wilful infringements, not only for a financial gain.	Criminal procedures and penalties shall be applied for wilful trademark counterfeiting or copyright piracy on a commercial scale. Members may provide for criminal procedures and penalties in other cases of IPR infringement, particularly where they are committed wilfully and on a commercial scale.

Source: Authors.

2.4.2 Japan–Singapore economic partnership agreement (EPA)

The Japan–Singapore EPA was signed in 2002. The IP chapter has only two pages, and its provisions are more flexible and oriented towards cooperation. For instance, the objective states that the two parties aim to develop cooperation in IP.[11] The first article in the IP chapter is about areas and forms of cooperation. It also gives priority to institution building. A joint committee on IP is established to facilitate the IP chapter's effective implementation (Article 97). It also emphasises facilitation for the use of the IP database (Article 98). The only 'hard' provision in this EPA is Article 98.1, which provides that 'Singapore shall, in accordance with its laws and regulations, take appropriate measures to facilitate the patenting process of an application filed in Singapore that corresponds to an application filed in Japan.'

Also, IP provisions in this FTA are more 'TRIPS defence' rather than 'TRIPS-plus'. For instance, Article 75.1 (f)(b) provides that TRIPS-compliant practices concerning IP are exempted from the prohibited performance requirement regarding the establishment, acquisition, expansion, management, operation, maintenance use, or possession of investment. Again, Article 86 also provides that national treatment in respect of IP rights is only applicable to the extent provided in TRIPS.

Like the US–Singapore FTA, IPR is also defined as categories of investment,[12] and specific types of IP are listed.[13]

2.4.3 Korea–Singapore FTA

Korea and Singapore signed their FTA in 2005. The IP chapter is also simple, with some provisions similar to the Japan–Singapore EPA. For instance, the provisions are TRIPS defence in nature. On enforcement, this FTA provides that 'the Parties shall, consistent with the TRIPS Agreement, provide for the enforcement of IPRs in their respective laws' (Article 17.3). It also focuses on facilitating cooperation in the area of IP (Article 17.5) and institution building (a joint committee to be established to facilitate implementation) (Article 17.9). It further includes a similar provision on patent filing facilitation as in the Japan–Singapore EPA.

One prominent provision in this FTA is the requirement for Singapore to designate the Korean IP Office (KIPO) as International Searching Authority (ISA) and International Preliminary Examination Authority (IPEA) under the Patent Cooperation Treaty (PCT). Although KIPO is one of the five biggest IP offices globally, along with the US Patent and Trademark Office, European Patent Office, Japan Patent Office, and the National Intellectual Property Administration of China (also known as the Chinese Patent Office), it is not the only one in East Asia. This designation did benefit Korea. However, from 2015, Singapore itself has become qualified as an ISA and IPEA under the PCT.

2.4.4 China–Singapore FTA

The 2010 bilateral FTA between China and Singapore did not mention IP. Since both countries are WTO members and are TRIPS signatories, not mentioning IP in an FTA means that TRIPS standards will automatically apply. When both parties upgraded their FTA in 2018, IP was not incorporated in the FTA either.

2.4.5 EU–Singapore FTA

The EU and Singapore signed their FTA in 2018. This FTA is not yet implemented. Its text has geographical indications (GIs) as one of the prominent issues. During the TRIPS negotiations, the EU attempted to establish a sui generis system to protect the GIs. However, the 'New World' countries led by the US contested this agenda. At the end of the TRIPS negotiations, GIs are protected at different levels: Article 22 provides a 'standard' form of protection for general products. In contrast, Article 23 provides stronger protection for wines and spirits. The difference between the two is that, according to Article 23 of the TRIPS Agreement, qualifiers such as 'kind', 'style', or 'like' cannot be used in the indication of the products. The EU started its negotiations of the deep-integration FTAs in 2006. The major objective for GI negotiation is to extend Article 23–level protection beyond wines and spirits, particularly agricultural products and foodstuffs. Specifically, the EU–Singapore FTA established a list of GIs for mutual recognition (Article 10.17). However, GIs' recognition is not 'mutual' as the EU listed 194 of its GIs to be protected in Singapore, while Singapore listed zero. Another objective of the EU is to give the GIs priority over trademarks.

2.4.6 Summary

In summary, Singapore is at the importing, rather than the exporting, end of IP regulation through FTAs. It has accepted high-level IP standards from the US and the EU but is not imposing higher standards on other countries (at least in the five FTAs we examined in this chapter). It defends TRIPS standards in its FTAs with China, Japan, and Korea. After the EU–Singapore FTA, the Intellectual Property (Border Enforcement) Act on 9 July 2018 implemented new treaty commitments concerning border measures. Major changes in the law empower customs offices to seize goods imported to and exported from Singapore upon request from rights holders. Previously, rights holders can only confiscate goods in the importation stage (Tan 2018).

2.5 Singapore's IP performance: making Singapore a brand

2.5.1 Ranked high in various IP-related indexes

As mentioned in Section 2.1, companies in Singapore are generally located at both ends of the smiling curve and, therefore, prioritise applications for patents, designs (related to R&D), and trademarks (related to branding and marketing). This section examines Singapore's overall IP performance. Instead of exploring individual parameters such as patent application, patent granting, and trademark registration, we analysed more systematic and complicated indexes, which will reveal the country's IP performance more comprehensively. In general, Singapore's IP performance is recognised as having achieved the highest protection level and established the most efficient supporting bureaucratic system. Specifically, it has been ranked high in various IP-related indexes (IPOS 2018):

i. *World Economic Forum's Global Competitiveness Report 2018*: Singapore is ranked third globally and top in Asia for having the best IP protection.
ii. *International Property Rights Index*:[14] Singapore is ranked fifth in the world. The index measures the strength of a country's property rights regime, including both intellectual and physical property rights.
iii. *US Global Intellectual Property Center's International IP Index 2018*: Singapore is ranked ninth in the world for its IP environment.
iv. *Bloomberg 2018 Innovation Index*: Singapore is ranked third in the world. The index scores economies using factors, including R&D spending and the concentration of high-tech public companies.
v. *Global Innovation Index 2018* by WIPO: Singapore is ranked the fifth most innovative nation globally and top in Asia. Singapore is ranked first in the world on the Innovation Input Sub-Index.

This part will first examine two of Singapore's IP performance indexes in more detail: WIPO's Global Innovation Index and the International IP index published by the US Chamber of Commerce. At the end, the performance of Singapore and other major ASEAN economies (Indonesia, Malaysia, and Thailand) will be compared and analysed to exhibit the uniqueness of Singapore in IP performance in the region.

WIPO's *Global Innovation Index 2018* measured both the input and output of innovation. The input indicators included institutions, human capital and research, infrastructure, market sophistication, and business sophistication. The outcome indicators included knowledge and technology outputs and creative outputs (WIPO 2018). Singapore ranked fifth among the 47 high-income countries and is the most innovative country in Southeast Asia and Oceania. Singapore's strengths can be found in the areas of institutions (first), human capital and research (first), and business sophistication (second). In particular, in terms of business sophistication, Singapore ranked very high in IP payments (first) and foreign direct investment inflows (first). An effective IP legal system guarantees these strengths and is essential to attracting talents and investment globally. Nonetheless, the weakness of Singapore's innovation system, including its IP system, lies in the creative outputs (or inability to lead to more creative outputs). It is lower than both the income group average and the regional average. It ranked 35th in Creative

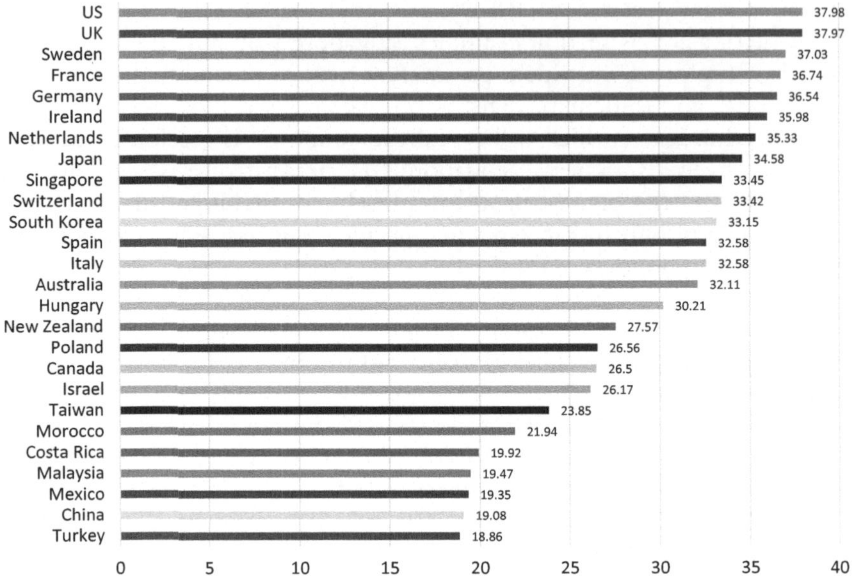

Figure 2.5 US Chamber of Commerce International IP Index 2018, Overall Scores.

Outputs globally for lack of creation from residents of the country. This can be seen in the following indicators: trademarks by origin (88th), industrial designs by origin (62nd), national feature films (38th), and printing and other media (70th).

The sixth annual International IP Index published by the US Chamber of Commerce divided IP performances into eight categories: category 1 – patents, related rights, and limitations; category 2 – copyright, related rights, and limitations; category 3 – trademarks, related rights, and limitations; category 4 – trade secrets and related rights; category 5 – commercialisation of IP assets; category 6 – enforcement; category 7 – systemic efficiency; and category 8 – membership in and ratification of international treaties.

Singapore ranked ninth in the overall scores of the US Chamber International IP Index 2018 (US Chamber of Commerce Global Innovation Policy Center 2018) (Figure 2.5). More specifically, Singapore ranked first in category 1 generally related to patents because of the newly added indicator of the participation in the patent prosecution highways. The IPOS had signed agreements with China, Mexico, and the European Patent Office. Singapore's copyright protection and system efficiency are also very close to the world's top five economies. However, in terms of trademarks, trade secrets, commercialisation of IP assets, and membership in international treaties, there is a gap between Singapore and the world's top five economies. The overall performance of Singapore is higher than the regional average.

2.6 Conclusion

To sum up, we observe a correlation between national IP performance and its position in the GVCs: the higher a country is located at the U curve, the higher its level of IP performance and vice versa. However, we do not have further evidence to establish a causal relationship between these two variables: whether higher IP protection causes a country or a firm to occupy a more profitable place in a GVC.

This correlation is complicated if we also consider the factor of foreign direct investment (FDI). The Southeast Asian countries and China have become the world's factory since the 1980s. Getting involved in the GVC has brought these countries large FDI inflows. They were also required to enhance their local capacities in various aspects. IP has been an essential prerequisite in the package of capacity building. The US has used various tools unilaterally (e.g. Special 301 Reports), bilaterally (incorporating IP into its FTAs), and multilaterally (framing IP as a trade-related issue and building it as a pillar of the WTO) to promote global IP standards.

It is crucial for developing Asian countries to think about their positions in the GVCs more strategically, particularly how to enhance their local capabilities required to sustain their long-term competitiveness. Taking from the Singaporean lesson, strategies that enable developing Asian countries to climb the smiling curve could include education and training of young people and IP specialists (patent examiners, patent attorneys, and IP lawyers and judges); functional and corruption-free legal system; responsive parliament to align statutory laws with current regional and global status; clear vision in negotiating and signing bilateral and regional trade agreements; governance transparency and long-term stability; favourable tax incentives; and a system to capture the best talents in the world, starting from the universities. Especially for other ASEAN countries, manufacturing activities are essential as they generate employment and trigger people's movement from rural to urban areas. Even Singapore has not abandoned or neglected this area and is moving towards smart manufacturing.

Notes

1 However, undoubtedly manufacturing secures middle-class jobs and creates networks of related industries (e.g. automobiles. For more discussion, see Kung-Chung Liu and Uday Racherla (eds.), *Innovation, Economic Development, and Intellectual Property in China and India – Comparing Six Economic Sectors* [Springer 2019]). Smart manufacturing could especially raise the bottom of the U curve upwards, closer to the other two ends. That is why India is promoting 'Make in India', and China has unveiled 'Made in China 2025'.

2 Literature on regulatory theories is abundant, see Drahos (2017). In the context of this chapter which focuses on global governance beyond states, regulation refers broadly to the means that guides individuals or institutions to behave according to formal or informal rules (Picciotti 2002).

3 According to Fujita (2018), foreign value-added indicates what part of a country's gross export comprises inputs that have been produced in other countries. The foreign value-added share is the share of the country's exports that do not add to its GDP.
4 https://wits.worldbank.org/countryprofile/en/country/SGP/startyear/1990/endyear/1994/indicator/NY-GDP-PCAP-CD
5 Specifically, the expert determination follows the WIPO Expert Determination Rules while the mediation follows the WIPO Mediation Rules.
6 According to Workman (2018), the major trading partners of Singapore are China: US$54 billion (14.5% of total Singapore exports); Hong Kong: $46 billion (12.3%); Malaysia: $39.6 billion (10.6%); Indonesia: $28 billion (7.5%); United States: $24.2 billion (6.5%); Japan: $17.1 billion (4.6%); Korea: $16.7 billion (4.5%); Taiwan: $16.6 billion (4.4%); Thailand: $14.7 billion (3.9%); Viet Nam: $12.3 billion (3.3%).
7 For this chapter, TRIPS-plus standards refer to IP standards that provide more extensive protection for IP compared with TRIPS or eliminate the flexibilities that are otherwise available in TRIPS.
8 In the area of trademarks, the amendment includes: (i) non-visual marks – a change in the definition of a trademark to remove the requirement of visual perceptibility as a precondition for registration. It is a TRIPS-plus standard in a sense that it eliminated a flexibility that is otherwise included in TRIPS; (ii) the addition of provisions on the dilution of marks – in the area of enforcement, the remedy of statutory damages was introduced. This often applies to cases where actual losses arising from the infringement may be difficult to prove or an account of profits equally difficult to obtain. Trademarks Act (Chapter 332) (Original Enactment: Act 46 of 1998), Revised Edition 2005. https://sso.agc.gov.sg/Act/TMA1998.
9 Most prominently, the copyright term is extended from 50 years to 70 years after the author's death.
10 Article 15.1 of the US–Singapore FTA recognises the following forms of investment: an enterprise; shares, stocks, and other forms of equity participation in an enterprise; bonds, debentures, and debt instruments and loans; futures, options, and other derivatives; turnkey, construction, management, production, concession, revenue-sharing, and other similar contracts; IPRs; licences, authorisations, permits, and similar rights conferred pursuant to applicable domestic law; and other tangible or intangible, movable or immovable property, and related property rights, such as leases, mortgages, liens, and pledges.
11 Article 1(a)(vii) Japan–Singapore EPA.
12 Article 72(a)(vi) Japan–Singapore EPA.
13 Article 72(a)(vi) provides that IPR includes trademarks, industrial designs, layout designs of integrated circuits, copyright, patents, trade names, indications of source or geographical indications, and undisclosed information.
14 The *International Property Rights Index* is the flagship publication of Property Rights Alliance. Available at: https://www.internationalpropertyrightsindex.org/.

Bibliography

AGC (2018), 'Overview of Functions', Last modified 8 October 2018, https://www.agc.gov.sg/our-roles/international-law-advisor/overview-of-functions2 (accessed 22 January 2019).

Baldwin, R. (2013), 'Global Supply Chains: Why They Emerged, Why They Matter, and Where They are Going', in D.K. Elms and P. Low (eds.), *Global Value Chains in a Changing World*. Geneva: WTO Publications, pp. 13–60.

BBC (2019), 'Dyson to Move Head Office to Singapore', https://www.bbc.com/news/business-46962093 (accessed 22 January 2019).

Chen, S-H. (2004), 'Taiwanese IT Firms' Offshore R&D in China and the Connection with the Global Innovation Network', *Research Policy*, 33(2), pp. 337–349.

De Backer, K. and S. Miroudot (2013), 'Mapping Global Value Chains', *OECD Trade Policy Papers* No. 159, Paris: OECD. doi: 10.1787/5k3v1trgnbr4-en.

Dedrick, J., K.L. Kraemer and G. Linden (2010), 'Who Profits from Innovation in Global Value Chains?: A Study of the iPod and Notebook PCs', *Industrial and Corporate Change*, 19(1), pp. 81–116.

Drahos, P. (2017), *Regulatory Theory: Foundations and Applications.* Canberra: ANU Press.

EDB Singapore (2017), 'Singapore Business Environment: Singapore Today', https://www.edb.gov.sg/content/dam/edbsite/news-and-resources/resources/singapore-business-environment/Singapore%20Business%20Environment%20-%20Singapore%20Today(June2017).pdf

EDB Singapore (2018), 'Medical Technology', https://www.edb.gov.sg/en/our-industries/medical-technology.html (accessed 22 January 2019).

Fujita, M. (2018), 'Global Value Chains in ASEAN: Singapore. ASEAN-Japan Centre', https://www.asean.or.jp/ja/wp-content/uploads/sites/2/Singapore-GVC_Paper-9.pdf (accessed 22 January 2019).

Helfer, L. (2004), 'Regime Shifting: The TRIPs Agreement and New Dynamics of International Intellectual Property Lawmaking', *Yale Journal of International Law*, 29, p. 1.

Heritage Foundation (2018), 'Index of Economic Freedom', http://www.heritage.org/index/country/singapore (accessed 22 January 2019).

Hsu, L. (2015), 'Free Trade Agreements: Singapore Legal Developments', *Research Collection School of Law*, https://ink.library.smu.edu.sg/cgi/viewcontent.cgi?article=4770&context=sol_research (accessed 22 January 2019).

IPOS (2018), 'Singapore's IP Ranking', https://www.ipos.gov.sg/about-ipos/singapore-ip-ranking (accessed 23 January 2019).

Jack, S. (2018), 'Dyson Chooses Singapore for New Electric Car Plant', *BBC News*, 23 October, https://www.bbc.com/news/business-45950377 (accessed 22 January 2019).

Kraemer, K., G. Linden and J. Dedrick (2011), 'Capturing Value in Global Networks: Apple's iPad and iPhone', https://pdfs.semanticscholar.org/9cb5/262a46e7c9131de43433b7c5f9b65386f8e2.pdf (accessed 22 January 2019).

Li, S., C. Hao and E.G. Pleggenkuhle-Miles (2010), 'Moving Upward in Global Value Chains: The Innovations of Mobile Phone Developers in China', *Chinese Management Studies*, 4(4), pp. 305–321.

MediaTek (2017), *Annual Report.* Taipei: MediaTek. https://cdn-www.mediatek.com/page/2017-English-Annual-Report_Final.pdf (accessed 22 January 2019).

Ministry of Law (2018), 'Intellectual Property Policy', https://www.mlaw.gov.sg/content/minlaw/en/our-work/intellectual-property-policy.html (accessed 22 January 2019).

Morck, R., B. Yeung and M. Zhao (2008), 'Perspectives on China's Outward Foreign Direct Investment', *Journal of International Business Studies*, 39(3), pp. 337–350.

Mudambi, R. (2008), 'Location, Control, and Innovation in Knowledge-Intensive Industries', *Journal of Economic Geography*, 8(5), pp. 699–725.

National Archives of Singapore (2017), 'Mediation Act to commence from 1 November 2017', Press Release, https://www.nas.gov.sg/archivesonline/data/

pdfdoc/20171101009/Mediation%20Act%20to%20take%20effect%20from%20 1%20November%202017.pdf (accessed 20 February 2021).

Nanto, D. (2008), 'The US-Singapore Free Trade Agreement: Effects after Three Years', *CRC Report for Congress*, 7 January 2008, https://fas.org/sgp/crs/row/RL34315.pdf (accessed 22 January 2019).

Picciotti, S. (2002), 'Introduction: Reconceptualizing Regulation in the Era of Globalization', *Journal of Law and Society*, 29(1), pp. 1–11. doi: 10.1111/1467-6478.00208.

Qualcomm (2018), *Annual Report*. https://investor.qualcomm.com/static-files/bde24726-605c-4118-92db-7190e0f58e53 (accessed 22 January 2019).

Qualcomm (2017), 'Qualcomm and TDK Announce Launch of Joint Venture', *San Diego Business Journal*, 5 February, https://www.sdbj.com/news/2017/feb/05/qualcomm-tdk-launch-joint-rf-venture/ (accessed 22 January 2019).

Sell, S. (2011), 'TRIPS Was Never Enough: Vertical Forum Shifting, FTAS, ACTA, and TTP', *Journal of Intellectual Property Law*, 18(2), p. 447.

Shin, N., K.L. Kraemer and J. Dedrick (2012), 'Value Capture in the Global Electronics Industry: Empirical Evidence for the "Smiling Curve" Concept', *Industry and Innovation*, 19(2), pp. 89–107.

Tan, S-A. (2018), 'Parliament: More Powers for Customs Officers to Seize Goods that Infringe Intellectual Property Rights', *The Straits Times*, 9 July 2018, https://www.straitstimes.com/politics/parliament-more-powers-for-customs-officers-to-seize-goods-that-infringe-intellectual (accessed 22 January 2019).

Timmer, M.P., A. Erumban, B. Los, R. Stehrer and G. de Vries (2014), 'Slicing Up Global Value Chains', *The Journal of Economic Perspectives*, 28(2), pp. 99–118.

Toh, M-H. (2017), 'Singapore's Participation in Global Value Chains: Perspectives of Trade in Value Added', in L.Y. Ing and F. Kimura, (eds.), *Production Networks in Southeast Asia*. New York: Routledge, pp. 138–160.

US Chamber of Commerce Global Innovation Policy Center (2018), *US Chamber International IP Index*, 6th edition, http://globalipcenter.wpengine.com/wp-content/uploads/2018/02/GIPC_IP_Index_2018.pdf (accessed 22 January 2019).

Wang, L.P. and F. Jia (2010), *Analysis on Supply Chain of Manufacturing Enterprise Product Service System, Emergency Management and Management Sciences (ICEMMS), 2010 IEEE International Conference* on 8–10 August 2010, Beijing, China.

World Bank (2018), 'Ease of Doing Business Rankings', http://www.doingbusiness.org/en/rankings (accessed 21 January 2019).

World Intellectual Property Organization (WIPO) (2018), 'Global Innovation Index: Singapore', p. 20. https://www.wipo.int/edocs/pubdocs/en/wipo_pub_gii_2018-profile42.pdf (accessed 22 January 2019).

Workman, D. (2018), 'Singapore's Top Trading Partners', http://www.worldstopexports.com/singapores-top-import-partners/ (accessed 22 January 2019).

WSJ Asia (2009), 'The Singapore Economic Model Works', https://www.wsj.com/articles/SB123369524433044773 (accessed 20 February 2020).

3 The challenges of digital economy and copyright protection in Indonesia

Poppy S. Winanti

3.1 Introduction

This chapter investigates the impact of the emergence of the digital economy on the protection of intellectual property rights (IPR), particularly copyright. Advanced technology has dramatically disturbed the current understanding of copyright protection. Technology has drastically reduced the cost of creating and distributing copyright work, which has lowered the cost of copyright infringement. This chapter intends to address the following questions: how does the digital economy affect copyright protection in developing countries? And how do the governments of developing countries respond to these challenges? In doing so, this chapter focuses on copyright protection in Indonesia and its policy in dealing with the challenges of today's digital economy. Therefore, this chapter is expected to provide policy recommendations for domestic reform and global rule-setting on IPR protection amid digital economy challenges.

The early 1990s saw the development of digitalisation and digital technologies that mainly refer to the digital economy. This has posed both new opportunities and challenges for global business. The report of the United Nations Conference on Trade and Development (UNCTAD) on information and communications technology (ICT) for development specifies that the new digital economy has emerged from

> ...a combination of technologies, mainly from the ICT space, that are becoming pervasive across mechanical systems, communications, infrastructure, and the built environment, and thus playing an increasingly important role, not only in social and political life, but in research, manufacturing, services, transportation, and even agriculture.
>
> (UNCTAD 2017, p. 2)

Despite this significant change, 'digital economy' has no generally agreed definition (Manyika and Lund 2016; IMF 2018; Gestrin and Staudt 2018). This chapter follows Gestrin and Staudt's definition of 'digital economy' as 'the broader economy as it undergoes the process of becoming increasingly digital' (Gestrin and Staudt 2018, p. 7). This chapter also employs the

DOI: 10.4324/9781003147657-4

IMF definition of digitalisation of economic activity 'as the incorporation of data and the Internet into production processes and products, new forms of household and government consumption, fixed capital formation, cross-border flows, and finance' (IMF 2018, p. 1).

The spread of the digital economy has posed new challenges for IPR protection since the digital economy has changed 'the way the products are created, the nature of products themselves, and how they are distributed' (Krishnan and Chakravarti 1998, p. 9). These may include 'ease of transmission, compactness, and multiple uses that pose problems for traditional IPR systems' (Krishnan and Chakravarti 1998, p. 11). This has created a mismatch between what can be protected under copyright and what is perceived by most people, such as lending a book differs from sharing a digital version of a book (Hargreaves 2011). Välimäki (2001) argued that the rise of the digital economy had created two competing views on IPR, either maximising the rights or the values. These two views reflect the debate between the legal aspect of IPR protection and the values of the strategic use of IPR at the expense of its protection. This chapter discusses further the dilemma faced by a developing country like Indonesia in responding and adapting to these challenges.

The rest of the chapter is organised as follows. Section 3.2 overviews the digital economy and its implications for IPR protection, particularly copyright. Section 3.3 reviews the historical aspect of copyright protection in Indonesia and how it is governed. This section also discusses the legal framework of copyright protection. Section 3.4 discusses Indonesia's policies in enhancing the digital economy and the contributions of the digital economy and copyright-based industries for economic development. Section 3.5 assesses the enforcement of copyright protection and Indonesia's performance in copyright protection compared to other ASEAN members. The last section concludes the discussion by highlighting the main findings and formulating policy recommendations for domestic reform on IPR protection in response to the digital economy.

3.2 Understanding the digital economy and its implications for copyright protection

As one of the IPR types, copyright originated in the printing press, with the assumption that it is not easily transferable (Krishnan and Chakravarti 1998). As briefly explained earlier, the appearance of the digital economy significantly impacts IPR protection, including copyright. Table 3.1 shows the characteristics of the digital economy that have affected IPR protection.

The rise of the digital economy with its characteristics (Table 3.1) has transformed the existing understanding of IPR that mainly focuses on the IPR protection's role to stimulate economic growth by protecting innovators from imitation, which will foster innovation. The digital economy has resulted in radical shifts in 'the ability to reproduce, distribute, control, and publish information' (National Research Council 2000, p. 3). As Ciocoiu

Table 3.1 Intellectual Property-Related Characteristics of the Digital Economy

Characteristics	*Description*	*Impact on IPR Protection*
Replication	The work in digital form can be replicated with nearly zero cost.	It is difficult for copyright owners to exercise control over the replication of their works and obtain compensation for unauthorised replication. This has challenged the principle that IPR rights are exclusive rights.
Ease of transmission, compactness, and multiple uses	Compared to paper versions of the works, digital works can be transmitted and used by multiple users and can be saved in a set of compact discs.	More difficult for copyright owners to exercise control over the transmission of their works and to obtain compensation for unauthorised and multiple uses. The sale of the first electronic copy can destroy the entire market.
Fixation of digital works	Works in digital form are easy and can be quickly modified by users.	The users can customise and modify the copyrighted works and sell them as new works.
Multimedia work	Multimedia work combines several different elements or types of works (text, sound, still images, and moving images) into a single medium.	Works protected by copyright will become less and less differentiated by type and more and more equivalent to one another because they will now be in the same medium.
Many and varied stakeholders	Advanced technology has facilitated the ability to self-publish electronically.	This may change the relations and the interaction between stakeholders, such as authors and traditional publishers.
Multiple actors, motivations, and strategies concerning IP	The traditional model (content produced and sold) is not the only model available with advanced technology. An example is developing an open-source software for enhance the community.	Since the actors are not homogenous, the IP policy must consider the heterogeneity of strategies of diverse actors for handling IP.

Source: Krishnan and Chakravarti (1998, pp. 10–11); National Research Council (2000).

(2011) argued, IPR protection could embrace different aspects in the digital economy since it also represents a digital right, network access, free speech, and cybernetic security. The digital era poses new threats for the existing copyright industries, which entail high fixed costs, such as newspapers and television. In the digital age, alternative ways of accessing content, which used to be the monopoly of those content industries, are widely available (WIPO 2015). With the growing significance of ICT, the context in which

IP operates has been extensively changed, including the characteristic of IPR rights as exclusive rights (OECD 2017). Under these circumstances, the ancient principles of IP protection, developed in a completely different technological context, may not be suitable in an emerging environment.

Consequently, new conceptual IPR protection arrangements are needed to regulate intellectual activities on the Internet (Ciocoiu 2011). In other words, IPR protection is not only about balancing between the protection of IPR owners' interests and the smooth diffusion of innovation for society. The existing IPR systems also need to be adjusted to respond to these new circumstances brought by advanced ICT.

3.3 An overview of copyright protection in Indonesia

This section overviews copyright protection in Indonesia. It discusses historical and cultural aspects, the mechanism under which copyright protection is governed, and the explanation of the legal framework of copyright protection.

3.3.1 The historical and cultural context of copyright protection in Indonesia[1]

This section discusses the historical and cultural background of IPR protection in Indonesia. It is important to illustrate that IPR protection did not have strong roots in the history of Indonesia's national laws before the Agreement on Trade-Related Aspects of Intellectual Property Rights (TRIPS Agreement) (Winanti 2011). Winanti (2011) further argued that IPR protection was mainly alien to Indonesia's national legislation before TRIPS. The main reason is that copyright protection conflicts with Indonesia's traditions and norms on IPR. Although IP legislation can date back to colonial period in 1844, those laws introduced under the Dutch colonial rule did not apply to native Indonesians.[2] Under the Dutch colonial rule, the indigenous Indonesians' legal system was *adat* (an extensive system of Indonesian customary norms), which did not recognise IPR protection. As a consequence, no Indonesian legal tradition protected IPR.

Winanti (2011) also argued that under unwritten *adat*, individual ownership of intellectual works or inventions is not recognised because knowledge is regarded as public property, and its main function is to benefit the public. Furthermore, since knowledge is also considered the common heritage of humankind, most traditions in Indonesian communities view that knowledge should be freely accessible and available to all (Butt 2008; Kusumadara n.d.). Such a notion conflicted with the Western-industrialised countries' tradition, which acknowledged IPR as part of individual rights (Gutowski 1999).

Winanti (2011) also explained that unlike the traditions of Western-industrialised countries, which regard commercialisation as the incentive for creativity, most Indonesian traditional communities prohibit the commercialisation of creative works because of their spiritual element; they are symbols of dedication and contribution to the community (Butt 2008). In this context, creative and innovative activities are considered part of the individual contribution to society's cultural and economic development. *Adat* also recognises that creativity and invention can be developed through the social benefits of creative work instead of material benefits for individual owners. In this regard, creativity and innovation are encouraged not through IP protection but the rapid and free dissemination of the invention and knowledge to society (Kusumadara n.d.). Winanti, therefore, concluded that this kind of norm is also contrary to the common understanding in Western-industrialised societies, which believe that material benefits from strong IPR protection are necessary to foster creativity and innovation (Marron and Steel 2000).

Unlike the Dutch Patent Act of 1910, which was formally abolished, the Indonesian government retained the Dutch Copyright Act of 1912 after independence. However, due to unstable economic and political conditions, this law was never effectively implemented. Furthermore, the Indonesian government, unable to fulfil its obligations due to the country's economic situation, formally withdrew its membership in the Berne Convention of 1958. As a newly independent developing country, the government argued that, if it retained its membership in the Berne Convention, Indonesia could not pay royalties to foreign copyright holders (Suwanto 1993). Considering the country's poor condition, the government also argued that society could copy expensive books freely to improve the quality of education (Antons 2000). This means that, as Winanti (2011) assessed, after independence until the early 1980s, Indonesia did not have any effective regulations concerning copyright protection, nor did it commit to any international obligation to provide for such purpose. As will be explained shortly, a significant change in copyright protection occurred only a few years later when the government amended its copyright law again in 1997 to respond to its TRIPS obligations.

3.3.2 Legal framework on copyright protection in Indonesia

Indonesia's first legal framework on copyright protection, Law No. 6, was introduced in 1982. This law was amended four times: in 1987 under Law No. 7; in 1997 under Law No. 12; in 2002 under Law No. 19; and the last one was enacted in 2014 under Law No. 28. The government also issued Presidential Decree No. 18/1997 to ratify the Berne Convention for the Protection of Literary and Artistic Works, invalidating its withdrawal in 1958. In the same year, the government ratified the WIPO Copyright Treaty through Presidential Decree No. 19/1997.

The first two laws on copyright in Indonesia did not meet the minimum requirement under the TRIPS Agreement. This also reveals that, as in many governments of developing countries, copyright protection was not the government's priority before the TRIPS Agreement. Indonesia's interest in copyright protection was mainly influenced by the TRIPS Agreement

Table 3.2 Indonesian Legal Framework on Copyright

		Before and During TRIPS Negotiations		*After Joining TRIPS*		
Items	*TRIPS Obligations*	*Before Negotiations (No. 6/1982)*	*During Negotiations (No. 7/1987)*	*During Transition (No. 12/1997)*	*After Enforcement (No. 19/2002)*	*After Enforcement (No. 28/2014)*
Subject matter coverage	Scientific, literary, and artistic works	Protected	Protected	Protected	Protected	Protected
	Computer programs, video recording, sound recording	Not protected	Protected	Protected	Protected	Protected
	Rental rights	Not protected	Not protected	Protected	Protected	Protected
	Related rights	Not protected	Not protected	Protected	Protected	Protected
	Database and optical discs	Not protected	Not protected	Not protected	Protected	Protected
Duration of protection other than photographic work and applied art	Life of author +50 years	Life of author +25 years	Life of author +50 years	Life of author +50 years	Life of author +50 years	Life of author +70 years
Duration of protection for performers and producers of phonograms	50 years	Not protected	Not protected	50 years	50 years	50 years

(*Continued*)

		Before and During TRIPS Negotiations		*After Joining TRIPS*		
Items	*TRIPS Obligations*	*Before Negotiations (No. 6/1982)*	*During Negotiations (No. 7/1987)*	*During Transition (No. 12/1997)*	*After Enforcement (No. 19/2002)*	*After Enforcement (No. 28/2014)*
Duration of protection for broadcasting organisations	20 years	Not protected	Not protected	20 years	20 years	20 years
Duration of protection for computer programs	50 years	Not protected	15 years	50 years	50 years	50 years
Eligible copyright holders	National treatment and Most-favoured-nation (MFN) principles	Only for Indonesian citizens and foreign works where the first publication of the creation took place in Indonesia	Granted national treatment and MFN principles	Granted national treatment and MFN principles	Granted national treatment and MFN principles	Granted national treatment and MFN principles
Enforcement	Requires civil and criminal enforcement but no minimum requirements	Included provisions for enforcement	Included provisions for enforcement	Included provisions for enforcement	Included provisions for enforcement	Included provisions for enforcement
TRIPS Compatibility	--	TRIPS-minus	TRIPS-minus	TRIPS-minimum	TRIPS-minimum	Beyond TRIPS

Source: Winanti (2011, 2019).

negotiations under the multilateral trading system in the late 1980s. With the enactment of Copyright Law No. 19/2002, Indonesia then started to display its interest in copyright protection and complied with its obligations under TRIPS.

The latest Copyright Law (No. 28/2014) can be regarded as beyond the TRIPS Agreement as it extends the duration and the scope of protected copyright. Law No. 28/2014 has several improvements compared to Law No. 19/2002. These include the coverage of copyright, the extension of copyright protection, and, more importantly, more detailed additional provisions regarding electronic information. Law No. 19/2002 covered only 12 items protected by copyright, but the most recent law covers 19 items:

i. Books, pamphlets, the layout of written published materials, and all other written materials
ii. Public talks, lectures, speeches, and other related creations
iii. Display tools made for education and science purposes
iv. Songs or music with or without lyrics
v. Dramas or musical dramas, dances, choreography, puppet shows, and pantomimes
vi. Art in all forms, such as paintings, pictures, carving, calligraphy, sculpture, and collage
vii. Applied arts
viii. Architecture
ix. Maps
x. Batik art or other patterns
xi. Photography
xii. Images
xiii. Cinematography
xiv. Translation, interpretation, adaptation, anthology, database, and other creations for the transferring of forms
xv. Translation, adaptation, arrangement, transformation, or modification of traditional cultural expression
xvi. Creation or data compilation, either in a format that a computer program or other media can read
xvii. Collection of traditional cultural expressions during the compilation of an original work
xviii. Video games
xix. Computer programs

Copyright Law No. 28/2014 extends the duration of protection from the author's life plus 50 years to the author's life plus 70 years. The law also extends protection from plus 20 years to 50 years for performers, producers, and broadcasting organisations. This law also incorporates new provisions on the means of control technology (Chapter VII), rights management information (Chapter II), and collective management (Chapters II and XII).

The collective management clause recognises the role of collective management societies in collecting and distributing royalties on copyrighted (and related rights) materials.

Copyright Law No. 19/2002 mentioned electronic information briefly in one article (Article 25.1), stating that electronic information will be protected. However, more detailed electronic information rules will be provided under government regulations. Copyright Law No. 28/2014 provides more guidance on electronic information. Article 7 explains the coverage of electronic information, which includes:

i. A work which appeared and is attached electronically in connection with the announcement of a creation
ii. Creator name, alias, or pseudonym
iii. As the creator of the copyright holder
iv. Period and conditions of use of a work
v. Number
vi. Information code

Chapter VII of Copyright Law No. 28/2014 contains provisions on 'means of control technology'. This chapter comprising three articles protects the 'means of control technology' that function to protect copyright and related rights. Chapter VII, Article 52.1 states that it is prohibited to damage, destroy, and eliminate the control of the technology used to protect copyright and related rights. Chapter VIII of Copyright Law No. 18/2014 covers provisions to protect the content of copyright and related rights in ICT. This chapter comprises three articles and contains provisions to prevent violations of copyright and related rights through technology-based information. Under this law, the Minister of Telecommunication and Information, with sufficient evidence, has the right to close down part or all of an Internet website's content that violates the electronic system's copyright or makes the electronic system service inaccessible. Within 14 days of the closure, the minister shall request a court warrant.

Another legal framework relating to copyright protection is Law No. 11/2008 on Electronic Information and Transaction. Even though this law, in principle, was enacted to deal with security and legal certainty on the use of Internet and electronic transactions, it also contains a chapter on copyright protection related to electronic information. The law defines electronic information

> as one or a collection of electronic data, including, but not limited to, writings, sounds, pictures, maps, designs, photos, electronic data interchange, electronic mails, telegram, telex, telecopy or the like, characters, symbols, or numbers, which have meanings or can be understood by people.
>
> (Chapter 1, Article 1.1)

An electronic transaction is defined as 'a legal act that is committed by the use of computers, computer networks, and/or other electronic media' (Chapter 1, Article 1.2). A specific reference for copyright protection is mentioned in Chapter VI (Article 25) that states 'electronic Information and/or electronic records that are created into intellectual works, Internet sites, and intellectual works contained therein shall be protected as Intellectual Property Rights under provisions of laws and regulations'.

As briefly discussed, there has been an attempt to expand the legal framework on copyright protection by providing a more detailed explanation of the coverage of electronic information both in Copyright Law No. 28/2014 and Law No. 11/2008 on Electronic Information and Transaction. Copyright Law No. 28/2014 also protects content copyright and related rights in ICT. However, other than these two laws, no other legal framework is available to provide rigorous protection for copyright-based industries. This indicates the Indonesian government's limited response in dealing with new challenges for copyright protection due to the advent and development of the digital economy.

3.3.3 The structure and mechanism of copyright protection administration

The administration of all IPR types in Indonesia, except for plant variety protection administered by the Ministry of Agriculture, is governed by the Ministry of Law and Human Rights. This is different from the common practice of IP administration in ASEAN and other developing countries where the IP office is usually under the jurisdiction of trade and/or commerce and industry-related ministries. The administration of IPR protection in Malaysia is governed by the Intellectual Property Corporation of Malaysia, Ministry of Domestic Trade, Co-operatives, and Consumerism. Similarly, the Department of Intellectual Property in Thailand is administered by the Ministry of Commerce. The administration of all types of IPR in India is governed by the Ministry of Commerce and Industry. In Brazil, copyright is administered by the Copyright and Intellectual Property Office, Ministry of Culture, whereas IP-related industrial property is governed by the National Institute of Industrial Property of the Ministry of Industry, Foreign Trade, and Services. Having almost all IPR protection administered by the Ministry of Law and Human Rights indicates the Indonesian government's stance on IPR protection. IPR protection is seen more as a legal business than a source of creativity and innovation that needs to be encouraged and protected. Consequently, the regulations on IPR protection are designed to ensure compliance and law enforcement instead of promoting creativity and stimulating innovation. The following section explains in more detail how IPR protection is governed in Indonesia.

IPR protection in Indonesia is administered by the Directorate General of Intellectual Property, Ministry of Law and Human Rights. The directorate general is divided into several directorates based on the types of IPR: Directorate of Copyright and Industrial Design; Directorate of Patent,

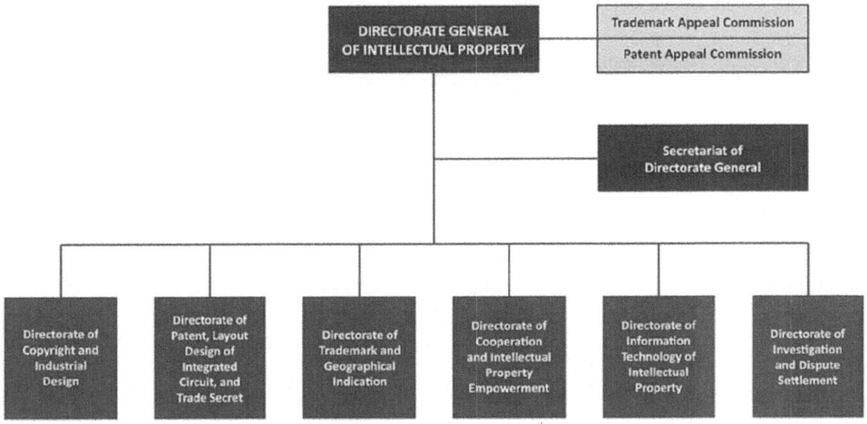

Figure 3.1 Indonesian Administration of IPR Protection.

Layout Design of Integrated Circuit, and Trade Secret; Directorate of Trademark and & Geographical Indication (Figure 3.1). Three other supporting directorates are the Directorate of Cooperation and Intellectual Property Empowerment, Directorate of Information Technology of Intellectual Property, and Directorate of Investigation and Dispute Settlement (Figure 3.1).

Figure 3.2 shows the sub directorates under the Directorate of Copyright and Industrial Design: Sub Directorate Division of Application and Publication, Sub Directorate of Industrial Design and Examination, Sub Directorate of Certificate and Documentation, and Sub Directorate of Legal Affairs and Collective Management Organization.

Like in most countries where no, or only voluntary, registration is required, copyright in Indonesia is also automatically protected. However, copyright registration is advisable to provide legal ownership, especially in the case of infringement. To streamline the procedure, the government introduced online procedures for copyright registration. Its online application is designed to be completed within one business day. However, this time limit is not applicable for fine arts, painting, applied arts, and sculpture, which require further verification (Figure 3.3).

Previous explanation exposes that before the TRIPS Agreement, copyright protection was not considered an important aspect of economic development in Indonesia. This is mainly because copyright protection was not in line with Indonesian society's tradition and culture, which perceives that knowledge should be freely accessible and available. With this understanding, the proliferation of knowledge is a symbol of dedication and contribution to the community. Therefore, the commercialisation of creative works is prohibited. This is different from Western-industrialised countries' tradition, which acknowledges IPR as part of individual rights and commercialisation of knowledge is needed to foster creativity and invention.

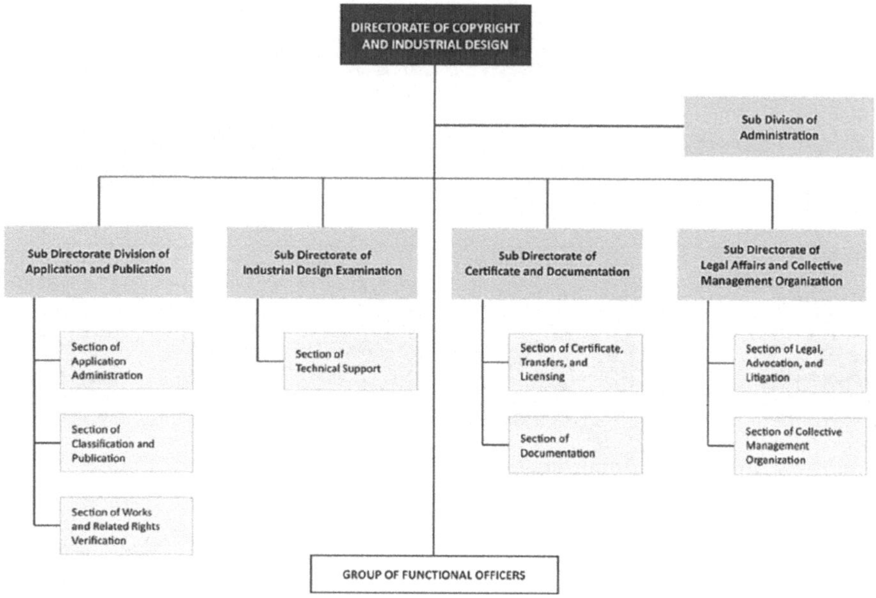

Figure 3.2 Indonesian Administration of Copyright Protection.

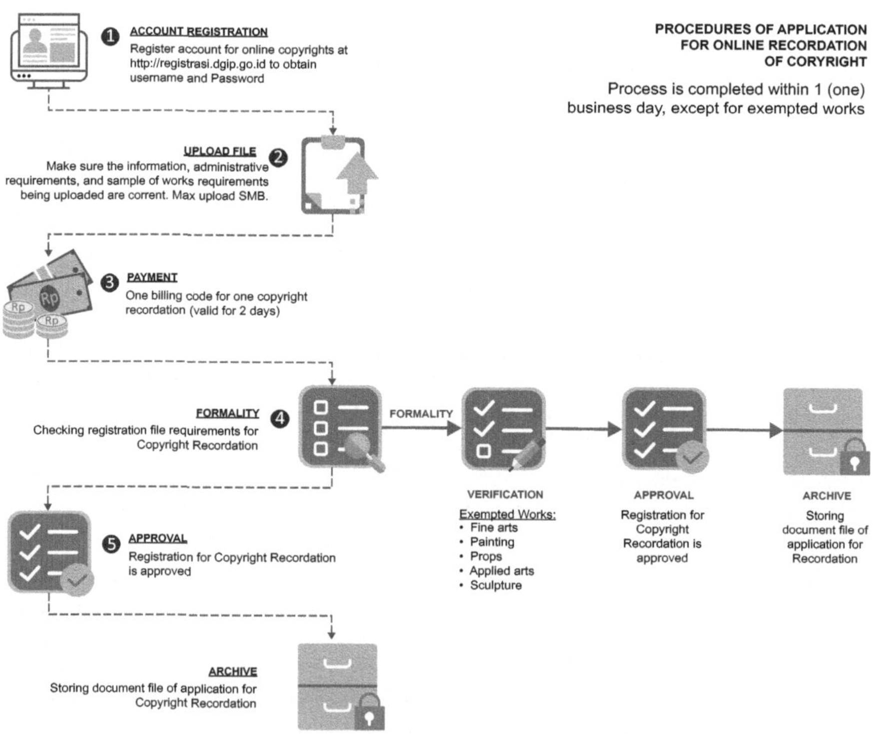

Figure 3.3 Procedures for Copyright Application in Indonesia.

Indonesia's interests in IPR protection, including copyright protection, have changed since the country was obliged to comply with the TRIPS Agreement. Indonesia considers IPR protection mainly its responsibility, as do the member countries of the World Trade Organization (WTO). Therefore, the country's response to its obligation to the TRIPS Agreement is highly influenced by its interests to comply with the TRIPS regime. This stance is also reflected in the design of IP administration in Indonesia managed by the Ministry of Law and Human Rights. Having IP administered by this ministry reflects the government's position towards IPR protection: that it is mainly a legal concern and not one that fosters creativity and innovation.

3.4 Indonesia's policies on the digital economy and the contribution of copyright-based industries for economic development

This section overviews Indonesia's policies on two important aspects related to copyright-based industries: digital economy and creative economy.[3] The government aims for Indonesia to become one of the largest economies by 2030, with the creative economy as its newest economic pillar (Badan 2018b). To achieve this aim, the government established the Indonesian Agency for Creative Economy in 2015, a government institution assigned to develop and foster the creative economy. This section also assesses the contribution of copyright-based industries to the country's economic development. The contribution of these sectors was calculated following the framework of the World Intellectual Property Organization (WIPO) on industry classification. Based on WIPO's framework, copyright-based industries are classified into four groups (WIPO 2015): (i) core copyright industries (industries that are fully engaged in the creation of copyright materials as the primary product);[4] (ii) interdependent copyright industries (industries that support and facilitate the creation of copyright works); (iii) partial copyright industries (industries that partially contribute to the creation of copyright works); and (iv) non-dedicated support industries (industries that facilitate the distribution of copyright works to consumers).

Based on Badan Ekonomi Kreatif (2018b), the creative economy has several sub-sectors: architecture, interior design, visual design, product design, film, animation and video, photography, craft, culinary, music, fashion, application and game developer, publishing, advertising, television and radio, performing arts, and fine arts. All these sub-sectors are copyright-based, and most of them are related to the digital economy.

Data from BPS Statistics Indonesia and the Indonesian Creative Board (Badan Ekonomi Kreatif 2017b) reveal that the creative economy consistently contributed on average around 7.4% to the total gross domestic product (GDP) between 2010 and 2016 (Figure 3.4). The data show that the creative economy's contribution to GDP reached the highest percentage of 7.66% in 2010.

Table 3.3 Indonesia's Sub-sectors of the Creative Economy based on WIPO's Framework on Copyright-Based Industries Classification

Creative Economy Category	*WIPO's Classification*
Architecture	Partial copyright industries
Interior design	Partial copyright industries
Visual design	Core copyright
Product design	Core copyright
Film, animation, and video	Core copyright
Photography	Core copyright
Craft	Partial copyright industries
Culinary	Partial copyright industries
Music	Core copyright
Fashion	Partial copyright industries
Application and game developer	Core copyright
Publishing	Core copyright
Advertising	Core copyright
Television and radio	Core copyright
Performing arts	Core copyright
Fine arts	Core copyright

Source: Author's assessment based on Badan Ekonomi Kreatif (2018b).

Figure 3.4 Contribution of the Creative Economy to Indonesia's GDP, 2010–2016 (%).

Data from the same report also demonstrate that the creative economy's contribution to Indonesia's total export increased from 8.56% in 2010 to 13.77% in 2016 (Figure 3.5). The biggest contribution to Indonesia's total export is from the apparel and/or fashion sub-sector, which reached US$10.90 billion in 2016, followed by craft, culinary, press and literature (Badan Ekonomi Kreatif 2018a).

Data from BPS Statistics Indonesia and the Indonesian Agency for Creative Economy (Badan Ekonomi Kreatif 2017a) confirm that copyright-based

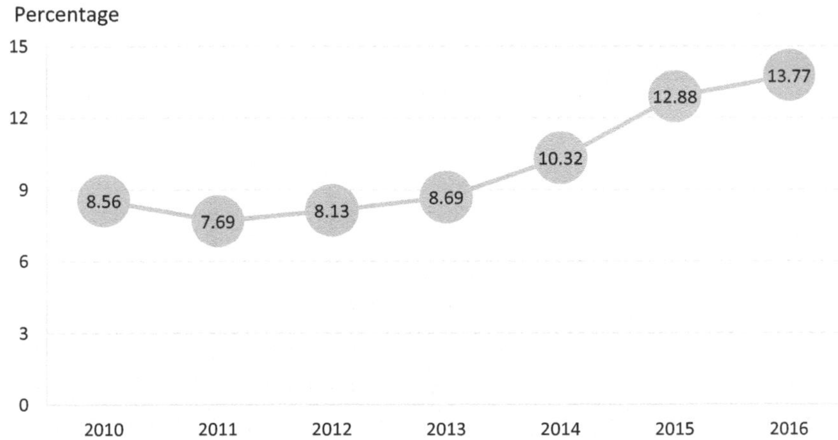

Figure 3.5 Contribution of the Creative Economy to Indonesia's Total Exports, 2010–2016 (%).

industries contribute to around 4% (IDR467 trillion) of Indonesia's total GDP (Table 3.4). The apparel sector (1.34%) has the highest share of the total copyright contribution to GDP. It is followed by handicraft (1.16%), radio and television (0.57%), and press and literature (0.46%). The data also illustrate that more than 8 million people, or 7.6% of total employment, work in these industries. Unfortunately, awareness to protect these creative works under copyright protection is still limited. Data from the Badan

Table 3.4 Contribution of Copyright Industries to Indonesia's GDP

Description of Industry	*Value (in trillion IDR)*	*% (to Indonesia's GDP)*
Total to GDP	467.11	4.04
Press and literature	53.61	0.46
Music, theatrical productions, and operas	6.22	0.05
Motion picture and video	1.36	0.01
Radio and television	66.30	0.57
Photography	3.84	0.03
Software and games	15.08	0.13
Visual and graphic arts	4.43	0.04
Advertising services	6.82	0.06
Apparel	154.68	1.34
Handicraft	133.80	1.16
Architecture	19.60	0.17
Interior design	1.36	0.01

Source: Badan Ekonomi Kreatif (2017b).

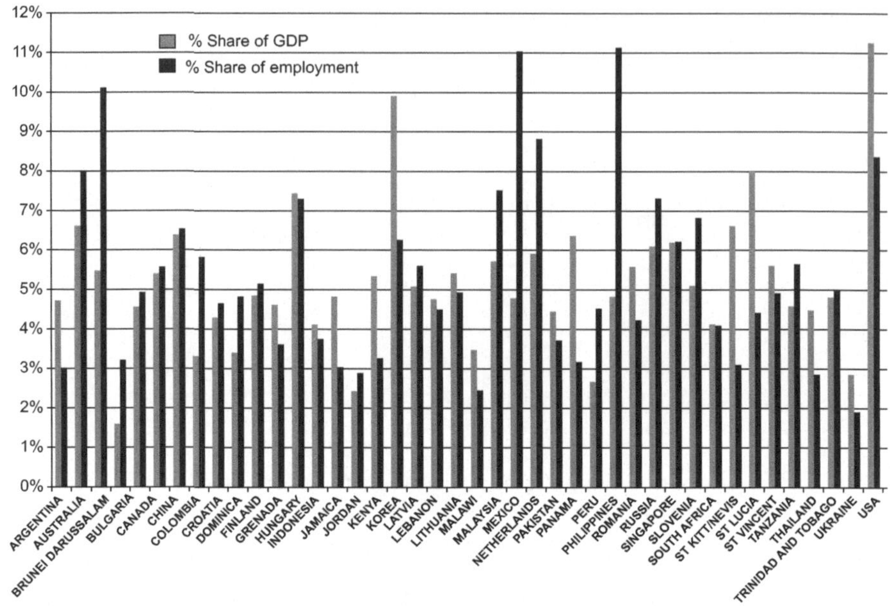

Figure 3.6 Overall Contribution of Copyright Industries to GDP and Employment.

Ekonomi Kreatif (2017b) shows that only around 11% of the total creative economy's work has copyright protection. Film, animation, and video is the biggest sub-sector with copyright protection (21.08%). The second sub-sector with copyright protection is culinary (19.75%), followed by TV and radio (16.59%).

In terms of the overall contribution of copyright industries to GDP and employment, Indonesia's position compared to other ASEAN members is slightly better than Malaysia and Thailand but still below Singapore (Figure 3.6). Compared to the Philippines where the industry contributes to more than 11% of total employment, the industry's contribution to employment in Indonesia is low.

Regarding the contribution of the copyright industries to GDP, Indonesia, along with Thailand and the Philippines, is still below the global average of 5.18% (Figure 3.7). Indonesia's performance is also far below Malaysia and Singapore, which have a higher percentage of copyright contribution to their GDP.

Based on the proportion between the share of GDP and national employment attributed to copyright industries, Indonesia's labour productivity is slightly above the world's average line (Figure 3.8). Compared to the other ASEAN members, Indonesia's labour productivity is lower than Thailand but way ahead of Malaysia, Brunei Darussalam, and the Philippines (WIPO 2014). In terms of the share of copyright-based industries for both GDP and employment, compared to Malaysia and Singapore, however, Indonesia is considered low (WIPO 2014).

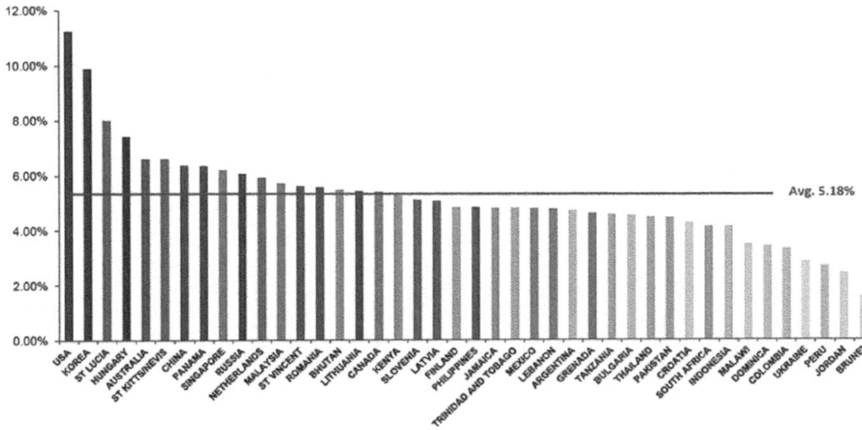

Figure 3.7 Contribution of Copyright Industries to GDP.

The previous discussion explains that the creative economy, which is mostly copyright-related, is growing. During the last decade, the creative economy has contributed to Indonesia's GDP and significantly increased to contribute to total export. Unfortunately, there is still lack of awareness of copyright protection in many industries. This may also be related to the historical and cultural aspects of the Indonesian community, which perceives copyright protection differently. As previously discussed, Indonesia's interests in IPR protection just developed after Indonesia had to comply with its TRIPS obligations. Compared to other ASEAN member countries, the copyright industry's contribution to Indonesia's economy in employment and GDP is low. Similarly, the industry's contribution to Indonesia's economy is also low compared to other ASEAN members. This is in line with previous findings that the country's response towards the challenges of copyright protection due to the digital economy's growth in terms of the legal framework is unsatisfactory.

3.5 Enforcement and performance of copyright protection

Compared with other ASEAN members, Indonesia ranked in the middle of the Property Rights Index from 2010 to 2020 (Table 3.5). Indonesia trailed behind Singapore, Malaysia, and Thailand but performed slightly better than the Philippines and Viet Nam and way ahead of Brunei Darussalam during the period.

Indonesia's relatively average performance in the Property Rights Index is supported by the fact that it had, along with Thailand, always been on the United States Trade Representative's (USTR) Priority Watch List between 2010 and 2017 (Table 3.6). Indonesia had remained on the USTR Priority Watch List while Thailand improved its watch list status in 2018. This reveals that the US government has viewed Indonesia as one with serious IPR

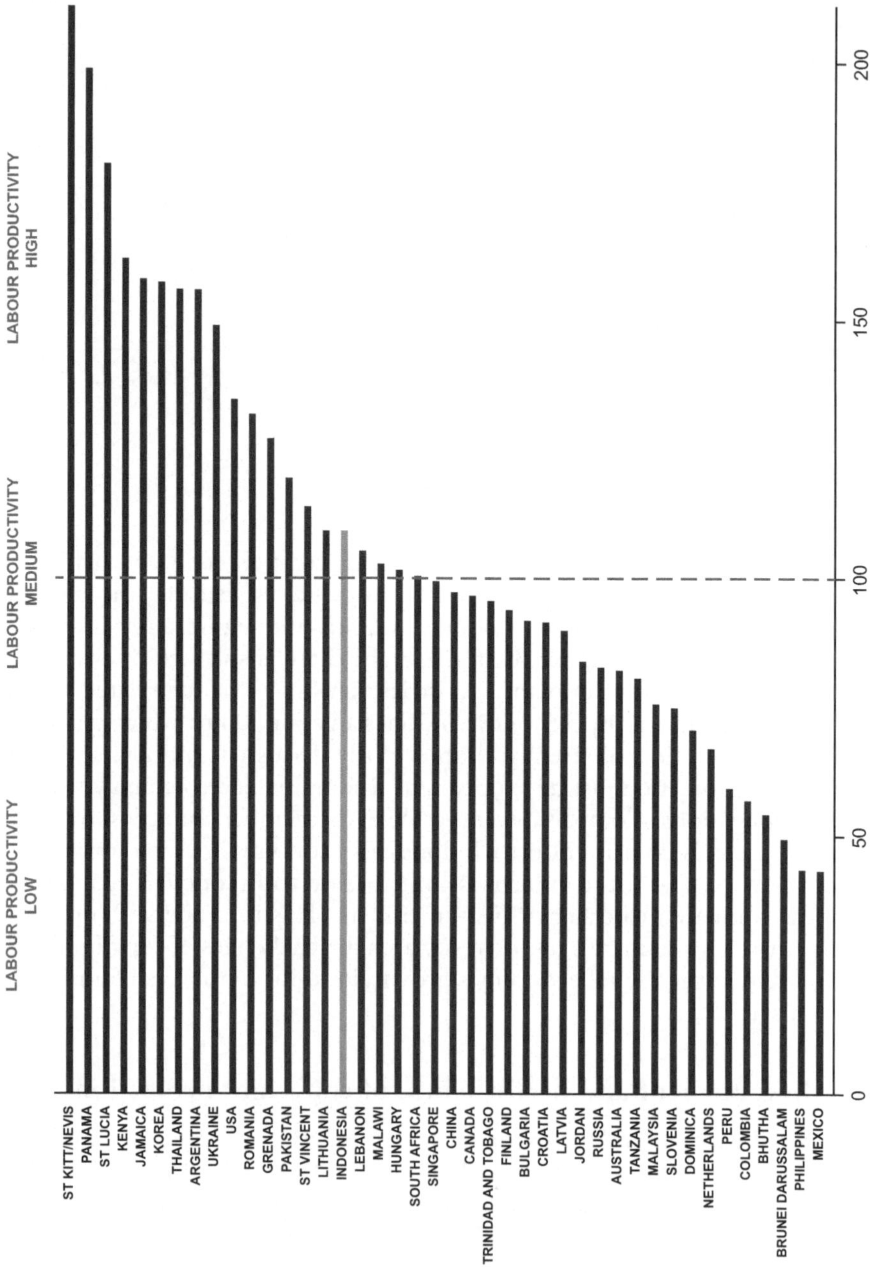

Figure 3.8 Labour Productivity Index for Copyright Industries.

Table 3.5 Property Rights Index: Indonesia and Some ASEAN Countries (2010–2020)

	2010		*2011*		*2012*		*2013*		*2014*		*2015*		*2016*		*2017*		*2018*		*2019*		*2020*	
	S	*R*	*S*	*R*	*S*	*R*	*S*	*R*	*S*	*R*	*S*	*R*	*S*	*R*	*S*	*R*	*S*	*R*	*S*	*R*	*S*	*R*
Singapore	8.2	8	8.3	3	8.3	4	8.1	7	8.2	5	8.1	5	8.1	6	8.3	7	8.4	5	8.4	4	8.4	3
Malaysia	6.7	42	6.1	44	6.4	38	6.5	33	6.5	27	6.6	28	6.8	26	6.6	32	6.4	34	6.6	31	6.7	30
Thailand	5.2	59	5.3	64	5.2	69	5.1	72	5.3	50	4.9	69	5.3	65	5.2	66	5.3	65	5.4	64	5.4	65
Indonesia	4.1	97	5	77	4.8	86	4.9	85	5	59	4.9	70	5	67	5.1	68	5.3	64	5.4	65	5.3	68
Philippines	4.5	80	4.7	87	4.7	87	5	80	-	-	5	65	5.1	63	5.1	67	5.2	70	5.3	67	5.3	69
Viet Nam	5.7	74	4.9	81	4.7	87	4.7	95	4.8	66	4.5	85	4.7	85	4.9	77	5	76	5	83	5.1	78
Brunei Darussalam	4.3	93	5.7	54	5.7	53	5.7	55	-	-	-	-	-	-	4.6	92	4.7	90	4.7	98	4.7	98

Notes: S = score, R = ranking.

Source: WIPO (2010–2020).

Table 3.6 ASEAN Member States in USTR Special 301 Report, 2010–2020

	2010	*2011*	*2012*	*2013*	*2014*	*2015*	*2016*	*2017*	*2018*	*2019*	*2020*
Singapore	Not on the list	Not on the list	Not on the list	Not on the list	Not on the list	Not on the list	Not on the list	Not on the list	Not on the list	Not on the list	Not on the list
Malaysia	Watch List	Watch List	Not on the List	Not on the list	Not on the list	Not on the list	Not on the list	Not on the list	Not on the list	Not on the list	Not on the list
Thailand	Priority Watch List	Priority Watch List	Priority Watch List	Priority Watch List	Priority Watch List	Priority Watch List	Priority Watch List	Priority Watch List	Watch List	Watch List	Watch List
Indonesia	Priority Watch List	Priority Watch List	Priority Watch List	Priority Watch List	Priority Watch List	Priority Watch List	Priority Watch List	Priority Watch List	Priority Watch List	Priority Watch List	Priority Watch List
Philippines	Watch List	Watch List	Watch List	Watch List	Watch List	Not on the list	Not on the list	Not on the list	Not on the list	Not on the list	Not on the list
Viet Nam	Watch List	Watch List	Watch List	Watch List	Watch List	Watch List	Watch List	Watch List	Watch List	Watch List	Watch List
Brunei Darussalam	Watch List	Watch List	Watch List	Not on the list	Not on the list	Not on the list	Not on the list	Not on the list	Not on the list	Not on the list	Not on the list

Source: USTR (2010-2020).

shortcomings. According to the USTR Special 301 Report 2018, Indonesia was still on the USTR's Priority Watch List due to insufficient and ineffective IP protection and enforcement. Based on the 2017 USTR Notorious Markets List, Indonesia was among the countries (along with Argentina, Brazil, Viet Nam, Chile, China) with rampant piracy using illicit streaming devices. This seriously threatens content creators, live performances, and other legitimate streaming. Indonesia has remained on the USTR Priority Watch List in 2019 and 2020, showing that the country still has an ineffective or inadequate IP enforcement system.

Economically, one motivation for IP protection is improving the country's capability in innovation. According to the Global Innovation Index (GII), Indonesia's general innovation performance is relatively low when compared to other ASEAN members. As shown in Table 3.7, Indonesia ranks below all other members except Cambodia (no data for the Lao PDR and Myanmar). The value of the domestic market scale is the highest contribution (with the value of 3,243 and ranked seventh) to Indonesia's innovation performance final score.

On the contrary, in almost all IPR-related indicators, the score can be considered low. Data from the GII 2018 exhibits that the score, for example, of online creativity indicator for Indonesia is only 3.4 and ranked 79th. This may indicate that innovation and IPR-related industries are still not the priority of the government. As Table 3.7 reveals, Indonesia's GII score did not change much in 2019 and 2020.

3.6 Conclusion: copyright reform for a digital economy

This chapter discusses how the digital economy affects IPR, particularly copyright protection, and how the government of a developing country responds to these challenges. In answering the first question on the impact of the digital economy on copyright protection, we may conclude that the digital economy's materialisation profoundly impacts copyright protection. The technological development in the digital era has expedited a new way of how copyrighted works are created, produced, shared, and accessed. Copyright protection will no longer be aimed only at providing adequate economic incentives for creativity; it must also facilitate new technology innovation and ensure widespread access. In this regard, the most difficult challenge in the digital economy age is designing copyright systems that can balance the rights of rights holders and users' needs (US Department of Commerce 2013). The logic of IPR protection is to monopolise ideas to provide incentives for creativity and innovation. In the digital economy, however, IPR can be inefficiently costly to enforce (Välimäki 2001) when consumers can reproduce the copyrighted products at zero marginal cost, and when free access to information and content is considered by many to be a right (Denton 2011). In this regard, it is much more crucial to 'maximise the value of their intellectual property, not the protection of it' (Välimäki 2001, p. 3). More importantly, the policy response to the digital economy's emergence

Table 3.7 GII: Indonesia and Some ASEAN Countries (2014–2020)

Country	*2014*		*2015*		*2016*		*2017*		*2018*		*2019*		*2020*	
	S	*R*	*S*	*R*	*S*	*R*	*S*	*R*	*S*	*R*	*S*	*R*	*S*	*R*
Brunei Darussalam	31.67	88	N/A	N/A	N/A	N/A	32.89	71	32.84	67	32.35	71	29.82	71
Cambodia	28.66	106	30.35	91	27.94	95	27.05	101	26.69	98	26.59	98	21.46	110
Indonesia	31.81	87	29.79	97	29.07	88	30.1	87	37.12	90	29.72	85	26.49	85
Malaysia	45.6	33	45.98	32	43.36	35	42.72	37	43.16	35	42.68	35	42.42	33
Philippines	29.87	100	31.05	83	31.83	74	32.48	73	31.56	73	36.18	54	35.19	50
Singapore	59.24	7	59.36	7	59.16	6	58.69	7	59.83	5	58.37	8	56.61	8
Thailand	39.28	48	38.1	55	36.51	52	37.57	51	38.00	44	38.63	43	36.68	44
Viet Nam	31.81	87	38.35	52	35.37	59	38.34	47	37.94	45	38.84	42	37.12	42

Notes: S = score, R = ranking.

Source: WIPO (2014-2020).

is, therefore, providing the right balance between enabling digital progress and addressing the risks.

On how the government of a developing country responds to these challenges, this chapter highlights the creative economy's contribution, including the copyright industry, to Indonesia's total GDP, employment, and export. The previous discussion indicates that the creative economy, which is mostly also copyright-related, is growing. During the last 10 years, the creative economy had contributed continuously to Indonesia's GDP; its contribution to total export likewise significantly increased. Unfortunately, only a few industries have copyright protection. Although Indonesia has been a WTO member and has complied with the TRIPS Agreement, the lack of awareness on copyright protection in its society is still prevalent. Lack of awareness of copyright protection in the creative economy may also be related to the Indonesian community's historical and cultural traditions, which perceive copyright protection differently. Furthermore, compared to other ASEAN member countries, the contribution of the copyright industry to Indonesia's economy in terms of employment and GDP is low. This is in line with previous findings that Indonesia's response towards the challenges of copyright protection due to the development of the digital economy in terms of the legal framework is also unsatisfactory. In conclusion, this chapter argues that significant reform is needed, including the strengthening of IPR protection by relevant ministries rather than by the Ministry of Law and Human Rights. As discussed, having the Ministry of Law and Human Rights administer IPR protection gives the perception that it is more of a legal issue than a source of innovation that fosters creativity.

Notes

1 This section on the historical and cultural context of copyright protection in Indonesia is based on Winanti (2011).

2 As quoted by Winanti (2011), the Dutch colonial rule classified the population into three different legal groups (the Europeans, foreign orientals, and indigenous Indonesians), each with its own legal system (Antons 2003, p. 16).

3 Indonesia's bill on creative economy defines creative economy as 'the materialization of added values from an intellectual property born of the human creativity, based on science, culture, and technology' (Badan Ekonomi Kreatif 2018b, p. 12).

4 WIPO's Guide on Surveying the Economic Contribution of the Copyright Industries (2015) further explains the definition of core copyright industries as 'industries which are wholly engaged in the creation, production and manufacture, performance, broadcasting, communication and exhibition, or distribution and sale of works and other protected subject matter' (WIPO 2015, p. 51).

Bibliography

Antons, C. (2003), 'Legal Culture and History of Law in Asia', in C. Heath (ed.), *Intellectual Property Law in Asia*. The Hague: Kluwer Law International, pp. 13–35.

Antons, C. (2000), *Intellectual Property Law in Indonesia*. The Hague: Kluwer Law International.

Badan, Ekonomi Kreatif (2018a), 'Infografis Ringkasan Data Statistik Ekonomi Kreatif Indonesia', Jakarta: Indonesian Agency for Creative Economy. http://www.bekraf.go.id/downloadable/pdf_file/180232-infografis-ringkasan-data-statistik-ekonomi-kreatif-indonesia.pdf (accessed 17 April 2019).

Badan, Ekonomi Kreatif (2018b). *Creative Economy Outlook 2019*. Jakarta: Indonesian Agency for Creative Economy.

Badan, Ekonomi Kreatif (2017a), 'Data Statistik dan Hasil Survei Ekonomi Kreatif'. Jakarta: Indonesian Agency for Creative Economy. http://www.bekraf.go.id/downloadable/pdf_file/170475-data-statistik-dan-hasil-survei-ekonomi-kreatif.pdf (accessed 19 April 2019).

Badan, Ekonomi Kreatif (2017b), *Ekspor Ekonomi Kreatif 2010–2016*. Jakarta: BPS Statistics Indonesia. http://www.bps.go.id (accessed 17 April 2019).

Butt, S. (2008), 'Intellectual Property in Indonesia: A Problematic Legal Transplant', in T. Lindsey (ed.), *Indonesia Law and Society*, 2nd ed. Sydney: Federation Press. pp. 620–635.

Ciocoiu, C.N. (2011), 'Considerations about Intellectual Property Rights, Innovation, and Economic Growth in the Digital Economy', *Economia Seria Management*, Volume 14, Issue 2, pp. 310–323.

Cornell University, INSEAD, and WIPO (2020), *The Global Innovation Index 2020: Who Will Finance Innovation?* Ithaca, Fontainebleau, and Geneva.

Cornell University, INSEAD, and WIPO (2019), *The Global Innovation Index 2019: Creating Healthy Lives – The Future of Medical Innovation*. Ithaca, Fontainebleau, and Geneva.

Cornell University, INSEAD, and WIPO (2018), *The Global Innovation Index 2018: Energizing the World with Innovation*. Ithaca, Fontainebleau, and Geneva.

Cornell University, INSEAD, and WIPO (2017), *The Global Innovation Index 2017: Innovation Feeding the World*. Ithaca, Fontainebleau, and Geneva.

Cornell University, INSEAD, and WIPO (2016), *The Global Innovation Index 2016: Winning with Global Innovation*. Ithaca, Fontainebleau, and Geneva.

Cornell University, INSEAD, and WIPO (2014), *The Global Innovation Index 2014: The Human Factor In innovation*, Second printing. Fontainebleau, Ithaca, and Geneva.

Denton, A. (2011), 'Intellectual Property Rights in Today's Digital Economy', *ITUNews*, September 2011, https://www.itu.int/net/itunews/issues/2011/07/38.aspx (accessed 25 May 2018).

Directorate General of Intellectual Property and Indonesian Ministry of Law and Human Rights (n.d.), 'Organizational Structure', http://en.dgip.go.id/organizational-structure (accessed 17 May 2019).

Gestrin, M.V. and J. Staudt (2018), *The Digital Economy, Multinational Enterprises, and International Investment Policy*. Paris: OECD. http://www.oecd.org/investment/investment-policy/The-digital-economy-multinational-enterprises-and-international-investment-policy.pdf (accessed 25 May 2018).

Gutowski, R.J. (1999), 'The Marriage of Intellectual Property and International Trade in the TRIPS Agreement: Strange Bedfellows or a Match Made in Heaven', *Buffalo Law Review*, 47, pp.713–762.

Hargreaves, I. (2011). 'Digital Opportunity A Review of Intellectual Property and Growth', https://assets.publishing.service.gov.uk/government/uploads/system/uploads/attachment_data/file/32563/ipreview-finalreport.pdf (accessed 20 August 2018).

IMF (2018), 'Measuring the Digital Economy', *IMF Policy Papers*, Washington, DC: International Monetary Fund. http://www.imf.org/external/pp/ppindex.aspx (accessed 25 May 2018).

Krishnan, A.S.A. and A.K. Chakravarti (1998), 'Intellectual Property Rights in the Ensuing Global Digital Economy', *Journal of Intellectual Property Rights*, 3(1), pp. 9–20.

Kusumadara, A. (n.d.), 'Problems of Enforcing Intellectual Property Laws in Indonesia', http://www.ialsnet.org/meetings/business/KusumadaraAfifah-Indonesia.pdf (accessed 1 December 2020).

Manyika, J. and S. Lund (2016), 'How Digital Trade is Transforming Globalisation', *E15 Initiative*, January 2016, Geneva: International for Trade and Sustainable Development (ICTSD) and World Economy Forum, www.e15initiative.org (accessed 20 May 2018).

Marron, D.B. and D.G. Steel (2000), 'Which Countries Protect Intellectual Property? The Case of Software Piracy', *Economic Inquiry*, 38(2), pp. 159–174.

National Research Council (2000), *The Digital Dilemma: Intellectual Property in the Information Age*. Washington, DC: The National Academies Press. https://doi.org/10.17226/9601 (accessed 10 August 2019).

OECD (2017), *OECD Digital Economy Outlook 2017*. Paris: OECD Publishing. http://dx.doi.org/10.1787/9789264276284-en (accessed 24 August 2019).

Property Rights Alliance (2020), *International Property Rights Index 2020*. Washington, DC: Property Rights Alliance.

Property Rights Alliance (2019), *International Property Rights Index 2019*. Washington, DC: Property Rights Alliance.

Property Rights Alliance (2018), *International Property Rights Index 2018*. Washington, DC: Property Rights Alliance.

Property Rights Alliance (2017), *International Property Rights Index 2017*. Washington, DC: Property Rights Alliance.

Property Rights Alliance (2016), *International Property Rights Index 2016*. Washington, DC: Property Rights Alliance.

Property Rights Alliance (2015), *International Property Rights Index 2015*. Washington, DC: Property Rights Alliance.

Property Rights Alliance (2014), *International Property Rights Index 2014*. Washington, DC: Property Rights Alliance.

Property Rights Alliance (2013), *International Property Rights Index 2013*. Washington, DC: Property Rights Alliance.

Property Rights Alliance (2012), *International Property Rights Index 2012*. Washington, DC: Property Rights Alliance.

Property Rights Alliance (2011), *International Property Rights Index 2011*. Washington, DC: Property Rights Alliance.

Property Rights Alliance (2010), *International Property Rights Index 2010*. Washington, DC: Property Rights Alliance.

Strange, R. and A. Zucchella (2017), 'Industry 4.0, Global Value Chains, and International Business', *Multinational Business Review*, 25(3), pp. 174–184.

Suwanto, F. M. (1993), 'Indonesia's New Patents Law: A Move in the Right Direction', *Santa Clara Computer and High Technology Law Journal*, 9, pp. 265–286.

UNCTAD (2017), *The New Digital Economy and Development*. Geneva: UNCTAD.

US Department of Commerce (2013), 'Copyright Policy, Creativity, and Innovation in the Digital Economy', https://www.uspto.gov/sites/default/files/news/publications/copyrightgreenpaper.pdf (accessed 17 May 2019).

USTR (2020), *2020 Special 301 Report*. Washington, DC: USTR.
USTR (2019), *2019 Special 301 Report*. Washington, DC: USTR.
USTR (2018), *2018 Special 301 Report*. Washington, DC: USTR.
USTR (2017a), *2017 Special 301 Report*. Washington, DC: USTR.
USTR (2017b), *2017 Out-of-Cycle Review of Notorious Markets*. Washington, DC: USTR.
USTR (2016), *2016 Special 301 Report*. Washington, DC: USTR.
USTR (2015), *2015 Special 301 Report*. Washington, DC: USTR.
USTR (2014), *2014 Special 301 Report*. Washington, DC: USTR.
USTR (2013), *2013 Special 301 Report*. Washington, DC: USTR.
USTR (2012), *2012 Special 301 Report*. Washington, DC: USTR.
USTR (2011), *2011 Special 301 Report*. Washington, DC: USTR.
USTR (2010), *2010 Special 301 Report*. Washington, DC: USTR.
Välimäki, M. (2001), 'Strategic Use of Intellectual Property Rights in Digital Economy – Case of Software Markets', https://pdfs.semanticscholar.org/72d4/05f7d8f-728236836d8505d331f7d8ad80113.pdf (accessed 20 December 2018).
Winanti, P.S. (2019). 'Regulatory Framework on IPR in Indonesia: Overview and Preliminary Assessment on the TPP's IP Chapter', in L. Chen, S. Urata, J. Nakagawa, and M. Ambashi (eds.), *Emerging Global Trade Governance Mega Free Trade Agreements and Implications for ASEAN*. London and New York: Routledge.
Winanti, P.S. (2011), External Pressures or Domestic Politics: Explaining Change in Developing Countries' Intellectual Property Legislation, PhD Thesis, University of Glasgow. http://theses.gla.ac.uk/2794/ (accessed 15 August 2016).
WIPO (2017), *World Intellectual Property Report 2017: Intangible Capital in Global Value Chains*. Geneva: WIPO.
WIPO (2015), *Guide on Surveying the Economic Contribution of the Copyright Industries*. Geneva: WIPO.
WIPO (2014), *Study on the Economic Contribution of Copyright and Related Rights Industries in Indonesia*. Geneva: WIPO.
WIPO, Cornell University, and INSEAD (2015), *The Global Innovation Index 2015: Effective Innovation Policies for Development*. Fontainebleau, Ithaca, and Geneva.
World Bank (2017), *Global Value Chain Development Report 2017: Measuring and Analysing the Impact of GVCs on Economic Development*. Washington, DC: World Bank Group.

4 Intellectual property and digital technology in Thailand

Opportunities and challenges

Jakkrit Kuanpoth and Chawana Huangsuntornchai

4.1 Introduction

This chapter aims to explore policy options to ensure that the protection of intellectual property (IP) contributes to promoting the digital economy. Specifically, it seeks to examine the legal issues associated with the protection of digital technology. It attempts to analyse digital technology issues, such as copyright for digital creations, by looking at Thailand's IP laws as they apply to digital technology. It also examines the situation relating to Thailand's current policy to facilitate the growth of the digital industry. This chapter further presents legal and socio-economic issues surrounding the protection of digital technology. The legal research will provide a comparative legal analysis of the factors and criteria that Thailand and other countries have adopted to protect digital works. The study will identify grey areas where urgent legislative reforms are needed to enhance protection. The socio-economic research will systematically review a set of case studies across product categories, such as virtual reality, social media, e-commerce, online services for entertainment content, and software development. Moreover, it will summarise a model framework of criteria for the coherent, effective, and efficient legal protection of digital technology.

The following section overviews Thailand's current IP regime, focusing on copyright law and digital technology protection. It then reviews the current situation of the Thailand 4.0 policy that the government adopted to share and advance a common understanding of the country's ongoing and future digital economy. For a comparative legal analysis of the factors, Section 4.4 examines the United States (US) and the European Union's (EU) laws on digital technology, including online distribution, virtual reality, platforms, and online services. The chapter concludes by analysing how the established legal principles can be applied in developing countries like Thailand as a policy tool to protect digital works and promote their digital technology policy.

4.2 Copyright and digital technology: a Thai context

Like most countries, Thailand has enacted laws to protect intellectual property rights (IPR) in almost all areas, particularly those required to be covered

DOI: 10.4324/9781003147657-5

by the Agreement on Trade-Related Aspects of Intellectual Property Rights (TRIPS) of the World Trade Organization (WTO). These include Patent Act 1979, Copyright Act 1994, Trademarks Act 1991, Plant Variety Protection Act 1999, Protection of Layout-Designs of Integrated Circuits Act 2000, Trade Secrets Act 2002, and Geographical Indications Protection Act 2003. All these laws have shared aims such as to provide a temporary monopoly for inventors, creators, designers, traders, and plant breeders to foster the development of a required technological base, to assist in the acquisition of foreign technologies, to protect against unfair competition.

4.2.1 *Historical development of the copyright law in Thailand*

Unlike Western countries, Thailand has not had a long period of legal development in the IP field. The first law to protect IP was the copyright law, which can be traced back to 1892 (Weeraworawit 1998). Copyright was first protected in Thailand under the Royal Proclamation of Vachirayan Library for the Protection of Literary Works R.S. 111. The proclamation prohibited the unauthorised reproduction of books published by the Vachirayan Library. Subsequently, Copyright Act 1901 was adopted to extend protection to all published materials upon registration. In 1931, Thailand, the then called the Kingdom of Siam, became a party to the Berne Convention by its ratification of the Berlin Act 1908. Copyright Act 1901 was then replaced by the Protection of Literary and Artistic Works Act 1931. The 1931 Act was adopted to bring Thailand's copyright up to the standards of the international convention. In 1978, the Protection of Literary and Artistic Works Act 1931 was repealed, and the new copyright law was adopted. Thailand's copyright law extended protection to sound recording and broadcast. The law also increased the penalties for copyright infringement. However, Copyright Act 1978 lasted only 16 years because it was replaced by Copyright Act 1994.

Copyright Act B.E. 2537 (1994), the current law, came into force on 21 March 1995. It was adopted during intensive external pressure demanding a complete overhaul of the country's IP laws. The 1994 Act was considerably influenced by rules and principles enshrined under the TRIPS Agreement. The new law also clarifies some ambiguous parts of the 1978 Act, especially whether computer programs were protected as literary work (Subhapholsiri 1996).

4.2.2 *Subject matter of copyright protection*

As a member of the Berne Convention and the TRIPS Agreement, Thailand protects foreign works under the principles of national treatment, domicile, and simultaneous publication. A foreign author can have copyright protection in Thailand on the following conditions:

i. He or she is a national of the country that is a member of any international agreement on copyright to which Thailand is also a member.
ii. He or she is in Thailand or in the country that is a member of any international agreement on copyright to which Thailand is also a member

throughout or most of the time of creating the work or at the time of the first publication of the work.

iii. The work is published for the first time in Thailand or in a country that is a member of any international agreement on copyright of which Thailand is also a member.

iv. The work is published in Thailand or in a country that is a member of any international agreement on copyright of which Thailand is also a member; it should be published within 30 days from the date of the first publication of the work.

Section 6 of the 1994 Copyright Act provides a catalogue of copyright works. It includes the creative works in the literary, dramatic, artistic, musical, audiovisual, cinematographic, sound recording, broadcasting, or any other work in the author's literary, scientific, or artistic sector, irrespective of the method or form of its expression. Unlike the previous law, which had no explicit provisions on computer programs, the present copyright statute protects computer programs as literary work. The 1994 Thailand Copyright Act defines the term 'computer program' as an instruction, a set of instructions, or any other material employed to enable the functioning of the computer or obtain a specific result, irrespective of the form of the language of the computer program.

According to Copyright Act 1994, the copyright holder has both economic and moral rights. While economic rights include the most recognised categories of rights as enshrined under the Berne Convention and the TRIPS Agreement, moral rights involve two major rights: paternity and integrity. Rental right is provided for computer programs, audiovisual work, cinematography, and sound recording.

Economic rights may be partly or wholly transferred to others. Moral rights are not transferable but may be inherited. After the author's death, the author's inheritor is entitled to enforce moral rights until the end of the copyright term. The copyright term is 50 years after the author's death, except for work of applied art whose period of protection lasts for 25 years. The 50-year term of the photographic, cinematographic, audiovisual, and broadcasting works starts from the creation or the first publication of the work.

Copyright infringement under Thai law is of two kinds: direct and indirect infringements. An internationally recognised fair use provision is stipulated by law, including educational purposes, private use, public interests, and so on.

Two interesting cases concern the fair use provision. These involved suits filed against book piracy. The proceedings resulted from foreign publishers' major policies to combat the unauthorised copying of textbooks, a booming business around Thai college or university campuses. In the first case, the Intellectual Property and International Trade Court ruled that the defendant who ran a photocopy shop did not infringe copyright by copying a textbook for students' use during their study.[1] According to the Copyright Act, the photocopy shop did not seek profit for copyright infringement, but it performed under a work-for-hire contract between the student and the shop. The shop acted as a representative of the student who benefited from the fair use exemption.

The second case produced a different result.[2] The defendant, who is also the owner of a photocopy shop, was found guilty of copyright infringement. The copyrighted work was copied at the defendant's initiative and was intended to be sold to customers. Thus, the copying of the work was not done for educational purposes. The defendant was not eligible for the fair use exemption.

4.2.3 Subject matter of neighbouring rights protection

Copyright Act 1994 does not use the term 'neighbouring rights'. The works universally classified as neighbouring rights, such as those of phonogram producers and broadcasting organisations, are considered copyright works in Thailand. The only right that receives special treatment under the copyright law is the right of performers. The term of protection for performers' rights is 50 years.

4.2.4 Protection of databases

Thai copyright law protects databases under Section 12. A compilation or assembling of data done with the permission of the copyright owner is a copyrighted work. The person who selects or assembles the data is the copyright owner of such works. However, the right shall not be prejudiced against the right subsisting in the data or material itself.

4.2.5 Originality requirements

Literary, dramatic, musical, or artistic works are only protected under the Act if they are original. However, the concept of 'originality' is not clearly defined or explained by the Act. In practice, the courts can interpret 'originality' as relating essentially to origin rather than to substantive considerations, such as novelty. Thus, a work is original if it originated from the author or creator and was not copied. While some labour and skill were expended in creating the work, courts have resisted arguments that the originality requirement should be interpreted as importing connotations of aesthetic quality or innovation.

Intellectual effort in creating a copyrighted work is required. In the United Kingdom, for example, this is defined in terms of 'labour, skill, and judgement'. This is often the only test applicable since, in this context, the quality or merit of a work is immaterial. However, the difficulty associated with this approach lies in deciding how much skill, and so on, is enough.[3] It was suggested that the criterion should be reduced to a harmonised level of 'not copied', that is, a computer program shall be protected if it is original in the sense of the author's intellectual creation.

The originality requirement is not an onerous one and does not mean that the computer program must be novel or unique in some respect. It merely means that it results from a modest amount of skill, labour, or effort and that it 'originates from the author'.[4] Compilations of existing information as in a street directory have been afforded copyright protection. Although many compilations have nothing original in their parts, the complete compilation may be original for copyright purposes.[5] In the light of these cases, virtually all computer programs will meet the originality requirement, even if the program comprises little more than an arrangement of commonly used subroutines. This is because the selection and structuring of those routines require a reasonable amount of skill and expertise.

It should not be overlooked that many modern computer programs are effective compilations of standard modules. Many algorithms and many subroutines are commonplace in the industry. They may have been placed or fallen into the public domain, or they may be de facto standard routines or algorithms. A program composed wholly or in part of such commonplace or unprotected algorithms and routines should nevertheless be protected as a compilation, provided it is original, and the creator demonstrated skill and labour in creating it. In other words, it is immaterial that the various elements comprising a collective whole were all copied from other sources, so long as the particular combination was itself not copied and involved the application of the compiler's skill, labour, and judgement.

4.2.6 Authorship

As with all literary works, the question of program authorship is to be solved in favour of the natural persons who created the work. Although the right to exercise exclusive rights may be assigned to another, the author retains at least the unalienable rights to claim paternity of his work. The first owner of the copyright in a work is usually its author. This is the case regardless of whose ideas underlie the work. This general rule is, however, subject to several significant exceptions. Of widest importance is the special rule that subject to contrary agreement, the first owner of the copyright in a work created by an employee during his or her employment is the employer, not the employee.

Copyright in a work created by a group of persons, which is usually the case in computer programs development, is to be exercised in common unless the persons concerned contract otherwise. Computer programs are frequently created by freelance programmers working on particular projects on behalf of the organisation that commissioned a given program. In such circumstances, unless the parties agree otherwise, the person or entity that causes the work to be created would generally wish to retain control over the program's exclusive rights.

A contractual provision for determining copyright ownership is essential when employing freelance staff or anyone not employed on a permanent employment contract. The contract should expressly state that the first copyright owner is the organisation and not the programmer. Also, there should be a written assignment of copyright signed by the freelance programmer. Of course, the fee charged will probably be greater because the freelance programmer might have envisaged using the program elsewhere. Suppose the contract is silent on such matters. The freelance programmer may later decide to test his ownership of the program by offering it to others or, worse still, claim that he will permit the continued use of the program only upon payment of a licence fee. These difficulties may arise especially when the program in question becomes more useful and successful than the parties originally envisaged (Bainbridge 1990).

An increasingly large number of programs are now generated using a computer (Bently and Sherman 2002). This means that program A is used to create programs B, C, and so on with some degree of human intervention to select the most appropriate means to achieve the objective. The question arises as to whether the authorship of these programs generated by the first computer program should reside with the first program's creator, or with the person who causes it to create other works. Since the first program is no different in its function from any other tool used to create a work, such as an instruction manual through which another work is created, it seems appropriate that the person who uses such a tool to generate programs should be considered the creator of those programs (Bently and Sherman 2002). In practice, such a person may be the computer operator. In England, the court held that random numbers selected by a computer for a newspaper competition called 'Millionaire of the Month' were protected by copyright.[6] Arguments that there was no human author and the list of numbers drawn by the computer were not protected by copyright were rejected by J. Whitford, who said that such a claim was as silly as saying that a pen could be the author of a literary work.

In works produced by or with the aid of a computer, the human skill can be found either in the person who entered information into the computer to produce the output, or in the work involved in writing the program used, or a combination of both.

4.2.7 Term of protection

Subject to certain exceptions, copyright in a literary, dramatic, musical, or artistic work lasts for 50 years from the end of the year the author dies (Bently and Sherman 2002). For a work of joint authorship, the 50-year period begins at the end of the year when the last known author dies. In the case of computer-generated work, copyright expires after 50 years from the end of the year the work was made. The latter rule is similar to the rules applying to sound recordings, films, broadcasts, and cable programs. The typographical arrangement of a published edition, which is itself a work for copyright purposes, is protected for a still-shorter term of 25 years from the end of the year of first publication. Thus, for a product such as a software package comprising multiple works, the copyright of the various parts will run out on several different dates. The duration of the copyright may depend, for example, on the life expectancy of various human contributors, the year when any computer-generated work was made, and the year the documentation was first published.

4.2.8 Infringement

A copyright can be given away, bought and sold, or left as an inheritance under a will as personal or movable property. An assignment or other transfer of copyright may be outright or may relate only to certain exclusive rights enjoyed by the owner. Thus, for example, an assignee may be given the right solely to translate a software package into a particular language. A transfer may also be limited to any part of the remaining term of the copyright. In practice, limited rights, such as for converting a program to be used in a particular operating system or for foreign language users, are more often granted by way of licence than by partial assignment. Where such a licence is exclusive, the right of copyright use will, in effect, be treated as the owner in terms of rights and remedies, and the distinction between such a licence and a corresponding assignment will be academic.[7]

A primary infringement occurs when a person directly commits an infringing act or authorises someone else. As their name suggests, secondary infringers are generally one stage removed from the relevant primary infringing acts. Still, they may be implicated by, for example, importing or distributing infringing copies without the consent of the copyright owner. A crucial distinction between primary infringers and secondary infringers is that the former can be liable for infringing copyright whether they realise they are doing so. Those in the latter category are only liable if they know or have reason to believe that they are committing an act of secondary infringement.

Space does not permit a full discussion of all acts constituting an infringement of the copyright in a work. The focus will be on the principal acts of so-called primary infringement, discussed as follows.

4.2.9 Copying

Thailand's Copyright Act B.E. 2537 (1994) provides that a copyright owner has the exclusive right to copy the work and authorise anyone else to do so. The Act provides that control over copying applies to the whole or any substantial part of a work, regardless of whether copying occurs directly or indirectly. Section 3 defines 'reproduction' as

> copying by whatever means, imitation, making of duplicate, making of printing block, recording of sound, recording of picture or both sound and picture from the original, from duplicate or from advertisement, which is a material part thereof, either wholly or partly,

and requires copyrights of computer programs to include 'copying or making of duplicate of computer program from any recording medium by whatever means which is a material part thereof, without having a description of a newly created work, either wholly or partly'.

For instance, if company B wrote a program independently that, by chance, turned out to be very similar to one written by company A, no copyright was infringed because A's program was neither copied nor adapted. Also, both A and B have a copyright in their respective programs.

The substantial similarity between programs, however, can suggest that one was copied from the other. This can shift the burden of proof to the defendant, especially if something suggests that copying may have taken place, such as access to the original program by the defendant. This means that instead of requiring the plaintiff to show that copying occurred, the defendant must show that he did not copy the plaintiff's work. Such a shift in the burden of proof can be exceedingly onerous to the defendant.

Unlike other literary work forms, a computer program cannot serve its purpose unless it is 'reproduced'. This 'reproduction' should not be confused with 'replication'. The program may be recreated in part or in whole as part of the computer's internal process which runs it. No second permanent copy of the program is made during this process. However, parts of the program will be 'reproduced' and stored in other parts of the computer memory during the program's operation. The temporary copying, moving, and storing operations may leave no trace once the machine's process is terminated. Thus, 'reproducing' in the traditional sense of producing a second permanent version of an original does not normally occur unless a 'backup' copy of the program is made.

Regarding all forms of copyright work, copying includes making transient copies. This implies that loading a computer program into a computer only to run the program is considered making a copy of the program, even though this 'reproduction' will be lost as soon as the computer is switched off. Loading the program is considered a restricted act in so far as it usually necessitates the program's reproduction in part or in whole. In this way, any unauthorised use of a computer program will infringe the copyright in that program.

In the future, programs may be more often contained in media that can be inserted physically into the computer, such as chips or an integral part of the hardware. In these circumstances, reproduction of the program may no longer be necessary. At present and because of the risk of unauthorised users entering and corrupting programs, loading should remain under the author's exclusive control.

Computer programs are especially vulnerable to copying by electronic means and unauthorised adaptation, destruction, or corruption, either for financial gain or political objectives. Computer programs controlling banking, military, or security operations must be protected against 'hacking' – that is, unauthorised entry into the system to remove, add, or change information contained in it. Such acts of fraud or sabotage can only be controlled if authors have broad and enforceable powers to protect programs against reproduction.

Backup copies of computer programs should be made. A backup copy will be needed if the original copy of the computer program is damaged or corrupted in any way. For example, it might be contaminated with a computer virus. If a computer program is used in a commercial environment, whether it be a word processing package, accounts system, or spreadsheet, the chances are that the original will fail at the worst possible moment.

4.2.10 Making adaptation

Copyright Act 1994 restricts the making of an adaptation of a work. Adaptation means, among other things, the translation of a literary work that is usually done from one human language to another. Adaptation of a literary work typically implies transforming a given text, such as a novel into another literary work like a play or an arrangement of a song.

In computer programs, the term 'adaptation' best describes the activities that involve work: whether the act is a translation from a humanly readable form into a machine-readable form, or from one programming language to another, or an adaptation of a program designed to perform one task so that it may perform another. A translation includes a version of the program that is converted into or out of a computer program language or code or into a different computer language or code, other than incidentally running the program.

A high-level source code computer program compiled (converted) into an object code program will be an adaptation of the source code program and is, therefore, a restricted act. At first sight, it would appear that the object code program, because it is a computer program, should be protected as a literary work in its own right. However, the elements of skill, labour, and effort will be missing from the object code version, which will have been created simply by using an appropriate compiler program. These elements will, of course, be present as regards the source code program. Therefore, object code programs should be protected as an adaptation of literary works.

The meaning of 'translation' seems too broad as it seems to catch a version of a source code program written in a different high-level language from that used for the original program. If a computer program was written using BASIC and someone then rewrote the program in COBOL, the latter would be an adaptation of the BASIC program because it was converted into a different computer language. But to produce a program in a different high-level language is not merely a question of translating the program instructions from one language to another as with spoken languages. The programmer would have to reduce the original program to its underlying concepts and ideas and, from those concepts and ideas (not from the computer program itself), develop a new version of the program in another high-level language.

The differences between the two programs could be as wide as those between *Romeo and Juliet* and *West Side Story*. As a basic principle, copyright should not protect ideas as such, only the expression or recording of those ideas. However, it seems that the new version of a program in a different high-level language will be an adaptation, regardless of the considerable amount of skill and effort required to 'translate' the program.

4.2.11 Distribution

Under traditional copyright protection for literary works, the author's exclusive rights comprise the right to control reproduction, adaptation, and translation of his work. The Berne Convention does not expressly give a right to control the distribution of works. However, the exclusives regarding reproduction are in practice exercised in most Berne Union countries to allow the author to determine how his work shall be put on the market.

Issuing copies of a work to the public is a restricted act and will infringe copyright if done without the copyright owner's permission. Regarding computer programs, the extension of this restricted act includes the rental of copies to the public. However, this restricted act is only relevant in the context of a particular work if copies of that work have not previously been circulated. The restricted act would apply to a situation where a person acquires a computer program unavailable to the public and then sells or rents copies of the program to the public.

Where a program is sold to the public, certain rights to use the property acquired should typically apply. These rights should include the right to use the program without further express authorisation from the rights holder. It should not be necessary to obtain the rights holder's authorisation to lend the program to a third party or use it on a given piece of apparatus or a given location. Similarly, loading, viewing, running, transmission, or storage should be taken as not requiring express authorisation of the rights holder, provided these acts are carried out to use the program and do not result in a second permanent replicate of the program. Similarly, any form of reproduction other than that required for use will not be permitted, particularly the making of a backup copy or a copy for private use.

4.3 Thailand 4.0: where it started

This section overviews the Thailand 4.0 policy and the importance of the Internet of Things, including opportunity trends in ten targeted S-Curve industries under the policy to share and advance a common understanding of the ongoing and future digital economy situation in Thailand. It is also important to first focus on Thailand's need to impose IP protection, which is a significant engine to drive economic growth.

In 2015, the National Reform Council of Thailand (2015) launched a new engine to drive economic growth, the so-called Thailand 4.0 policy. This is the fourth model following the first Thailand 1.0 model on agriculture, the Thailand 2.0 model on light industry, and the Thailand 3.0 model on heavy and exporting industries. The current Thailand 4.0 focuses on innovation. This policy comprises three key elements: (i) productive growth engine, (ii) inclusive growth engine, and (iii) green growth engine (National Reform Council of Thailand 2015). The council believes that the policy will drive the country to escape the middle-income trap, and fix the inequality and imbalance in Thai society. The policy resembles that of other developed countries, such as the 'Nation of Makers' of the United States (White House of President Barack Obama 2015), 'Design in Innovation' of the United Kingdom (Technology Strategy Board 2015), 'Make in India' (2016), and the 'Creative Economy' of the Republic of Korea (UNCTAD 2017).

Under the Thailand 4.0 model, it is necessary to improve the national economic structure from 'comparative advantage' to 'competitive advantage'. Then the domestic industries will move from 'value-added industries' to 'value creation industries' in five clusters (National Reform Council of Thailand 2015). These clusters are the bio-based, renewable, engineering and design, wellness, and creative economic industries (National Reform Council of Thailand 2015). These five clusters are based on Thailand's natural and cultural advantages, such as biodiversity and cultural diversity.

The country needs to balance at least four dimensions: economic wealth, environmental wellness, social well-being, and human wisdom (National Reform Council of Thailand 2015). The balanced development should rely on the Thai development approach, the 'Philosophy of Sufficiency Economy' – whatever is insufficient needs to be filled, whatever is enough needs to be stopped, and whatever is excessive needs to be shared. At the micro-level, the filling, stopping, and sharing make people have their guarantee during socio-economic stability, leading to social power where people unite. At the macro level, the filling, stopping, and sharing make Thailand ready for global responsiveness, increased national competitiveness, and local inclusiveness.

The transition to the value creation industry of Thailand's 4.0 policy highlights the advancement of procedures. The agricultural sector, for example, includes smart farming. This means that farmers will be wealthier and become entrepreneurs. Small and medium-sized enterprises should have new efficient and effective startups. In the service sector, the change from traditional services to high-value services should be applied. The food, agriculture, and biotechnology cluster should develop new startups that use agricultural or food technologies. In the healthcare and medical technology cluster, Thailand needs to develop and apply health and medical technology. Businesses like spas should be promoted. The advancement in robotics technology will be enhanced with the use of mechanical, robotic, and electronic technologies. Digital technology, the Internet, artificial intelligence, electronic finance, e-Marketplace, and e-Commerce must be widely developed and used, along with other clusters, such as the creative industry, culture, high-value service, lifestyle business, and so on.

The Thailand 4.0 policy also refers to the importance of the Internet of Things. It also focuses on ten targeted industries for opportunities and investment in the country. Earlier, Thailand navigated the first five S-Curve businesses: next-generation automotive, intelligent electronics, advance agricultural and biotechnology, food processing, and tourism (Phichagonakasit 2019). Later in 2018, new S-Curve industries aimed to advance Thailand's competitiveness and speed up new industrial economic growth through technology innovation. The five new S-Curve businesses are (i) digital, (ii) robotics and automation, (iii) aviation and logistics, (iv) biofuels and biochemicals, and (v) medical hub.

According to Phichagonakasit (2019), the Thai government aims to attract foreign investment in the Internet of Things (IoT) and artificial intelligence sectors in Thailand). IoT expenditures in Thailand concentrate on the manufacturing and logistics industries rather than agriculture. However, about 40% of employment and 10% of Thailand's gross domestic product is accounted for by the agriculture sector. The industrial and manufacturing units in the robotics and automation businesses are also in demand because of the low operating costs in automation. Furthermore, several blockchain providers in the aviation and logistics businesses are interested in investing in Thailand to become a regional logistics hub. Its logistics in several ports, including airways, waterways, or railways, are expected to connect soon. This connection requires technology integration and carriers to achieve the goal. The investment in biofuels and biochemicals is attractive since Thailand is known as the world's leading agricultural producer and exporter (Phichagonakasit 2019). Biofuels are made from sugarcane and related agricultural products, which are abundant in the country. Last but not least is the S-Curve medical hub business. As Thailand has begun to include robotics in the medical community, this new business opportunity might be of interest to foreign investors equipped with medical technologies.

From a legal viewpoint, three pieces of legislation have been enacted by or proposed to the National Legislative Assembly to drive the Thailand 4.0 economic policy. These are the Electronic Transaction Act,[8] the Personal Data Protection Act,[9] and the Cyber Security Act.[10] These laws aim to deal with activities such as gaining unauthorised access to specific computers, altering data, or impeding access to computers. They also attempt to prevent unauthorised use of and interference with a computer system. For example, under the Cyber Security Act B.E. 2562, attacking a computing device by breach of a security mechanism to collect, alter, or destroy data or information, or install vulnerabilities to obtain an illegal benefit is prohibited and considered a criminal offence. Although legislation criminalises such activities, there may still be practical difficulties regarding how unlawful activities can be effectively detected and prosecuted.

Previously, no law governed data protection in Thailand. Various regulations in line with the business sector, such as telecommunications, healthcare, banking, and the credit bureau, protected specific personal data. The Personal Data Protection Act, which the National Legislative Assembly approved on 28 February 2019, is the first law on data governance. Most of the basic principles and concepts of Thailand's data protection law were drawn from the EU's General Data Protection Regulation. Any businesses that collect data from Thai residents must follow the Personal Data Protection Act. Notably, companies must ensure that a data subject's consent is secured before personal data is collected, disclosed, used, or transferred.

The adoption of digital laws reflects Thailand's policy for the need to balance the privacy of individuals or corporations and the public freedom of information and freedom of expression. Like most countries, however, Thailand is still struggling to draw the line between what level of sensitive information should be treated as private property and what level should not be treated as such. Since the country still lacks experience in implementing digital technology laws, how those new laws will help drive the Thailand 4.0 model to achieve its objectives remains to be seen. Thailand could learn from more experienced countries and governments in jurisdictions that have supported such legislation and thoroughly reviewed its effectiveness. The following section will address some interesting examples of how Europe and the US have used their digital technology laws.

4.4 Digital technology and laws – lessons learned from Europe and the US

All developed nations already have various laws which, to a greater or lesser extent, are aimed at or can be used to regulate digital technology and protect valuable digital information against unauthorised interference. This section addresses laws and regulations on technology-related activities, including online distribution, virtual reality, platforms, and online services. The US and European experiences are used as illustrations.

4.4.1 Online distribution

Online distribution refers to distribution of contents in a digital manner (USLegal n.d.), such as materials presented online in the form of news articles or any other information that can be distributed as electronic copies. Unlawful distribution of information has existed for ages. Still, it has become more troublesome in recent years due to the emergence of new forms of services, helped by faster and more reliable Internet communications. According to the World Intellectual Property Organization (WIPO), owners of content have lost millions of dollars in revenue caused by the unauthorised distribution of digital content (WIPO 2002). Leaving this issue unsolved, makers of creative works, such as content creation distributors, academics, software developers, and so on, might lose their incentives to innovate original works. In the worst-case scenario, this issue may lead to failure of the 'marketplace of ideas' (Oster 2015, p. 17) where truth cannot be found in a place where public debate is prohibited because the best idea is yet to be found and one may have no incentive to contribute.

In *Authors Guild v Google* case,[11] the US Courts of Appeal decided whether it is legal to duplicate digitally whole books without authorisation. The Court of First Instance ruled that Google has the right to fair use in digitally copying books without permission because it intends to inform the public of the claimant's books. The Second Circuit agreed with the former court and found that

> The purpose of the copyright is highly transformative, the public display of text is limited, and the revelations do not provide a significant market substitute for the protected aspects of the originals. Google's commercial nature and profit motivation do not justify denial of fair use.[12]

The court balanced the advantages and drawbacks of the main purpose of academic books – that they need to be distributed to benefit society. However, if academic books were transformed into other kinds of literary works, it would be interesting to see how the court would develop the solution.

Another interesting case is the *Infopaq International v Danske Dagblades Forening* decision.[13] The European Court of Justice (ECJ) decided whether authors have an exclusive right to authorise or prohibit reproduction of their works. The court ruled that the authors have such right to authorise or prohibit reproduction under Article 2(a) of Directive 2001/29.

According to the ECJ:

> Article 2(a) of Directive 2001/29 [the Information Society Directive] provides that authors have the exclusive right to authorise or prohibit reproduction, in whole or in part, of their works. It follows that protection of the author's right to authorise or prohibit reproduction is intended to cover 'work'. It is, apparent from the general scheme of the Berne Convention and Article 2(5) and (8), in particular, the protection of certain subject matters as artistic or literary works presupposes that they are intellectual creations.

Note that the European case is different from *Authors Guild v Google* case because the content creator in the second case lost interest in the reproduction. In the former case, the online distributor circulated online information to support the original author.

4.4.2 Virtual reality

Virtual reality (VR) is a new form of computer-generated experience where the user can interact with artificial objects on-screen by wearing equipment. Merriam-Webster dictionary defines VR as an artificial environment or surrounding experienced through sensory stimuli provided by a computer and in which one's actions partially determine what happens in the environment. Currently, in Thailand, VR is applied mainly for entertainment rather than for business and productivity purposes. Hence, it might be too soon to make an economic impact assessment on this type of technology.

VR also concerns IP, which might lead to legal disputes. For example, when new VR gadgets are invented, the issue of patent protection comes into play. VR advertisement involves replication and the use of brand names, logos, and other trademark-related signs. VR technology in Thailand is still in an infancy state. The experiences of other countries should be examined.

In the *ZeniMax Media v Oculus* case,[14] the US District Court had to decide, among other things, whether Oculus misappropriated the trade secrets of ZeniMax and whether Oculus used codes that infringed on ZeniMax's copyright. On the misappropriation of trade secrets, the court decided that the plaintiff failed to provide sufficient evidence to prove damages. The court further explained that 'even if there had been sufficient evidence regarding Plaintiff's damages, Plaintiffs' claim would still fail because the evidence is insufficient to prove any alleged damages were proximately caused by the Defendants' act of false designation'.[15] VR innovation is a developing process of past technology. Thus, it benefits society provided that the former inventors will enjoy benefits if they can provide sufficient evidence that such technology is part of their trade secret. Another claim involves the infringement of plaintiffs' copyright. The court found that it is difficult to prove copyright code infringement in computer software. However, the plaintiffs referred to the Abstraction-Filtration-Comparison (AFC) test, an analysis system to break down a computer program into particles and compare ZeniMax and Oculus codes. Finally, there was enough similarity, resulting in copyright code infringement. Oculus was ordered to pay US$50 million for such infringement. This means that understanding the complexity of technology is essential for lawmakers and the courts. However, although the US has advanced technology, the jury accepted the complexity in applying the AFC test. If such a situation arises in Thailand, it is interesting to see how judges would tackle the issue.

4.4.3 Platforms

Platforms refer to online applications that allow individuals to contribute to a particular ecosystem or marketplace. Mostly, it is free of charge. According to the European Commission, the online platforms in the digital economy have grown into a wide-ranging set of activities, including online advertising platforms, marketplaces, search engines, social media and creative content outlets, application distribution platform, communications services, payment systems, and other platforms (European Commission 2016). Such platforms play an essential role in the daily life of people. Well-known platforms include eBay, Amazon, Airbnb, and Uber. Platforms also have an economic role in the digital economy (Oxera 2015). An online marketplace's existence cuts the costs of creating, distributing, acquiring, and providing goods and services. Consumers can conveniently choose any options, varieties, and varieties of products with bargaining power. At the same time, business operators have more opportunities to expand their market, reduce costs, advertise, and cooperate through repeated interaction. Due to the advent of this technology, the problem of IP rights unavoidably follows.

In the *Scarlet Extended SA/SABAM* case,[16] the Court of Justice of the EU had to decide whether Scarlet, an Internet service provider, had the right to address a filtering system for electronic communications for an unlimited period and at its expense against unlawful use committed by its customers. The court stated that 'holders of intellectual property rights may apply for an injunction against intermediaries, such as ISPs, whose services are being used by a third party to infringe their rights'[17] and 'intermediaries to take measures aimed not only at bringing to an end infringements already committed against intellectual property rights using their information society services but also at preventing further infringements'.[18] Consequently, the court found that the filtering system imposed on an Internet service provider did not conform with Articles 8 and 11 of the EU Charter of Fundamental Rights. The filtering system only benefited copyright holders in musical works. However, it harmed the Internet service provider and Internet users' rights to protect personal data and freedom of expression.[19]

Another interesting case provided by the ECJ is *Bonnier Audio v Perfect Communication Sweden*.[20] The court had to decide whether public distributors infringed the exclusive rights of publishers to reproduce certain audiobooks. In this case, the distributors transferred and shared data between computers connected to the Internet. The ECJ concluded that 'legislation must be regarded as likely, in principle, to ensure a fair balance between the protection of intellectual property rights enjoyed by copyright holders and the protection of personal data enjoyed by Internet subscribers or users'.[21]

Internet platforms increasingly play a key role in this digital era. Consequently, IP infringement seems to increase at the same time. Many factors need to be considered alongside IP literacy such as human rights, including freedom of expression, right to privacy, personal data protection, and so on. While the European court relied on the principle of proportionality to weigh the conflict of interests between both parties, how Thai courts will answer these questions in the Thai legal context remains to be seen.

4.4.4 Online services

One fundamental technological development relating to IP protection is the use of computers and digital networks to provide services on the Internet. Online services have emerged from the advent of globalisation and the IoT in the digital era, such as an Internet service provider, an email provider, a news provider, an entertainment provider, a search engine, an e-commerce site, a financial site, and so on. Legal protection is required to protect various encryption systems used to control the dissemination of the works against the manufacture and distribution of decoding tools. Legal protection is also required for rights management information, which is necessary to attach to the works when transmitted.

In the decision on *Innoweb v Wegener*,[22] the Court of Justice of the European Union decided whether the claimant was reusing the plaintiff's database for Article 7(1) of the Database Directive when it made the dedicated meta-search engines (DMSEs) available to the public. The court found that

> that reutilisation involves a substantial part of the contents of the database concerned, if not the entire contents, since a dedicated meta-search engine such as that at issue in the main proceedings makes it possible to search the entire contents of that database, like a query entered directly in that database's search engine.[23]

The court concluded that legal protection of databases must be interpreted so that an operator who makes content available on the Internet, such as a DMSE, must be liable when a substantial part of the database was reutilised.

The court further acknowledged that only a small number of results may be shown, but not the entire database content.

Online service technology has already impacted Thai society. In 2013, the Online News Providers Association of Thailand (SONP) filed a lawsuit against Apple, Inc. to the Central Intellectual Property and International Trade Court of Thailand. The court found that Apple, Inc. infringed IPR and trademark, allowing illegal news applications to be available for download in AppStore.[24] Apple, Inc. agreed to pay compensation. This is the first case that the association of Thai news gathered to sue Apple, Inc., stopping unauthorised news in its application. Such applications comprised *THAINEWs+*, *Tiny–Thai News Reader*, *Thai News Reader*, *EveryNews*, and *Thai Newspaper*. Both parties, however, concluded a mediation agreement leading to the SONP to withdraw the case.

This *SONP v Apple, Inc.* case promoted understanding of IP rights in the news because news facts have no IP rights. However, news analyses, pictures, and their structure might be protected as copyright works under the law. Thus, using such information on the Internet without authorisation in any form would be considered an infringement.

Undoubtedly, how the country will use digital technology to drive its Thailand 4.0 policy depends mostly on how it can implement the laws, including the IP law, to prevent online infringement.

4.5 Concluding remarks

The promotion of innovative digital technology presents the IP system with a unique set of challenges. Digital technology shares some characteristics with the innovations generally protected by patents and others with innovations protected by copyright. Nevertheless, a unique combination of patent, copyright, and trade secret law has emerged to protect the technology. This chapter argues that the existing system of rights is inconsistent with the first principles of the IP system. It shows how the combination of protections available to technology developers provides a suboptimal incentive structure for innovation. This chapter does not contend that the existing IP regime has failed to generate a vibrant digital industry. However, it shows how unfunctional protective regimes could prevent knowledge dissemination and mitigate commercial competition.

Even though protected works require creativity and possibly devotion, the product outcome is merely a set(s) of 'data' in a machine-readable format presented by an electronic device. The cost of reproduction is therefore often low (Posner and Landes 1989). Decisions on intellectual infringement cases rely heavily on a case-by-case basis. However, failing to provide an effective solution to the digital-related infringement issue will prevent society from benefiting from this new technology in many ways. The author might lose the incentive to make his or her work public and more likely circulate the work privately to reduce the risk of copying (Posner and Landes 1989). The infringer, on the other hand, enjoys benefits from illegal, yet hassle-less, reproduction. While consumers enjoy the product at a lower price, such a price might not reflect the creation's actual cost. As a result, society might face difficulties in fostering innovations or creations.

Attempting to protect digital works by excessively expanding the scope of exclusive rights might harm society. Overprotection may hamper individuals' right to access information that constitutes the 'marketplace of ideas' that help reveal truths for society's sake. By contrast, balancing IP with many other values becomes a huge burden to lawmakers and government authorities. Judges inevitably require a thorough understanding of social science and economics to make fateful decisions. Otherwise, Thailand's ambition to promote the digital economy might turn out to be fruitless.

Notes

1 Judgement of the Central IP&IT Court, Case No. (Black) Aor 326/2542; Case No. (Red) Aor 784/2542, *The Intellectual Property and International Trade Law Forum: Special Issue 1999*, Bangkok, 1999, pp. 534–48.
2 Judgement of the Central IP&IT Court, Case No. (Black) Aor 372/2542; Case No. (Red) Aor 785/2542, *The Intellectual Property and International Trade Law Forum: Special Issue 1999*, Bangkok, 1999, pp. 549–56.
3 In Germany, *Südwestdeutsche Inkasso v Bappart and Burker, Computer GmbH Federal Supreme Court* 1985 held that programs must represent an individual, original, creative achievement, exceeding the average skills displayed in developing computer programs.
4 *University of London Press v University Tutorial Press Ltd.*, [1916] 2 Ch 601.
5 *Macmillan & Co. Ltd v K&J Cooper* (1923) 40 TLR 186.
6 *Express Newspaper Plc V Liverpool Daily Post & Echo Pl* (1985), 1 WLR 1089.
7 An exclusive licensee has, except against the copyright owner, the same rights and remedies in respect of matters occurring after the grant of the licence as if the licence had been an assignment.
8 Electronic Transactions Act B.E. 2544 (2001).
9 Personal Data Protection Act B.E. 2562 (2019).
10 Cybersecurity Act B.E. 2562 (2019).
11 *Authors Guild, Inc. v. Google Inc.*, No. 13-4829-cv (US Court of Appeals for the Second Circuit), 16 October 2015.
12 Ibid., p.46.
13 *Infopaq International v. Danske Dagblades Forening*, C-5/08 [2009] ECR I-6569.
14 *ZeniMax Media Inc. et al. v. Oculus VR, Inc. et al.*, No. 3:14-cv-01849-P (US District Court for Northern District of Texas), 2 February 2017.
15 Ibid., p.15.
16 *Scarlet Extended SA v Société Belge des Auteurs, Compositeurs et Éditeurs SCRL (SABAM)* (C-70/10) [2011] E.C.R. I-11959 (24 November 2011).
17 Ibid., para. 30.
18 Ibid., para. 31.
19 The Court of Justice of the European Union also followed this argumentation and came out with the same conclusion in *Belgische Vereniging van Auteurs, Componisten en Uitgevers CVBA (SABAM) v Netlog NV* (C-360/10) (2012) E.C.R. I-0000 (16 February 2012).
20 *Bonnier Audio AB v Perfect Communication Sweden AB* (C-461/10) [2012] EUECJ (19 April 2012).
21 Ibid., para. 60.

22 *Innoweb BV v Wegener ICT Media BV and Wegener Mediaventions BV*, (C-202/12) [2013] (19 December 2013).

23 Ibid., para. 53.

24 *Thairath Online* (11 December 2013), 'Apple, Inc. Agreed to Pay Compensation of IP Infringement submitted by the Online News Providers Association', https://www.thairath.co.th/content/388662 (accessed 29 December 2018) (Thai version); and *Posttoday* (11 December 2013), 'Apple, Inc. Agreed to Pay Compensation: IP Infringement Case submitted by the Online News Providers Association', https://www.posttoday.com/social/general/264215 (accessed 29 December 2018) (Thai version).

Bibliography

Bainbridge, D.I. (1990), *Computers and the Law*. London: Pitman Publishing.

Bently, L. and B. Sherman (2002), *Intellectual Property Law*. 4th ed. New York: Oxford University Press.

European Commission (2016), Communication from the Commission to the European Parliament, the Council, the European Economic and Social Committee and the Committee of the Regions–Online Platforms and the Digital Single Market Opportunities and Challenges for Europe, COM/2016/0288 final, 25 May 2016.

Made in India (2016), 'Make in India: The Vision, New Processes, Sectors, Infrastructure, and Mindset', http://www.makeinindia.com/article/-/v/make-in-india-reason-vision-for-the-initiative (accessed 27 December 2018).

Merriam-Webster (n.d.), 'Virtual Reality', https://www.merriam-webster.com/dictionary/virtual%20reality (accessed 28 December 2018).

National Reform Council of Thailand (2015), *Visions and Strategies to Thailand Reform and The Modification of Governmental Mechanism*, https://www.parliament.go.th/ewtadmin/ewt/parliament_parcy/download/parcy/001.pdf (in Thai) (accessed 27 December 2018).

Oster, J. (2015), *Media Freedom as a Fundamental Right*. New York: Cambridge University Press, p. 17.

Oxera (2015), 'Benefits of Online Platforms', October 2015, https://www.oxera.com/wp-content/uploads/2018/07/The-benefits-of-online-platforms-main-findings-October-2015.pdf.pdf (accessed 29 December 2018).

Phichagonakasit, L. (2019), 'Thailand 4.0: Opportunities in the S-Curve 10 Targeted Industries', *Asia IoT Business Platform: Driving Digitalisation Ecosystems in ASEAN*, 1 July 2019, http://iotbusiness-platform.com/blog/thailand-4-0-opportunities-in-the-s-curve-10-targeted-industries/ (accessed 27 December 2019).

Posner, R.A. and W.M. Landes (1989), 'An Economic Analysis of Copyright Law', *The Journal of Legal Studies*, 18(2), pp. 325–363.

Subhapholsiri, D. (1996), *Copyright Law*. Bangkok: Nithitham Publishing House.

Technology Strategy Board (2015), 'Innovate UK: Design in Innovation Strategy 2015–2019', https://www.gov.uk/government/publications/design-in-innovation-strategy-2015-to-2020 (accessed 27 December 2018).

UNCTAD (2017), 'Strengthening the Creative Industries for Development in the Republic of Korea', UNCTAD/DITC/TED/2017/4, Geneva: UNCTAD.

USLegal (n.d.), 'Digital Distribution Law and Legal Definition', https://definitions.uslegal.com/d/digital-distribution/ (accessed 28 December 2018).

Weeraworawit, W. (1998), 'Copyright in Thailand', *Intellectual Property and International Trade Law Forum* 1998, pp. 46–60.

White House of President Barack Obama (2015), 'Nation of Makers', https://obamawhitehouse.archives.gov/nation-of-makers (accessed 27 December 2018).
WIPO (2002), 'Intellectual Property and Small and Medium-sized Enterprises (SMES)', www.wipo.int/edocs/mdocs/sme/en/wipo_ip_bkk_/wipo_ip_bkk_02_5_b.pdf (accessed 28 December 2020).

5 Copyright protection in Malaysia

Development and challenges of the digital economy

Nurhidayah binti Abdullah and Hanira binti Hanafi

5.1 Introduction

As the global economy increasingly develops, the protection of intellectual property rights (IPR) has become a critical issue for advanced economies and emerging markets. Many emerging Asian economies, including Malaysia, have made significant progress in developing, implementing, and consolidating their domestic IPR systems. At the same time, the global economy is undergoing a digital transformation that is moving towards the 'digital economy'. It is self-evident; every day, borderless online connections are happening globally among people, businesses, devices, data, and processes. Business is conducted in a new paradigm shift; it is moving away from the traditional way of business at a breakneck speed through the Internet and the World Wide Web. In this regard, the connection between IPR and the digital economy is very close. Recently, Malaysia also became the first country to establish a digital free trade zone, a special trade zone providing a state-of-the-art platform for small and medium-sized enterprises (SMEs) to promote e-commerce. Mara Warwick, World Bank Country Director for Brunei Darussalam, Malaysia, Philippines, and Thailand commented that 'Malaysia is doing many things right to promote its digital economy as a new engine of growth – ranging from digitizing the delivery of public services to broadening connectivity to promoting digital entrepreneurship' (World Bank 2018a).

One of the mechanisms to promote the digital economy is protection, which acts as an armour for its development and challenges. The focus of the discussion is on copyright, one of the elements of IPR. The issue under discussion will be on the creative industry as it constitutes the current economic trend and falls under copyright.

The outline of this chapter is as follows. Section 5.2 provides the landscape of the country, specifically its economic background. Section 5.3 discusses the background of IPR protection in Malaysia, followed by the local and international regulatory framework in Section 5.4. Section 5.5 focuses on copyright in the creative industry, including its development and challenges. Section 5.6 concludes and provides policy recommendations.

DOI: 10.4324/9781003147657-6

5.2 Economic background of Malaysia

Historically, Malaysia had moved from a highly agrarian and commodity export–intensive economy towards a more open and diversified economy with robust performance. The change in policy to foster new industries, among others, benefited Malaysia in terms of a gradual decline in income inequality and increasing participation of the Bumiputera (Malays and indigenous groups) in the urban and modern economy. The government started promoting export-oriented industrialisation, with a strong emphasis on manufacturing activities; production of microelectronics products; and exports of tin, rubber, palm oil products, and crude oil. From 1960 to 2016, Malaysia enjoyed favourable real gross domestic product (GDP) growth averaging at 6.4%, attributable to policies that sustained rapid and comprehensive economic growth (World Bank, 2018b). In 2016, real GDP was 4.2% and reached 5.9% in 2017 (Department of Statistics Malaysia, 2017). Apart from global demands, strong and robust domestic demand accelerated economic growth, which corresponded with the increment of employment rate at 3.0% annually, and 7.9% of capital stock increment annually from 1960 to 2016 (World Bank 2018c). Today, Malaysia is synonymous with the production and exportation of electrical and electronics products, totalling about 37% of gross exports in 2017 (Department of Statistics Malaysia, 2017).

Malaysia was not spared the Asian financial crisis in 1998 but remained steadfast by adopting controversial and unconventional policies to stride the trouble. Malaysia chose to fortify macroeconomic policies and strengthen its financial sector by making it more resilient, especially the local currency bond markets. Pre-emptive measures were taken, and the authorities were on high alert for any risks and irregularities in the markets. The policies proved relatively successful, reducing external risks on a domestic economy while stabilising and promoting resilience in the economy. Market resiliency and strong domestic demand mitigated the effect of the 2008 global financial crisis, as well as accelerating its recovery.

Additionally, global value chains (GVCs) have become a dominant feature of world trade and investment, encompassing developing, emerging, and developed economies. The process of producing goods, from raw materials to finished products, is increasingly fragmented and is carried out whatever necessary skills and materials are available at competitive cost and quality. Due to its openness to trade, Malaysia was also deeply involved in GVCs, specialising in the final stages of the production process during the 1990s. The participation was driven by efficiency gains whereby the production spreads across countries (Han and Hwa 2017). From a regional perspective, GVCs in ASEAN are currently manifesting the growth and spread of international and regional production networks in the region. These networks comprise both transnational corporations and local firms as producers, and they form several value chains. Production value chains created in ASEAN spread into several ASEAN countries including Malaysia, forming regional value chains (RVCs), and may go beyond the region, forming GVCs. Although the formation of GVCs and RVCs could differ by industry or product, generally speaking, ASEAN member countries have intensified their production networks by importing more and more intermediate products and integrating these products into their export products, thus establishing value chains. Furthermore, these export products have been increasingly reintegrated into exports from other countries as intermediate products (Masataka 2019).

The efforts to diversify the economy have benefited the country by boosting growth; increasing job opportunity and productivity; accessing worldwide markets more; exchanging capital, knowledge, and technology; enhancing the business environment; and enlarging the GVCs. Gross national income per capita reached US$9,650 in 2017, and Malaysia is projected to attain high-income status in the next decade (World Bank 2017). Furthermore, policies advocating the business-friendly environment have been recognised globally in Malaysia's 18th rank in the World Bank's Ease of Doing Business 2016 index (World Bank 2015).

Against the backdrop of the commendable achievements accumulated over the years, fears of the future remain high. The objective of securing a high-income nation status by the next decade is hampered by growing anxiety on the effect of economic growth on the improvements in living standards and cost of living. The government believes that harnessing Industry 4.0 and digitalising the economy might bring solutions or options to the table. By harnessing the digital economy's potential, the government believes that becoming a developed nation is possible within the prescribed period. To survive the coming decades, Malaysia must embrace the digitalisation of the economy and prepare its workforce with the right mindset and skills appropriate for the digital economy.

5.3 An overview of IPR protection in Malaysia

Various government agencies strive to translate the government's aspirations into working policies, assistance, and standards, including the Ministry of Domestic Trade, Co-operatives, and Consumerism (MDTCC), the Intellectual Property Corporation of Malaysia (MyIPO), and the National Intellectual Property Policy (DHIN). The MDTCC took steps to enhance Malaysia's enforcement regime, including active cooperation with rights holders on IPR enforcement matters, ongoing training of prosecutors for specialised IPR courts, and the reestablishment of a Special Anti-Piracy Taskforce in 2013. MyIPO was established in March 2003 to regulate matters relating to IP. Over time, online registration and IP courts were introduced and developed. The government also introduced the DHIN to leverage IP as a new growth engine to improve economic and social prosperity. Agencies such as MyIPO and Intellectual Asset Management were established. These comprise three value chains – IP creation, IP protection, and IP commercialisation.

The commitment to IPR was put under the responsibility of multiple ministries and government agencies such as the Ministry of Communication and Multimedia Malaysia; Malaysian Administration Modernisation and Management Planning Unit; Ministry of Domestic Trade, Co-operatives and Consumerism; and the Ministry of Home Affairs, supported by the Royal Malaysia Police and MyIPO.

The genesis of the economy's digitalisation can be traced to the establishment in 1996 of the Malaysia Digital Economy Corporation (MDEC), formerly known as the Multimedia Development Corporation. It functions as an advisory arm to the government in matters including legislation, policies concerning the growth and proliferation of local technology firms, investment, and the development of Cyberjaya. The creation of Cyberjaya, modelled after Silicon Valley, brings aspirations to integrate and support the high-tech industry, being the country's science park of sorts. Apart from Cyberjaya, in 1996, MDEC also established the Multimedia Super Corridor (MSC) to unite, amalgamate, and manage digital development in the country. Firms receiving MSC status enjoy incentives in the form of exemptions from local ownership rules, recruitment of knowledge employees abroad, the liberty to acquire capital worldwide, tax breaks, and research and development grants.

As pointed out earlier, MDEC is tasked with promoting the digital economy and entrepreneurship in the country. The agency aims to attract foreign investors, support local technological talents, promote a digital-friendly environment, and foster more inclusive technology adoption. The MSC, the brainchild of MDEC, is one of the efforts to provide stimulus and incentives to increase and manage digital improvement in the country, with business firms situated inside the area being blessed with benefits associated with the program.

5.4 Regulatory framework

This section highlights the regulatory framework of IPR protection in Malaysia. IP protection in Malaysia comprises patents, trademarks, industrial designs, copyright, geographical indications, and layout designs of integrated circuits (MIDA 2019). The discussion includes the local statutes relevant to IPR protection and later preceded by international commitments.

5.4.1 Laws related to IPR protection in Malaysia

Several local statutes relevant to IPR protection in Malaysia include statutes on patents, trademarks, industrial designs, copyright, geographical indications, and layout designs of integrated circuits. All statutes fall under the jurisdiction of MyIPO, a corporation established to facilitate all IPR-related matters. Malaysia is also a member of the World Intellectual Property Organisation and a signatory to the Paris Convention and the Berne Convention, which govern IPR.

Patent Act 1983 (Act 291) and the Patents Regulations 1986 govern patent protection in Malaysia. This Act regulates the registration and procedures related to patents, which also include the rights of patent owners. The

Act also provides several offences which include falsification of registered and unregistered patent agents, where any breach of this Act may expose one to fine and imprisonment.

Trademark protection is governed by the Trademarks Act 2019 and the Trademarks Regulations 1997. The Act protects registered trademarks and service marks in Malaysia. Other people or enterprises cannot merely use the trademarks registered by its proprietor or authorised user. Legal action against this breach of the law may be initiated against abusers. Once registered, the tenure of protection is up to ten years and is renewable every ten years thereafter. The owner also enjoys the right to deal or assign a licence to its use. This Act also covers matters related to conventions and international arrangements, namely, convention countries and the Paris Convention.

The protection of industrial designs in Malaysia is governed by Industrial Designs Act 1996 and Industrial Designs Regulations 1999. Industrial Designs Act 1996 provides registration procedures and grants the rights of registered industrial designs as personal property capable of assignment and transmission through the law's operation. Registered industrial designs are protected for an initial period of five years which may be extended for another two five-year terms, thus providing total protection of 15 years. Besides, there is also a provision on offences related to falsification of registration where the punishment may include imprisonment and fine.

The Copyright Act 1987 provides comprehensive protection for copyrightable works. The Act outlines the nature of works eligible for copyright (which includes computer programs), the scope of protection, and how the protection is accorded. Copyright protection for literary, musical, or artistic works is for the duration of the life of the author plus 50 years after his death. In sound recordings, broadcasts, and films, copyright is protected for 50 years after the works are first published or made. The Act also protects the performer's rights in a live performance, which shall continue to remain in effect for 50 years from the beginning of the calendar year following the year of the live performance. A unique feature of the Act is the inclusion of provisions for its enforcement.

Part VIA of the Act prohibits the illegal filming and recording of films in theatres. These should help control and eventually prevent film piracy. The punishment for any breach may extend to a fine of 100,000 Malaysian ringgit (RM) and five years' imprisonment. Amendment was made in October 2003 to provide enforcement officers of the MDTCC with the power to arrest and arrest without a warrant. They are appointed to enforce the Act; they have rights to enter any premises suspected of having infringing copies and to search and seize infringing copies and contrivances.

The Layout Designs of Integrated Circuits Act 2000 protects the layout designs of integrated circuits. The layout design is deemed original if it is a result of the creator's intellectual efforts. The layout design of an integrated circuit does not require registration. The tenure of protection is up to ten years from the date of its commercial exploitation or 15 years from the date of creation if not commercially exploited. The owner who enjoys the protection may take legal action against any abuse of his or her rights. Besides, their rights, which can be transmitted or assigned either partly or wholly through assignment, licence, testamentary instrument, and delegation by operation of law, are considered personal property. The Act is consistent with the Agreement on Trade-Related Aspects of Intellectual Property Rights or TRIPS Agreement. It aims to provide a guarantee to investors in Malaysia's electronics industry and ensure the growth of technology in the country.

The Geographical Indications Act 2000 protects any production of goods based on their origin. A given quality, reputation, or other characteristics of the goods are essentially attributable to their geographical origin. Section 2 of the Act specifies the meaning. The word 'goods' is further clarified under the Act's same section to include any natural or agricultural or handicraft product. Section 14 provides that any person may contest the registration of geographical indication if it is found, among others, to be inconsistent with public order and morality or if the goods do not fall under the meaning provided under Section 2. The registration period is conferred up to 10 years and can be renewed, subject to the conditions provided by the Act.

5.4.2 Malaysia's commitment to international IPR standards

Generally speaking, Malaysia adequately protects both local and foreign investors. Its IP laws conform to international standards and are reviewed by the TRIPS Council periodically. Even local statutes stated earlier provide an international commitment to convention countries, particularly on copyright matters. Copyright Act 1987 provides comprehensive protection for copyrightable works. At the international level, Malaysia has shown strong support for IPR protection, too. The country is also a member of the World Intellectual Property Organization (WIPO) and a signatory to the Paris Convention and the Berne Convention. It is also a signatory to the TRIPS Agreement signed under the auspices of the World Trade Organization. In December 2011, the Malaysian Parliament passed amendments to the copyright law designed to comply with, among other things, the WIPO Copyright Treaty and the WIPO Performance and Phonogram Treaty, to define Internet service provider liabilities, and prohibit the unauthorised recording of motion pictures in theatres. Malaysia subsequently acceded to the WIPO Copyright Treaty and the WIPO Performance and Phonogram Treaty in September 2012.

The Global Intellectual Property Center Index is a study that helps governments and businesses better understand the concrete benefits of robust IP systems. The 2015 edition maps the IP regimes of 80 countries, including five ASEAN nations – Indonesia, Malaysia, Singapore, Thailand, and Viet Nam. Malaysia improved its score in the copyright, related rights, and limitations category from 3.53 in 2014 (Pugtach et al. 2014) to 3.78 in 2015 (Pugtach et al. 2015]), and 4.28 in 2018 (Pugtach et al., 2018). As the 2012

Copyright Act was amended, enforcement was ongoing and had gathered traction. Raids on alleged operators of pirated online materials and websites, such as jiwang.org (*The Star* 2013) and syok.org, had been conducted since 2013 (Kam Jia Yi and Jusoh 2016). Furthermore, the launch of 'Ops Semak Tulen', an anti-software piracy campaign, had included up to 20,000 businesses under the radar of the authorities.

5.4.3 Free trade agreement: Comprehensive and Progressive Agreement for Trans-Pacific Partnership (CPTPP)

The Trans-Pacific Partnership Agreement (TPPA) is a trade agreement between 12 Pacific Rim nations: Australia, Brunei Darussalam, Canada, Chile, Japan, Malaysia, Mexico, New Zealand, Peru, Singapore, the United States (US), and Viet Nam. It was signed on 4 February 2016 in Auckland, New Zealand. In light of the US withdrawal from the TPPA, the remaining 11 member countries decided to pursue the realisation of the agreement under the CPTPP. The CPTPP is one of the largest free trade agreements in the world. It will provide enhanced market access to key Asian markets and increased participation in the agreement by providing accession provisions to countries wishing to join the CPTPP.

One of the main issues discussed in the CPTPP is IPR, particularly of pharmaceuticals. An analyst claimed that IPR would allow pharmaceutical firms to raise the value of trade through higher prices and not more goods (Govind 2018). The production of generic drugs would be delayed and would have serious consequences on the standard of healthcare in Malaysia. Twenty-two of the IPR provisions are from the CPTPP. These are US-centric and have little relevance for the remaining member countries. Article 18 of the CPTPP provides regulations and legal principles about copyright. The bulk of the provisions under Section H are almost identical to Malaysia's Copyright Act, save in some matters, especially the suspended rights (Table 5.1). Each of the 11 countries in the CPTPP has its laws and regulations to handle copyright infringements. Therefore, there is no need to impose one global standard (Abdul Ghani Azmi et al. 2018).

Furthermore, the TPPA also has stronger criminal copyright provisions, taken from the Anti-Counterfeiting Trade Agreement. Article 18.77 outlines the jurisprudence of such criminal liability:

> Each Party shall provide for criminal procedures and penalties to be applied at least in cases of willful trademark counterfeiting or copyright or related rights piracy on a commercial scale. In respect of willful copyright or related rights piracy, 'on a commercial scale' includes at least: (a) acts carried out for commercial advantage or financial gain; and (b) significant acts, not carried out for commercial advantage or financial gain, that have a substantial prejudicial impact on the interests of the copyright or related rights holder in relation to the marketplace.

Table 5.1 The Suspended Rights

a) Article 18.63 (Term of protection for copyright and related rights)	An increase in the term of the copyright period, from 50 years to 70 years. Malaysia's Copyright Act provides for 50 years for the right to subsist.
b) Article 18.68 (Technological protection measures)	The section concerns the technological protection measures and unauthorised circumvention of the measures. The Copyright Act does provide for such protection, although without the operative words engaged willingly and for the purpose of commercial advantage or financial gain.
c) Article 18.69 (Rights management information)	Akin to the technological protection measures, Malaysia's Copyright Act does have provisions for the Rights Management Information (RMI), and the penalty associated with unauthorised removal or alteration of the RMI. The footnote to Article 18.69 paragraph 1(a)(i) suggests that knowledge requirement may be dispensed with, culminating in the effect that the knowledge requirement may be irrelevant in prosecuting the offence. Dispensing with the knowledge requirement is harsh and may open up prosecution for otherwise unintentional alteration or removal of the RMI.
d) Article 18.79 (Protection of encrypted program–carrying satellite and cable signals)	The article is concerned with any manufacture, assembly, modification, import, export, sell, lease, or distribution of a device of the system, knowingly or having reason to know that such device can decode an encrypted program–carrying satellite signal without the authorisation of the lawful distributor of such signal.
e) Article 18.82 (Legal remedies and safe harbours)	This article tries to impose a single method in dealing with liability on the part of service providers and the issues of safe harbours.

Source: Authors.

The net effect of the provisions seems to suggest that even if the crime committed is not for commercial advantage or without any financial gain, it can still be prosecuted as long as it causes a substantial prejudicial impact on the interests of the copyright or related rights holder in relation to the marketplace (Abdul Ghani Azmi et al. 2018). Recklessly disregarding the chances that the material used might be a violation can raise the presumption of intentional violation. Moreover, knowledge can be constructive or implied; a total disregard of the copyright and indiscriminate sharing of the material can be construed as wilful. This is a departure from our stand, which is the requirement of *mens rea* (knowledge of wrongdoing).

Furthermore, the term 'commercial scale' could be extended to include acts 'not carried out for commercial advantage or financial gain but which have a substantial prejudicial impact on the interest of the copyright or related rights holder in relation to the marketplace'. On the point of criminal liability for aiding and abetting, even an innocent intermediary may be subjected to a criminal penalty, if US jurisprudence were to be interpreted. As a consequence, there is a reasonable risk that the local law has cast Malaysian criminal net a bit too far (Abdul Ghani Azmi et al., 2018, p. 472).

Strictly for copyright, there is no indication that ratifying the CPTPP will accord the country better and greater power in combating copyright violations. The 2012 amendment to the Copyright Act indicates that Malaysia is heading towards the right path. With the suspension of some of the more substantial articles in the agreement, the CPTPP is but a tamer version of the Trans-Pacific Partnership (TPP) Agreement, as most of the suspended articles leaned towards the US's agenda and interest. It is all the more reason not to ratify as Malaysia has its own version of the suspended articles.

Despite the IPR issue, another contentious issue that Malaysia would have to grapple with would be the TPP's investor–state dispute settlement provisions. These provisions would allow foreign companies to sue host country governments for loss of profits, including future profits, due to policy changes that promote national interest. The arbitration by these tribunals would override national laws and judiciaries in the country. The agenda on state-owned enterprises (SOEs) will likely affect Malaysian SOEs because many of them emphasise public welfare instead of profit maximisation. Currently, many SOEs can operate without profit, with non-commercial assistance being provided to them to ensure business sustainability. On the contrary, the TPP prohibits non-commercial assistance to SOEs, thus, adversely affecting competition. This will undoubtedly affect many SMEs in the country that form the economy's backbone.

In short, no narrative is compelling for Malaysia to ratify the CPTPP as we continue to enjoy the benefits of free trade agreements with many countries in the CPTPP. There is still no concrete confirmation as to when or will Malaysia accede or ratify the CPTPP. Deputy Minister Ong Kian Ming gave a somewhat cryptic answer on whether Malaysia will ratify the CPTPP. Earlier, in an interview with the *South China Morning Post*, Minister Darell Leiking indicated that signing the CPTPP may involve lengthy deliberations, and non-ratification is still in the picture. He suggested that Malaysia seek bilateral agreements, however, as an alternative (Jaipragas 2019). Until today, the position towards the CPTPP in Malaysia remains uncertain.

5.5 Copyright and the digital economy in Malaysia

This section highlights the matters related to the development of copyright protection in the digital era, including the development of copyright and the creative industry in Malaysia. Further discussion also includes the challenges of copyright protection in the digital economy, which small and medium-sized industries face as they are actively involved in the creative industry sector.

5.5.1 Development of copyright and creative industry in Malaysia

Copyright is a branch of many forms of IPR that is important due to the advancement of the Internet of Things. It protects the creative industries – music, film, television, publishing, games, and software. Digital technologies, the companies that exploit them, and the business models they facilitate are all potentially affected by copyright (ITU News 2011).

The creative industries receive much protection from copyright as it is the best mechanism to protect them. The creative industries 'are those whose products originate from individual creativity, skill, and talent and which have a potential for wealth and job creation through the generation and exploitation of IP' (Barker and Lee 2017, pp. 21–37). The National Creative Industries Policy (or *Dasar Industri Kreatif Negara* [DIKN]), issued in 2009, is the only articulation of a comprehensive policy on creative industries implemented by the government. The DIKN aims to empower the creative industries based on creativity and innovation – thus contributing to a high-income economy – and uphold the nation's cultural heritage (Rais 2011). In Malaysia, the creative industries are categorised into Multimedia Creative Industry, Cultural Arts Creative Industry, and Cultural Heritage Creative Industry (Table 5.2).

Creative agencies comprise many agencies, schemes, and programs. The Ministry of Communication and Multimedia Malaysia (known as Kementerian Komunikasi dan Multimedia Malaysia [MCMM]) and the Prime Minister's Office, which oversees the Economic Transformation Programme whose goals are closely aligned with *Wawasan 2020*, mostly implement the creative industry policy. Under the MCMM are three important agencies: Multimedia Development Corporation (now MDEC), National Film Development Corporation Malaysia (Perbadanan Kemajuan Filem Nasional

Table 5.2 Classification of the Creative Industries

Multimedia Creative Industries	• Film and TV • Advertising • Design • Animation and Digital Content
Cultural Arts Creative Industries	• Crafts • Visual Arts • Music • Performing Arts • Creative Writing • Fashion and Textiles
Cultural Heritage Creative Industries	• Museum • Archives • Restoration • Preservation

Source: Malaysian Communications and Multimedia Commission (2009).

Table 5.3 Economic Data about the Creative Multimedia Cluster in Malaysia

Year	*Revenue (billion RM)*	*Exports (million RM)*	*Jobs*
2008	3.2	132	7,724
2009	4.028	186	7,028
2010	4.84685	255.98	8,086
2011	6.07	363.46	9,183
2012	6.99	490	11,070
2013	6.39	430	10,170
2014	7.10	500	10,515
2015	7.24	850	10,639
2016	7.60	1,170	10,916
2017	7.91	1,420	11,590

Source: MDEC (2015).

Malaysia [FINAS]), and the Malaysian Communications and Multimedia Commission.

Table 5.3 refers to the economic data on the creative multimedia cluster. It depicts an increase in revenues, exports, and job opportunities, particularly after launching the National Creative Industries Policy in 2009. The revenues increased from RM3.2 billion in 2008 to RM7.91 billion in 2017, showing tremendous growth in nine years. In 2017, the export sales (in terms of financial performance) recorded the highest at RM1,420 billion. Also, job opportunities significantly increased in the industry, particularly in 2012 (11,070) and 2017 (11,590).

According to the 2016 *Kuala Lumpur as a Cultural and Innovative City Report*, Kuala Lumpur's contribution to GDP is expected to increase through a five-year action plan – from RM11.2 billion in 2016 to RM19.4 billion by the end of 2021. Communications and Multimedia Minister Datuk Seri Salleh Said Keruak, who launched the report, said the creative economy is one of the world's most rapidly growing sectors.

> It is highly transformative in terms of income generation, job creation, and export earnings. At the same time, it also generates non-monetary value that reflects a nation's capacity to express itself artistically and creatively through its home-grown culture and heritage – be it film, music, literature, theatre, and the arts, which can be shared with the world,

Salleh said before launching the report.[1] One example is Les Copaque, a company that benefited from various government-sponsored facilities such as tax incentives, market access, and availability of low-cost yet high-quality computing technology that could render animation on par with Hollywood counterparts. The MDEC, a government-linked company, played a major role in supporting Les Copaque financially and logistically through pioneer incentives, apart from individual investors' backing. Similarly, another successful Multimedia Super Corridor-status company is Rhythm and Hues, an American visual effects and animation company based in California, but whose subsidiary is based in Cyberjaya, Malaysia. A company team is made up almost entirely of Malaysian talents from local universities and colleges. One of its successful files was *The Life of Pi* that won an Oscar award for visual effects (Sukumaran 2013).

The creative industry is not problem-free despite its tremendous growth in coping with the digital economy era. The industry itself is exposed to various copyright infringement cases, which include piracy of music, film, television programs, publications, games, and software. Furthermore, SMEs, the most relevant actors in the creative industry, also face challenges – such as financial constraints and ignorance of the importance of IPR protection – in coping with the digital era and copyright protection. The details of the challenges of the digital economy and copyright protection are discussed in the following section.

5.5.2 Challenges of the digital economy and copyright protection

5.5.2.1 Lack of awareness

Based on Ch'ng (2015), more movie directors are incorporating special effects and computer graphics in their movies, blurring the line that divides animation from live action. Barker and Lee (2017) argued that little emphasis seems to be given to addressing problems in how creative industries are structured, regulated, or operated. According to the Economic Transformation Plan, there is a lack of IPR awareness, competency, and capacity as the local content creation companies must reach out to the global market to ensure sustainable growth. The creative sector's key challenges include the low level of industry exposure, profile, and reputation; lack of awareness; and regulation enforcement (Harris et al. 2012).

5.5.2.2 Lengthy and time-consuming procedures

SMEs may be reluctant to protect their products or innovation through IP protection as they might think that IP systems are esoteric, involve too much hassle, and time-wasting (Gee et al., 2007). The narrative stems from inadequate knowledge of IP systems in Malaysia. SMEs find the IP system irrelevant to their business strategy and costly and complex to utilise. Fees associated with IP registration often forced newcomers to shy away from protecting their products or services through formal means. Thus, small companies may perceive that the IP protection benefits do not outweigh the costs that could be incurred to register their products or innovation. The perception that financial assistance from the government and the private sector can be hard to secure amplifies the problems (Idris 2003). SMEs may find delays in registration as an obstruction in finding potential licensees or partners to exploit an invention.

5.5.2.3 Ignorance of the importance of IPR protection

Ratzenböck (2004) noted that the creative sector, which depends on digitalisation and mainly comprises small-scale ventures, finds it hard to grow and develop globally. These small-scale ventures are challenged in securing the latest and modern technologies, which is paramount in innovation, mainly due to the inability to make a significant investment or be financially robust. Forty-three percent of innovative firms in Malaysia conceded that securing financial assistance would be a major obstacle, based on the Malaysian Innovation Survey of 2005–2008 (World Bank 2010). As for the SMEs, their inadequate legal, technical, and scientific expertise internally may hamper efficient IP management and governance, in addition to the complex IP system and limited access to legal guidance.

This may lead to ignorance of the importance of IPR protection. An invention that is not protected is exposed to the risks of being lost to bigger competitors that are financially robust and stable to market the invention at a cheaper rate, leaving the inventor without any reward for the effort. Such is the significance of IP for SMEs. IP, when registered and protected, could become a source of income and profit for SMEs. IP enables SMEs to turn their innovation and creativity to financial strength to fund further innovation. Apart from becoming business assets, IP products can be licensed, commercialised, or sold to generate more market share and profit margin (Idris 2003). In essence, firms that denounce IPR may risk losing not only their short-term profits but also any future earnings that capitalise on the IP itself.

5.5.2.4 Financial constraints

Md Nor et al. (2016) remarked that Malaysian SMEs faced difficulties in financing their innovation processes. Problems arose concerning financial assistance both from the government and the private sector. The high interest rate or profit charged, intricate loan process, and outright rejection of promotional packages contributed to hardships in financing innovation. Moreover, the SMEs noted that a lack of skilled human capital and employees, infrastructures, and technology would be detrimental to their creation. Stiff competition and weak competitiveness were other factors cited that would impede innovation.

Azizi (2010) indicated that low moral awareness on respecting IP rights, reflected from the proliferation of pirated software, caused a setback in the IP right. Purchasers should refrain from undertaking transactions when the price or terms of sale of the goods are inordinately low or 'too good to be true'. This strongly suggests the goods are not genuine. Distributors and rights holders should cooperate to have procedures and practices to verify their customers' (usually retailers') legitimacy or reputation to ensure that IPR-infringing goods are not mixed with genuine goods at the point of sale (Hung 2007). It is also to make the public aware that the manufacture and the trafficking of counterfeit and pirated products, including the import and export of such products, are illegal and may result in severe civil and/or criminal penalties (WIPO Magazine 2005). To overcome counterfeit and/or pirated goods, protecting supply chains requires close public–private sector collaboration. Both must work in concert to identify infringing goods and prevent them from entering the marketplace and international channels of commerce. In this interplay, SMEs should actively endeavour to ensure the security of their production and distribution chains. Indeed, close cooperation between the public and the private sectors is essential to secure supply chains and protect consumers and rights holders (Sukarmijan and Sapong 2014). Even though the industry has been developing well, especially on the export market, there are still challenges that need much attention, such as awareness and enforcement issues.

Malaysians doing business, particularly online sales, can easily bring counterfeit products comprising textiles and leather products, for example, from Viet Nam into Malaysia. Many scarves are imitations of Duck, Ariani, Bokitta, and the like. Furthermore, customs officers do not have specific training to identify counterfeit products. They are just interested in collecting customs duties on imported goods.

5.6 Policy recommendations

5.6.1 Strengthen enforcement and coordination between government agencies

Despite Malaysia's success in improving IP enforcement, key issues remain: the widespread availability of pirated and counterfeit products, the high rate of online piracy, and continued problems with book piracy. Therefore, continuous coordination among agencies – the MDTCC; the royal police; and customs authority – is pivotal in combating the problem, particularly in the digital era.

5.6.2 Create a talent pool to promote compliance and registration

Creating a highly qualified talent pool is extremely important to assist and facilitate the compliance and registration of IPR, particularly among SMEs. Providing relevant advice related to registration, licensing, owners' rights, and enforcement is essential to reduce uncertainty. The pool may comprise government agencies, lawyers, and relevant stakeholders.

5.6.3 Increase social awareness through social media

Nowadays, social media plays a vital role in educating or nurturing people on the importance of IPR protection, especially copyright issues. Many copyright issues are related to the awareness of people themselves to avoid copyright infringement or piracy. Undoubtedly, social media platforms, such as

Facebook, Twitter, WhatsApp, and YouTube, are approachable platforms to increase awareness, being the current mode of disseminating information. A similar approach as in cinemas – where an advertisement on piracy is shown before a movie starts – can be adopted in social media as a platform to convey the message.

5.6.4 A balance between domestic and international laws and the CPTPP

The legal protection given to copyright is parallel with international copyright protection, as discussed earlier. However, on the current issue of the CPTPP on IPR protection, Malaysia is still unsure whether to accede or ratify the CPTPP. A balance is needed to weigh its benefits and advantages. Many copyright provisions in the CPTPP are almost identical to Malaysian domestic law, which gives similar protection. Many of its provisions refer to American copyright laws, thus impeding the sovereignty if it is not well protected.

5.7 Conclusions

In conclusion, copyright protection is synonymous with the 'creative industry'. It aims to protect the industry's creativity and innovation. Recently, interest towards Malaysia's creative industry has been rising, contributing to many innovations, and boosting the economy in parallel with the booming digital economy era. Undoubtedly, infringement or piracy issues are the main hindrance to success, despite many successful stories. Government assistance is always at the end of the tunnel should the firms be ready to fight for it. Thus, to strengthen the enforcement section, it is recommended to increase social awareness through social media, provide a talent pool for promoting compliance and registration, and offer an avenue to protect its growth and development. Although Malaysia has not yet ratified the CPTPP, its mood is lukewarm due to the CPTPP's requirements on the domestic reform. Despite that, Malaysia is doing well in its bilateral dealings. Domestic laws' commitment is in line with international standards, which is adequate to give protection even without the CPTPP.

Notes

1 https://www.thesundaily.my/archive/creative-economy-boost-gdp-BUARCH524702

Bibliography

Abdul Ghani Azmi I.M., G.H. Heng, S.T. Pek, and P.S. Cheng (2018), 'Trans-Pacific Partnership Agreement Minus One and Enhanced Criminal Penalty for Online Copyright Piracy: Malaysia's Options', *Journal of World Trade*, 52(3), pp. 461–477.

Azizi, M.Q. (2010), 'Ismail Sabri: Kesedaran mengenai Harta Intelek Penting', *mStar Online*, 22 April, www.mStar.com.my.

Barker, T. and Y.B. Lee (2017), 'Making Creative Industries Policy: The Malaysian Case', *Kajian Malaysia*, 35(2), pp. 21–37.

Ch'ng, C.C. (2015), 'Does Malaysia's Animation Industry Have A Future?' *Penang Monthly*, https://penangmonthly.com (accessed 5 January 2019).

Department of Statistics Malaysia (2017), 'Economic Census – Usage of ICT by Businesses and e-Commerce', November. www.dosm.gov.my (accessed 5 January 2019).

Gee, H.L., I.M. Abdul Ghani Azmi and A.R. Alavi (2007), 'Impact of the Intellectual Property System on Economic Growth: Fact-Finding Surveys and Analysis in the Asian Region, Country Report – Malaysia', *WIPO-UNU Joint Research Project*, Geneva: WIPO-UNU.

Govind, S. (2018), 'CPTPP Spells Trouble for ASEAN, Particularly Malaysia', *Khmer Times*, https://www.khmertimeskh.com/50562547/cptpp-spells-trouble-for-asean-particularly-malaysia/ (accessed 5 January 2019).

Han, L.M. and T.B. Hwa (2017), 'Global Value Chains and the Drivers of Exports in Malaysia', *BNM Quarterly Bulletin*, second quarter, pp. 18–20.

Harris, H., K.A. Aziz, and M. Norhisham (2012) 'Success Strategies of SMEs in the Creative Sector in Malaysia: A Case Study of Les Copaque', *International Journal of Management Practice*, 5(3), pp. 287–299.

Hung, T.V. (2007), *SMEs and Supply Chains.* Macao: National Office of Intellectual Property of Viet Nam.

Idris, K. (2003), *Intellectual Property A Power Tool For Economic Growth.* Switzerland: World Intellectual Property Organization.

ITU News (2011), 'Intellectual Property Rights in Today's Digital Economy', http://www.itu.int/net/itunews/issues/2011/07/38.aspx (accessed 5 January 2019).

Jaipragas, B. (2019), 'Malaysia Won't Be Pressured into CPTPP: Trade Minister Darell Leiking', *This Week in Asia*, https://www.scmp.com/week-asia/politics/article/2182574/malaysia-wont-be-pressured-cptpp-trade-minister-darell-leiking (accessed 5 January 2019).

Kam Jia Yi, A. and S. Jusoh (2016), 'A Macro Analysis of the Intellectual Property Rights in ASEAN Countries', *SEANET Perspectives*, Issue No. 8, April, Kuala Lumpur: Southeast Asia Network For Development, https://www.researchgate.net/publication/303882232_A_Macro_Analysis_of_Intellectual_Property_Rights_in_ASEAN_Countries/download (accessed 5 January 2019).

Masataka, F. (2019), 'Global Value Chains in ASEAN: A Regional Perspective', *Paper* 1 (Revised), Tokyo: ASEAN-Japan Centre.

Malaysian Communications and Multimedia Commission (2009), *Policy of National Creative Industry.* Kuala Lumpur: Malaysian Communications and Multimedia Commission. www.mcmc.gov.my/pdf/dikn.pdf (accessed 5 January 2019).

MDEC (2015), *MSC Malaysia Annual Industry Report 2014.* http://www.mscmalaysia.my/ sites/default/files/pdf/downloads/2014-MSC-Malaysia-Annual-Industry-Report.pdf (accessed 5 January 2019).

MIDA (2019), 'Intellectual Property Protection', http://www.mida.gov.my/home/intellectual-property-protection/posts/ (accessed 5 January 2019).

Md Nor, N.G., A.B. Bhuiyan, J. Said, and S.S. Alam (2016), 'Innovation Barriers and Risks for Food Processing SMEs in Malaysia: A Logistic Regression Analysis', *Geografia-Malaysian Journal of Society and Space*, 12(2), pp. 167–178.

Pugtach, M., R. Chu and D. Torstensson (2018), *Unlimited Potential – GIPC International IP Index* (6th ed.). Washington, DC: US Chamber of Commerce's Global Intellectual Property Center.

Pugtach, M., R. Chu, and D. Torstensson (2015), *Unlimited Potential – GIPC International IP Index* (3rd ed.). Washington, DC: US Chamber of Commerce's Global Intellectual Property Center.

Pugtach, M., R. Chu, and D. Torstensson (2014), *Charting The Course – GIPC International IP Index* (2nd ed.). Washington, DC: US Chamber of Commerce's Global Intellectual Property Center.

Rais, Y. (2011), 'Dasar Industri Kreatif Negara Mampu Lonjak Ekonomi dan Sosiobudaya Negara', http://www.carigold.com/portal/forums/archive/index.php/t-278062.html (accessed 3 December 2018).

Ratzenböck, V. (2004), *An Analysis of the Economic Potential of the Creative Industries in Vienna*. Vienna: Chamber of Commerce Vienna.

Sukarmijan, S. and O. Sapong (2014), 'The Importance of Intellectual Property for SMEs: Challenges and Moving Forward', *UMK Procedia*, 1, pp. 74–81.

Sukumaran, T. (2013), 'Malaysian Team Behind Life of Pi's Oscar Win', *The Star*, 25 February, http://www.thestar.com.my/news/nation/2013/02/25/malaysian-team-behind-life-of-pis-oscar-win/ (accessed 5 January 2019).

WIPO Magazine (2005), 'Intellectual Property, Innovation and New Product Development', July–August, pp. 6–10.

World Bank (2010), *National Innovation Survey 2005–2008*. Washington, DC: World Bank.

World Bank (2015), 'Malaysia Among Top 20 Best Economies and First Among Emerging East Asia Economies for Ease of Doing Business', Press release, 28 October, https://www.worldbank.org/en/news/press-release/2015/10/28/malaysia-among-top-20-best-economies-and-first-among-emerging-east-asia-economies-for-ease-of-doing-business (accessed 5 January 2019).

World Bank (2017), *Malaysia Economic Monitor – Navigating Change*, 18 June, document1.worldbank.pdf (accessed 5 January 2019).

World Bank (2018a), 'The Digital Economy: Unlocking its Full Potential to Drive Malaysia's Development', https://www.worldbank.org/en/news/press-release/2018/09/12/the-digital-economy-unlocking-its-full-potential-to-drive-malaysias-development (accessed 5 January 2019).

World Bank (2018b), *Malaysia's Digital Economy: A New Driver of Development*. Washington, DC: World Bank.

World Bank (2018c), *World Development Indicators, The Conference Board Total Economy Database*. Washington, DC: World Bank.

6 Assessing IPR protection in the semiconductor and electronics industry in the Philippines

Challenges and opportunities in the global value chain

Christopher E. Cruz, Kenbert Alan I. Ting and Peter Immanuel D. Tenido

6.1 Introduction

Many studies have already recognised the important role of intellectual property (IP) in economic development. The World Intellectual Property Organization (WIPO 2011, p. 3) reported that 'firms are investing historically unprecedented amounts in the creation of intangible assets – new ideas, technologies, designs, brands, organisational know-how and business models'. WIPO further reported that 'lasting economic growth relies on continuous technological progress' (WIPO 2015, p. 7) and that 'intellectual property incentivises innovation … and promotes technology markets' (WIPO 2015, p. 14). These studies indubitably show that IP has become one of the major drivers of innovation, which, in turn, helps spur economic growth and development. This is especially true today, with the emergence of global value chains (GVCs).

The role of IP in economic development has been more pronounced with the advent of the GVCs in the manufacture of goods and services. Unlike the manufacturing ecosystem of the 20th century, which is predominantly limited to a few locations, the production of goods and services in the 21st century is now turning global. For example, the production of a car needs the design from Germany, the technology from Japan, and the workers from Thailand. Each stage in the process *adds* value to the end-product – and this value may give rise to IP created by each contributor to the production process. With the growing dependence of nations on each other in developing and manufacturing products and services, the contribution in the GVCs of developing countries in the ASEAN region becomes more prominent. This has resulted in greater calls for IP protection in the global market.

In the Philippines, the main driver for economic growth has been the semiconductor and electronics industry for several decades. Before the Philippines became the centre of business process outsourcing in the region in 2000 with the boom of the call centre industry, the country's major contribution to the global market was in the semiconductor and electronics

DOI: 10.4324/9781003147657-7

industry. With exports reaching US$32.7 billion in 2017 and US$34.9 billion in 2018 (Lachica 2019), the industry was expected to continue its development with a steady growth rate of 6% in 2019. As one of the flagship industries, it behooves us to ask whether intellectual property rights (IPR) are relevant to the Philippines' semiconductor and electronics industry. Given the industry's importance to the Philippine economy and its contribution to the GVCs, does IPR play a role in its growth and development?

Studies on the role of IPR protection in various Philippine industries, including the semiconductor and electronics industry, are limited. This is probably due to the low level of IP awareness and utilisation in the country in general. Why is this so? This chapter will attempt to answer this question and determine the role of IP in the growth and development of the Philippines' semiconductor and electronics industry. It will also discuss the industry's role in the GVCs and the challenges the industry faces in the 21st century.

To put the inquiry in context, there will be a brief discussion on the Philippines' economic structure, performance, and development plan in general, and the semiconductor and electronics industry in particular. There will also be a discussion of the Philippines' legal and regulatory environment related to IPR protection to determine whether the Philippines has the legal infrastructure to protect IP in the semiconductor and electronics industry. The chapter will conclude with policy recommendations on how the semiconductor and electronics industry can move forward and benefit from a sound IPR protection system in the Philippines.

This chapter seeks to determine IP awareness and utilisation in the semiconductor and electronics industry in the Philippines. It also seeks to know whether IP is a factor in making business decisions in such industry. Finally, it aims to determine whether strategic IP management is relevant in the Philippine semiconductor and electronics industry in facing GVC challenges.

The semiconductor industry has been one of the main drivers of the Philippine economy for many decades. This is mainly due to the country's strategic location in ASEAN, competitive labour costs, and skilled workers. With production shifting to the global market because of the emergence of GVCs, the competitiveness of the country's semiconductor and electronics industry is put to the test. While IPR protection is essential in any industry, its importance is further highlighted in today's Industry 4.0 with the emergence of GVCs. Is the semiconductor and electronics industry in the Philippines ready to meet this challenge? Does IPR protection make a difference in the semiconductor and electronics industry in the Philippines? How can IPR protection help this industry be competitive and relevant in the GVCs?

Studies on the relationship of IP to economic development are not new. However, few studies have been made on its application to individual developing states like the Philippines, particularly in the semiconductor and electronics industry. Hence, this study will focus on IP's role in this industry's growth and development in the Philippines. This study draws on several sources of information: a review of the literature available for

GVCs and the electronics and electrical sector; a focus group discussion involving representatives of Philippine firms participating in the electronics sector, including some members of the semiconductor and electronics industry of the Philippines; and international and national trade data from the Philippines.

6.2 The semiconductor and electronics industry in the Philippine economy

The Philippines is one of the world's fastest-growing economies with average annual GDP growth of more than 6% from 2012 to 2017, and a GDP per capita that increased 15.3% from US$2591.63 in 2012 to US$2988.90 in 2017 (Statista 2019a, 2019b). With about 105 million population, the World Bank (2018) expects the country to progress from a lower-middle-income country to an upper-middle-income one in the medium term. In the *2018 Global Competitiveness Report* prepared by the World Economic Forum (WEF 2018), the Philippines was ranked 56th out of 140 economies, up from 68th in the previous year. In terms of innovation capacity, that is, the 12th pillar of WEF's Global Competitiveness Index (2018), the country ranked fourth among ASEAN member states, behind Singapore (14th), Malaysia (30th), and Thailand (51st) and ahead of Indonesia (68th) and Viet Nam (82nd).

The Philippine economy's rapid growth in the past few decades seems to be attributed to its evolution from an agricultural-based economy to one dependent on an export-oriented services sector (Duke CGGC 2016a). To further drive economic development, the Philippine government has been exploring the revival of the country's manufacturing sector (Duke CGGC 2016b). To this end, with assistance from the US Agency for International Development/Philippines Science, Technology, Research and Innovation for Development (STRIDE) program, the Philippine Department of Trade and Industry Board of Investments commissioned the Duke Center on Globalization, Governance & Competitiveness (Duke CGGC) to prepare a series of GVC analyses for several manufacturing sectors, one of which is the electronics and electrical equipment sector. GVC analysis of a targeted sector provides an understanding of the sector's potential competitiveness globally. It also guides the sector in improving its position in the GVCs (Duke CGGC 2016b).

6.2.1 Electronics and electrical supply chains

The electronics and electrical industries supply a wide range of component, intermediate, and final products that feed into different end markets – from computers, communications, and consumer products to more sophisticated equipment used in automotive, medical, industrial, and aerospace applications. Further, current technology trends towards the Internet of Things, automated devices, robotics, and artificial intelligence have resulted in the growing ubiquity of smart devices, creating more opportunities for electronics and electrical firms. World exports by the electronics and electrical industry reached US$2.9 trillion in 2014, with final electronic products and electronic components accounting for more than two-thirds of the export value (Department of Trade and Industry 2017). The semiconductor industry, in particular, is characterised by a highly specialised and globally dispersed value chain that arose from consumer-driven demand for better products and services (Nathan Associates Inc. 2016).

The electronics sector is one of the pioneering industries to adopt the GVC production model (Duke CGGC 2016b). Activities in the global electronics and electrical supply chains can include the supply of inputs and raw materials needed to make electronic and electrical components; research and development (R&D); design; component manufacturing; assembly; testing; packaging; and marketing, distribution, and sales. Each activity in the GVC requires some specialisation and contributes to the final product's competitive edge (Nathan Associates Inc. 2016).

Different countries tend to specialise in various activities in the semiconductor GVCs (Table 6.1). Arguably, focus and specialisation in select GVC activities can promote technological stewardship and national industrial competitiveness, and make efficient use of local (e.g. natural, financial, and human) resources (Nathan Associates Inc. 2016).

The benefits of participating in the GVCs include increased employment; development of human resources and skills; lawful access to sophisticated foreign technology and critical process knowledge, global markets for goods and capital; and overall economic growth (Nathan Associates Inc. 2016).

Asia has become an important geographic end market in the global electronics and electrical supply chains due to the shift of production to the region and the growing Asian consumer market. The semiconductor market in the Asia-Pacific region has grown to over US$194 billion in 2014, with China, Hong Kong, Taiwan, and Japan among the large and vital semiconductor markets (Nathan Associates Inc. 2016).

Table 6.1 GVC Activities and Countries that Specialise in Them

GVC Activities	*Countries*
Semiconductor design High-end manufacturing	Canada, European countries, United States (US)
Semiconductor equipment Raw materials	Japan, US, European countries
Manufacturing, assembly, testing, packaging	China, Taiwan, Malaysia, other Asian countries
Semiconductor R&D	Canada, China, Germany, India, Israel, Singapore, Republic of Korea, United Kingdom, US

Source: Nathan Associates Inc. (2016).

6.2.2 The Philippines in the global electronics and electrical supply chains

Electronics firms in industrialised nations began relocating their production facilities to the Philippines in the mid-1970s to control increasing production costs. The Philippine electronics industry has grown and overtaken agriculture as the leading export-earning industry within two decades. According to the Semiconductor and Electronics Industries in the Philippines Foundation, Inc., the largest organisation of foreign and Filipino electronics companies in the Philippines,[1] the electronics industry accounted for 52.02% of total commodity exports from the Philippines in 2017. Also, 3.2 million workers were employed in the same year by about 420 multinational corporations and Filipino-owned semiconductor and electronics firms operating out of the Philippines.

In terms of trade, Philippine export values for goods and commercial services reached US$63.233 billion and US$35.586 billion in 2017, respectively (WTO 2019). Non-agricultural products from the electronics and electrical equipment industry dominate export goods (WTO 2019). The Philippines was the ninth largest global exporter of electronic circuit components in 2017, contributing to about 3% of the industry's GVCs (Biolena 2018). Top electronics contract manufacturers with manufacturing facilities in the Philippines include Cal-Comp, SIIX, and IMI. Main ASEAN competitors in the electronics and electrical sector are Malaysia and Viet Nam.

More than half of 2017 Philippine exports went to Hong Kong, the US, China, Singapore, and Japan, partly benefiting from its participation in regional trade agreements, such as the ASEAN Free Trade Area (FTA) signed in 1992, the ASEAN–Japan FTA signed in 2008, the ASEAN–China FTA, and the ASEAN–Korea FTA effective 2010. Additionally, the Philippines is one of the 29 signatories to the Information Technology Agreement (ITA) launched in 1996. The agreement removed tariffs on information and communications technology (ICT) products, including semiconductors, computers, and telecommunications equipment. Ezell and Wu (2017) argued that ITA accession could bolster national employment by (i) making a country more attractive for ICT goods production, (ii) expanding participation within ICT GVCs, (iii) growing local ICT industries, (iv) making local exporters more globally competitive, and (v) reducing the costs paid by local firms for ICT goods. According to the authors, growth in global two-way ITA trade (total of imports and exports), which increased fourfold from US$1.26 trillion in 1996 to US$5.6 trillion in 2014, can be attributed to falling prices for crucial ICT hardware inputs and the effects of the ITA itself.

The Philippines is not yet an active participant in more profitable segments of GVCs. Most of its contributions to GVCs narrow in the component stage (semiconductor assembly and testing activities). The country has not yet been able to get involved in more profitable GVC stages, such as product development, consumer research, branding, and marketing (Duke CGGC 2016c). For instance, no semiconductor wafer fabs exist in the country. The government had targeted the integrated circuit design (with IP content) sector as a priority investment area in the 2017 Investment Priorities Plan. The Semiconductor and Electronics Industry of the Philippines, Inc. also identified this sector in 2018 as a niche area in its industry road map.[2] However, the country's involvement in this sector is still very limited.

The country's relatively small GVC value-added may be attributed partly to low investments in R&D, loss of engineering talent to other countries that hamper functional upgrading efforts (Department of Trade and Industry 2017), and a small pool of engineering graduates compared with other disciplines. In electronics and electrical manufacturing establishments, about three-quarters of employees work in production as operators and technicians. These workers typically finished secondary education and have some additional technical and/or vocational training. Engineers and scientists (about 10% of the workforce) are needed for process and product development and inventory and supply chain management (Duke CGGC 2016c). The absence of specialised technical talent at the PhD level was mentioned as impacting firms' abilities to introduce innovations in their products and services (Duke CGGC 2016c; RTI International 2014). The middle-income trap, which essentially means middle-income economies are finding it hard to transition to high-income economies due to lack of participation in innovative and creative GVC activities, is a hotly debated issue in GVC participation by developing economies. This is especially since the importance of low-skilled labour as a factor of production decreases as GVCs become more knowledge-intensive and more reliant on automation (WTO 2017; Lund et al. 2019).

To address the lack of specialised technical talent, the Department of Science and Technology has a 'Balik Scientist Program' which 'seeks to encourage highly trained overseas Filipino scientists and technologists, experts, and professionals to return to the Philippines and share their expertise to accelerate the scientific, agro-industrial, and economic development of the country'.[3] They have helped solve problem areas where experts residing in the country are scarce.

On the other side, a cost-competitive, educated, and English-speaking workforce is one of the country's competitive advantages (Department of Trade and Industry 2017). Out of 2,353 higher education institutions in the country, four – the University of the Philippines, Ateneo de Manila University, the University of Santo Tomas, and De La Salle University – made it to the top 200 of the 2018 Quacquarelli Symonds Asia University Rankings (Commission on Higher Education 2018). The University of the Philippines and De La Salle University also made it to the Times Higher Education World University Rankings 2019 and 2020. Further, Republic Act 10931, or the 'Universal Access to Quality Tertiary Education Act', was signed on 3 August 2017. It aims to waive school fees to provide every Filipino an opportunity to earn higher education and a degree in state and local universities and colleges.

Most Philippine electronics and electrical firms tend to be manufacturing branch plants of foreign multinational corporations (i.e. few are

Filipino-owned firms). Electronics and electrical investments account for a significant portion of all foreign direct investment (FDI) (Department of Trade and Industry 2017). The said Philippine sector's participation in the GVCs can thus be attributed to FDI supporting the sector (Francisco et al. 2018). Moreover, foreign investors will also require a robust IP regime to protect their IP investments.

Identified as a key advantage to electronics firms (Duke CGCG 2016c) is the Philippine Economic Zone Authority (PEZA), attached to the Philippine Department of Trade and Industry. PEZA is the government agency that promotes investments, extends assistance, registers, grants incentives, and facilitates the business operations of investors in export-oriented manufacturing and service facilities inside export-processing zones (EPZs). The key benefits of operating in EPZs include income tax holidays, tax- and duty-free imports, simplified import and export procedures, and special visas for employees (Duke CGCG 2016b).

Nevertheless, countries should not rely too much on EPZs to improve participation in GVCs. GVC participation may be limited to those that operate in the EPZs. Small domestic firms continue to face high transaction costs that would deter their participation in the GVCs (WTO 2017).

6.3 The Philippine IP regime

A well-crafted and enforced IP legal and regulatory system is vital in making IP a contributor to economic development in the GVCs. While the Philippines has legal and regulatory mechanisms in place, their implementation and enforcement leave much to be desired. In the 2019 National Trade Estimate Report of Foreign Trade Barriers, the Office of the United States Trade Representative reported that although IP protection has improved, online piracy, counterfeit drugs, inadequate provisions in the patent law, slow investigation of IP-related cases, and inexperienced courts still hound the country (Rosales 2019). Nevertheless, the Philippines is committed to improving IPR protection and enforcement in the country. Through the efforts of the Intellectual Property Office of the Philippines, the government continues to maintain a robust environment for IP protection. Since 2014, the United States Special 301 Report has excluded the Philippines from the annual list of economies with weak IPR enforcement.

To overview the Philippine legal and regulatory system for IPR protection, the following is a discussion of (i) the IP treaties to which the Philippines is a party, (ii) domestic laws on IP, (iii) the government agencies that implement them, and (iv) administrative and judicial remedies.

6.3.1 Treaties

The Philippines is a party to numerous IP treaties. Among them are the Paris Convention for the Protection of Industrial Property, the Berne

Convention for the Protection of Literary and Artistic Works, the Patent Cooperation Treaty, the Budapest Treaty, the WIPO Copyright Treaty, the WIPO Performances and Phonograms Treaty, the Marrakesh Treaty, the Madrid Protocol, and the Agreement on Trade-Related Aspects of Intellectual Property Rights (henceforth TRIPS Agreement). Under its obligations to the TRIPS Agreement, the Philippines passed its primary law on IP that placed the country closer to its ASEAN neighbours in the area of IP legislation. In 1998, a comprehensive IP law, the Intellectual Property Code of the Philippines,[4] took effect pursuant to the country's commitment to the TRIPS Agreement.

6.3.2 Domestic laws

IP laws in the Philippines date back to the time of her colonisers in the 19th century. However, only in the late 20th century did the country have a comprehensive law on IP in a single code. In 1998, the Intellectual Property Code of the Philippines (Republic Act 8293), the main law on IP, took effect, providing for the different types of IPR protection, including patents, trademarks, and copyright. It established the Intellectual Property Office of the Philippines (IPOPHIL). Republic Act 10372 amended Republic Act 8293 in 2012 through the following changes, among others: (i) the creation of the Bureau of Copyrights, (ii) the grant of visitorial powers to the Director General of the IPOPHIL, and (iii) the mandate for all universities and schools to have an institutional IP policy. Also, the following laws complement the Intellectual Property Code in protecting IP-related rights in the Philippines (Tables 6.2 and 6.3).

6.3.3 Government agencies

At the forefront of the advocacy for IP protection and enforcement is the Intellectual Property Office of the Philippines (IPOPHIL). Its mandate is to administer and implement state policies declared in the Intellectual Property Code (Section 5, RA 8293). This mandate includes examining patent applications, registering technology transfer agreements, promoting IP, adjudicating IP disputes, and coordinating with other government agencies in IPR protection.

The Optical Media Board is another government agency responsible for enforcing IPR, particularly in the optical media industry. It conducts investigations and raids on infringers of optical media like CDs and DVDs. Another agency that enforces IPR is the Bureau of Customs. It is the gatekeeper of the country in curbing the import of infringing goods.

To help in the enforcement efforts, the Philippine National Police (PNP) and the National Bureau of Investigation (NBI) assist in enforcing IPR through raids and prosecuting cases in court. The PNP and the NBI have dedicated units that handle IP-related cases in coordination with IPOPHIL

Table 6.2 Laws Complementing the Philippine Intellectual Property Code

Law	*Description*	*Lead Agency*
Protection of Layout-Designs (RA 9150)	Amends RA 8293 by protecting layout-designs (topographies)	Intellectual Property Office of the Philippines (IPOPHIL)
Cheaper and Quality Medicines Act (RA 9502)	Amends RA 8293 by providing, among others, flexibilities in the parallel importation of pharmaceutical products and the Bolar provision in patents	IPOPHIL
Philippine Competition Act (2015) (RA 10667)	Provides an anti-competition policy and prohibits anti-competitive agreements and practices	Philippine Competition Commission
Cybercrime Prevention Act (2012) (RA 10175)	Provides for crimes committed online and, on the Internet, like cybersquatting and identity theft	Cybercrime Investigation and Coordinating Center (CICC)
Anti-Camcording Act (2010) (RA 10088)	Prohibits and penalises unauthorised use, possession, and control of audiovisual recording devices and unauthorised recording of movies and other works	Philippine National Police, National Bureau of Investigation and Optical Media Board (OMB)
Philippine Technology Transfer Act (2009) (RA 10055)	Inspired by the Bayh-Dole Act of the United States, it provides the framework and support system for ownership, management, and commercialisation of IP created by universities and R&D institutions, and funded by the government	IPOPHIL, Department of Science and Technology (DOST)
Food and Drug Administration Act (2009) (RA 9711)	Provides for the strengthening, upgrading, and rationalising of the regulatory capacity of the former Bureau of Food and Drugs of the Philippines	Food and Drug Administration (FDA)
Optical Media Act (2003) (RA 9239)	Prohibits the unauthorised and illegal manufacture, replication, importation, and exportation of optical media like CDs and discs	OMB, IPOPHIL
Philippine Plant Variety Act of 2002 (RA 9168)	Provides for the sui generis protection of new plant varieties consistent with the TRIPS Agreement	National Plant Variety Protection Registrar

(*Continued*)

Table 6.2 (Continued)

Law	*Description*	*Lead Agency*
Anti–Money Laundering Act (2001) (RA. 9160)	Defines the crime of money laundering and provides penalties for its violation (including its amendments)	Anti–Money Laundering Council (AMLC)
Electronic Commerce Act (2000) (RA 8792)	Provides for the legal use of electronic documents and penalties for non-compliance	Department of Trade and Industry (DTI)
Special Law on Counterfeit Drugs (1996) (RA 8203)	Prohibits counterfeit drugs and provides penalties for its violation	FDA
Consumer Act (1992) (RA 7392)	Provides for the rights and obligations of consumers in business transactions	DTI
Food, Drugs and Devices and Cosmetics Act (RA 3720)	Provides for the safety and purity of food, drugs, and cosmetics made available to the public	FDA
Use of Stamped or Marked Bottles, Boxes, Casks, Kegs, Barrels, and Other Similar Containers (RA 623)	Makes it unlawful for any person without the consent of the registrant of a bottle, box, etc. to use it without the consent of the registered owner	DTI, IPOPHIL

Source: Authors, referring to Hechanova (2018).

and the Optical Media Board. Likewise, non-governmental organisations, cause-oriented groups, and academe help raise awareness of the importance of IPR protection. The establishment of innovation and technology support offices in 2011 in universities and R&D institutions has helped increase collaboration among the government, industry, and academe.

6.3.4 Administrative and judicial remedies

Administrative cases for IPR protection are filed with the Bureau of Legal Affairs (BLA) of IPOPHIL. It has original jurisdiction over *inter partes* cases (opposition and cancellation of patents, trademarks, and petition for compulsory licensing) for claims for damages not less than ₱200,000.00. Decisions of the BLA Director are appealable to the Office of the Director General, then to the Court of Appeals, and finally to the Supreme Court.

For civil and criminal actions, the special commercial courts (regional trial courts) have jurisdiction over IPR cases. The Rules of Procedure for Intellectual Property Rights Cases govern the proceedings, supplemented by the Rules of Court of the Philippines. Its decisions are appealable to the Court of Appeals, and then finally to the Supreme Court.

Table 6.3 Laws Complementing the Philippine Intellectual Property Code – Recent Treaties and Laws

Treaty/Law/Regulation	*Description*	*Lead Agency*
Nagoya Protocol (2015)	Sharing of benefits from utilisation and access to generic resources (Supplement to Convention on Biological Diversity)	Department of Environment and Natural Resources (DENR)
Patent Prosecution Highway with Japan (2018), United States Patent and Trademark Office, Korean Intellectual Property Office, European Patent Office	Bilateral Agreements for Patent Prosecution	Intellectual Property Office of the Philippines (IPOPHIL)
ASEAN Patent Examination Cooperation Programme (ASPEC) (2014)	Regional Patent Cooperation Project for the ASEAN for Search and Examination results	IPOPHIL
IPOPHIL Memo Circular 17-010 (1 August 2017)	Amendments to Trademark Rules and Regulations	IPOPHIL
IPOPHIL Memo Circular 17-010 (1 August 2017)	Expediting Trial of Cases for Violation of IP Laws	IPOPHIL
IPOPHIL Memo Circular 17-010 (1 August 2017)	Amendment to Rules and Regulations on Patents on Revival of Applications	IPOPHIL
Data Privacy Act of 2012 (RA 10173) (September 2012)	Privacy of Data and Establishment of the National Privacy Commission	National Privacy Commission
Philippine Design Competitiveness Act (RA 10557) (May 2013)	Promoting Design Industry by Registration with IPOPHIL	IPOPHIL
Philippine Competition Act (RA 10667) (July 2015)	Regulating and Prohibiting Monopolies and Anti-Competition Activities	Philippine Competition Commission (PCC)

Source: Authors, referring to Hechanova (2018).

6.4 State of IP protection in the Philippines

6.4.1 Patenting activity in ASEAN

According to Clarivate Analytics (2016), patenting activity from ASEAN increased more than 40% from 2012 (~30,000 applications) to 2014 (~42,000 applications). This sudden increase was noteworthy since from 2005 to 2012, the volume of patent applications each year had remained

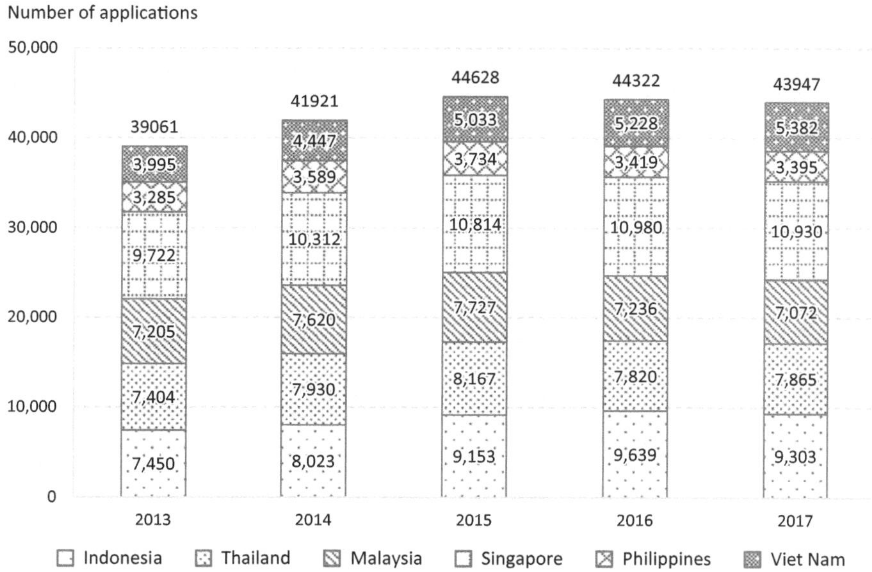

Figure 6.1 Patent Applications (Direct and PCT National Phase Entries) in ASEAN-6 (2013–2017), Total Count by Filing Office.

steady at about 30,000. Patent applications in the region have been stable at about 43,000 applications from 2013 to 2017 on average. However, an 11% growth was still observed in that period, from ~39,000 applications in 2013 to ~44,000 applications in 2017 (Figure 6.1).

In terms of origin, most patent applications in Indonesia, Malaysia, the Philippines, Singapore, Thailand, and Viet Nam (ASEAN-6) are filed by non-residents (Figure 6.2). The rising number of non-resident patent filings suggests interest from foreign companies entering the region's fast-growing markets and exploiting business opportunities. The number of resident filings, however, has been increasing in 2013–2017. This increase may suggest growing innovation capacity and/or a stronger push for IP protection and utilisation for countries in the region.

6.4.2 Patenting activity in the Philippines

In the 2018 edition of the *Global Competitiveness Report* published by the WEF, the Philippines placed 67th out of 140 countries and fourth out of nine ASEAN member states included in the ranking for innovation capability. Innovation capability, one of the 12 Pillars of the Global Competitiveness Index 4.0 used in the report, captures a country's ability to generate knowledge, encourage collaboration across diverse points of view, and turn ideas into new products and services. IP – particularly patent applications and trademark applications – constitutes two out of the ten components under innovation capability (WEF 2018).

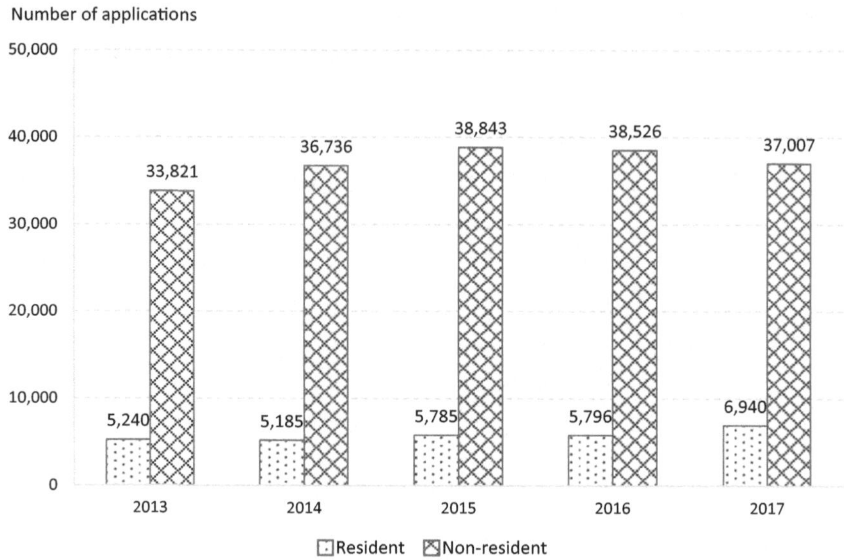

Figure 6.2 ASEAN-6 Patent Applications, Resident and Non-resident Count by Filing Office.

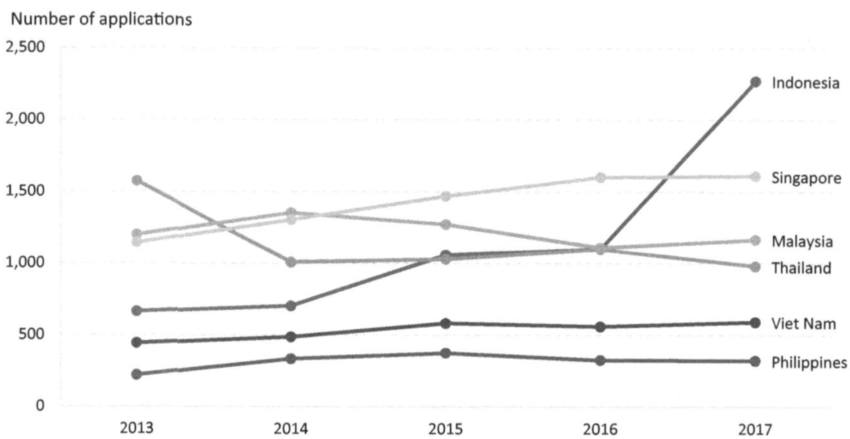

Figure 6.3 Number of Resident Patent Applications in ASEAN-6 (2013–2017).

WIPO statistics show that patenting activity in the Philippines is relatively low. Figure 6.3 plots the number of resident patent applications in ASEAN-6 from 2013 to 2017. Applications in the Philippines remained relatively steady at an average of 316 applications, reached their peak in 2015 with 375 applications, then dropped to 323 applications in 2017.

The number of non-resident patent applications in the Philippines also lags that of other ASEAN-6 states. From 2013 to 2017, non-resident patent applications in the Philippines averaged at 3,169, reached its maximum in

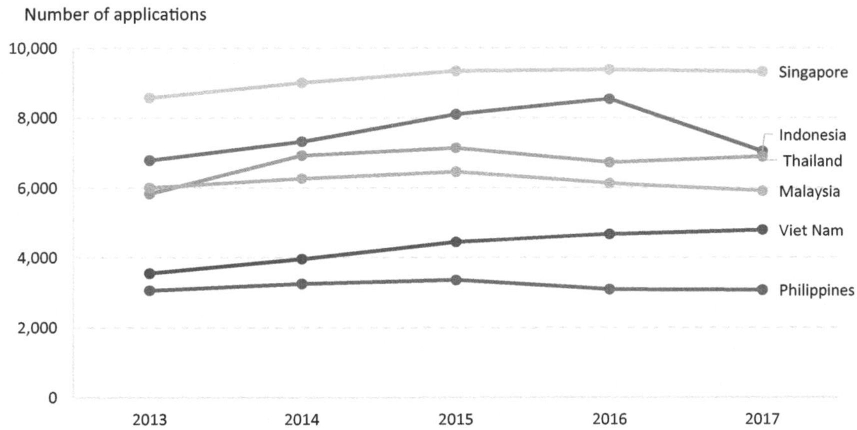

Figure 6.4 Number of Non-resident Patent Applications in the ASEAN-6 (2013–2017).

2015 at 3,359 applications, then decreased to 3,072 applications in 2017 (Figure 6.4). Every year within these five years, the Philippines consistently had the lowest number of resident and non-resident patent applications among ASEAN-6. Figure 6.5 shows that the total patent applications from 2013 to 2017 constituted only 8% of the total number of patent applications in ASEAN-6 within that period. The low number of filings has been

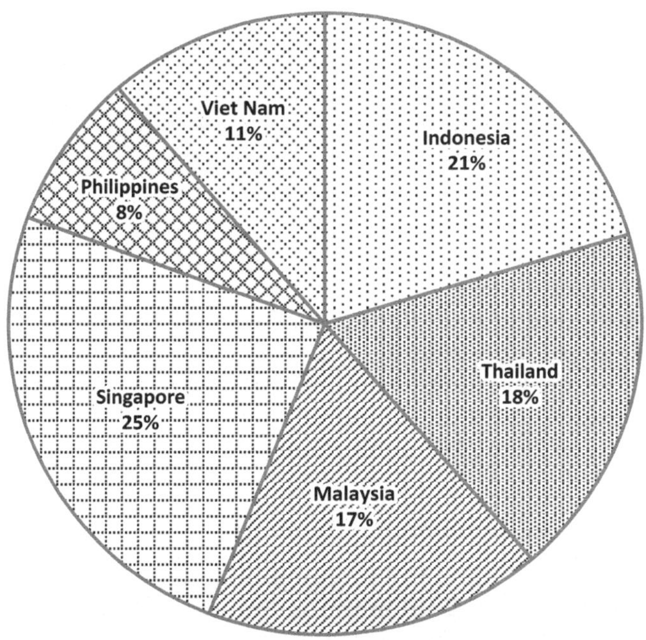

Figure 6.5 ASEAN-6 Countries Share of Patent Applications (2013–2017).

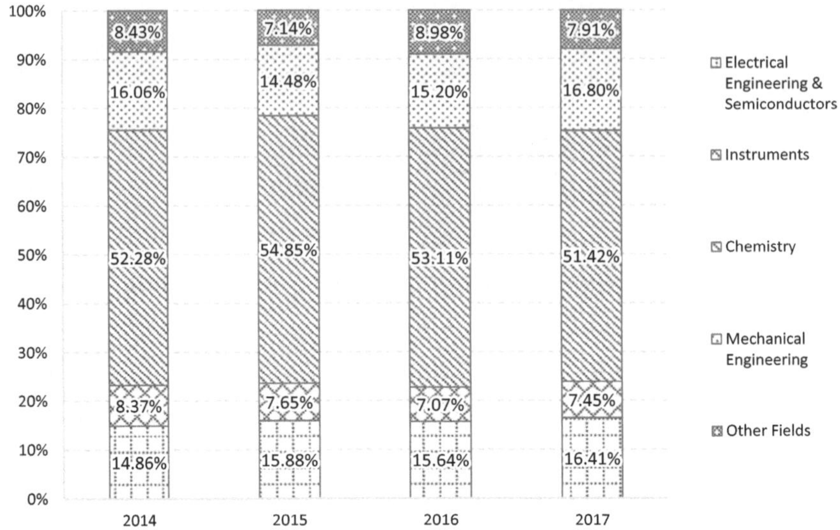

Figure 6.6 Philippines Patent Publications, by Technology Sector (2014–2017).

attributed to various factors, including the lack of awareness on or under-appreciation of the Philippine IP system (Tayao-Juego 2018) and the firms' preference to protect innovations through trade secrets (Quimba et al. 2017).

6.4.3 Patenting activity in the Philippines, by field of technology

In terms of the volume of patent publications, the most innovative technology sector in the Philippines is the chemistry sector, constituting about 52% of patent publications in the Philippines from 2014 to 2017, based on data from the WIPO IP Statistics Center (Figure 6.6). The technology classifications are based on the International Patent Classification and Technology Concordance Table (Schmoch 2008). Meanwhile, the share of Philippine patent publications classified into the electrical engineering and semiconductors technology sectors gradually increased from 14.86% in 2014 to 16.41% in 2017. Figure 6.7 delves deeper into these technology sectors. The total number of patent publications in these sectors appears to have increased from 222 publications in 2014 to 421 publications in 2017. However, a drop is observed between 2016 (498 publications) and 2017 (421 publications).

6.4.4 IP protection and innovation in the Philippines

The Philippines ranks 49th in knowledge and technology outputs in the *Global Innovation Index 2018* prepared by Cornell University, INSEAD, and WIPO. IP protection has been cited as an incentive contributing to a positive business environment that prompts firms to invest in operations in

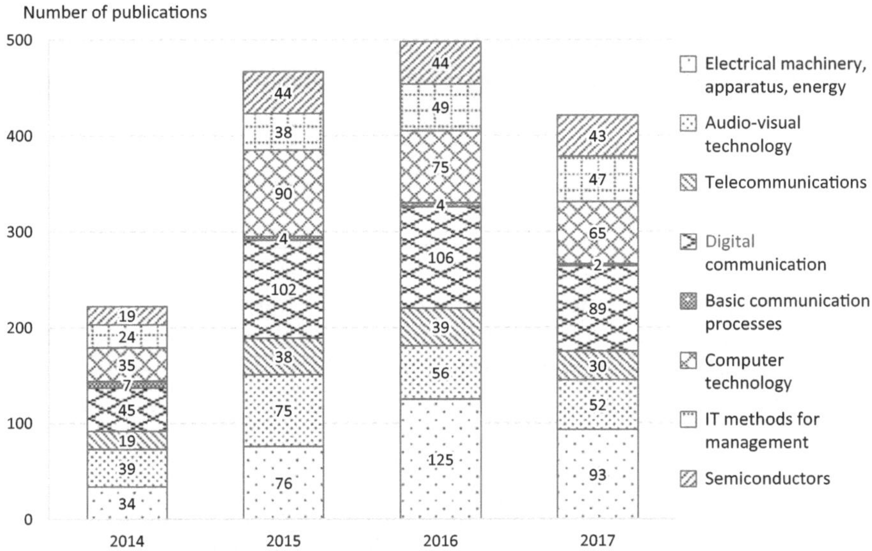

Figure 6.7 Philippines Patent Publications in Electrical Engineering & Semiconductor Technology Sectors (2013–2017).

a country and promotes its participation in the GVCs (Nathan Associates 2016). However, a lack of Patent Cooperation Treaty (PCT) filings and relatively few scientific and technical articles were cited in the *Global Innovation Index 2018* as weaknesses of the Philippines in terms of innovation outputs. As previously discussed, the Philippines does not actively participate in more innovative and profitable GVC segments that generate IP. This may explain the low propensity for filing PCT applications and for publishing scientific and technical articles. The Philippine Development Plan 2017–2022 also noted the absence of a vibrant IP culture as a challenge (NEDA 2017).

There are reports of multinational corporations' regional and global engineering R&D centres in several industries, suggesting evidence of local innovative activity (RTI International 2014). In her study of ten firms in the Philippine electronics industry, Reyes-Macasaquit (2010) found evidence of local innovative activities directed at product and process upgrading. Nevertheless, private companies seldom file local patents for their innovations and are comfortable maintaining their technologies as trade secrets (RTI International 2014).

The Board of Investments and the PEZA offer pioneer status to investment areas involving the manufacture, processing, or production – not merely assembly or packaging – of a product that is 'new' and never been produced in the Philippines commercially. Patents may be supplied as evidence that the product is 'new'. The income tax holiday for pioneer status is six years, compared to four years for a non-pioneer status.

There is increasing awareness among Philippine universities and government research units of the importance of building IP portfolios. However,

IP ownership and control and revenue-sharing issues are some reasons the industry prefers consulting arrangements with faculty over direct collaborative arrangements and technology transfer arrangements with universities (RTI International 2014). Such consulting engagements, which can be lucrative for contracted faculty, result in IP ownership by the contracting firms without going through tedious negotiations with universities (RTI International 2014). Reyes-Macasaquit (2010) also found, from a survey of Philippine electronic firms, that sources of knowledge and new technologies come primarily from technology transfer with multinational corporations; personnel recruitment; adoption of foreign technology; and participation in conferences, trade fairs, and exhibitions. The majority of the respondents did not deem important linkages with universities, R&D institutes, and information obtained from patents.

6.5 Findings and discussion

To confirm the available data and know first-hand the answers to the questions posed in this study, the researchers organised a focus group discussion (FGD) on 15 January 2019 at the De La Salle University Laguna Campus, Philippines. Six companies participated in the FGD, three of which are from the semiconductor and electronics industry of the Philippines. The FGD aimed, among others, to (i) inform the industry about IP and its importance in business; (ii) get the insights and perspectives of companies in the semiconductor industry on the value of IP in their business; (iii) determine if semiconductor and electrical companies in the Philippines have IP initiatives, strategies, and policies; and (iv) serve as an opportunity for interaction between industry representatives and members of the academic community.

Table 6.4 briefly describes the six semiconductor and electrical companies and the organisation to which they belong that participated in the FGD. The companies are not named but are instead described according to specialisation and growth in their innovation. The FGD was a good mix of companies from different backgrounds and perspectives.

Based on the answers and comments of the representatives of the participating companies from the semiconductor and electronics industry, the FGD resulted in the following findings categorised into three main themes: (i) human capital, (ii) company concerns, and (iii) government support.

6.5.1 Theme 1: human capital

6.5.1.1 Filipinos got talent

All respondent companies agree that Filipinos are very talented and are at par with their foreign counterparts in terms of skill, creativity, and dedication to work. Respondent companies think that Filipinos, beaming with a sense of nationalism, can contribute more to the GVCs if they have enough resources

Table 6.4 Description of the Participating Semiconductor Companies

Company	*Company Description*
A	• A Japanese semiconductor company and a world-class supplier of semiconductor products, such as packaging and test services • It has facilities and sub-companies in Asia, Europe, and America
B	• A start-up company producing nanomaterials as additives for different polymers • This company focuses on R&D of nanotechnology into several applications, like electronics and semiconductors
C	• One of the top electronic manufacturing services (EMS) providers in the Philippines • A Filipino-owned global manufacturing company
D	• One of the leading pioneers of innovation, new technologies, and new markets in the world • This company has pioneered numerous electronics and electrical products through the years
E	• A Philippine-based company that belongs to the semiconductor microelectronics manufacturing industry • The company's expertise is in high levels of cutting, grinding, production, and process engineering
F	• An electronic component manufacturing company specialising in magnetic technology using in-house developed materials • It has more than 30 linked countries across the globe
G	• Largest organisation for the semiconductor and electronics industry in the Philippines catering to foreign and local companies • It aims to make the industry, its markets, and the Philippines as a whole, a globally competitive business avenue for their innovation and technologies developed

Source: Authors.

and support. In particular, company E believes that the Filipino's talent is on process innovation – for example a task normally done in three days can be done by Filipinos in a day. However, the challenge is how to keep the Filipino talent in the Philippines, considering the better opportunities abroad. The proverbial 'brain drain' of Filipino talent has left the Philippines with mostly non-skilled workers in the manufacturing sector. This has hampered the efforts of Filipino companies from contributing more to the higher-level activities in the value chain.

6.5.1.2 Grant of patent incentives to employees

One respondent company shared that one way to motivate employees to stay in the company and continue innovating is to give incentives to patent applications. With the meagre salary, a patent incentive program for employees motivates engineers and scientists to pursue patenting activities.

6.5.2 Theme 2: company concerns

6.5.2.1 Lack of strategic IP management

Most respondent companies, except for two, lack IP strategies to coincide with their business strategies. They do not find it meaningful yet to pursue these activities as all, except for one, respondents are multinational companies. This has resulted in an uncoordinated and sporadic approach to IP protection at the firm level. Most companies do not consider IP a valuable business asset in the Philippines, although they do so abroad.

6.5.2.2 Need to improve and update the companies' IP management practices

Considering that most respondent companies do not have IP strategies, it is not surprising that IP road maps, processes, policies, audit mechanisms, and budget allocation do not exist. However, one respondent company has most of these components because it is a multinational company whose parent company gives premium to IP management. Companies F and B have documentation, storage, and records processes in their IP. Very few have entered into licensing agreements, and the primary documents they have are non-disclosure agreements. These companies see the need to expand their IP management activities.

6.5.2.3 Low IP awareness and knowledge in the industry and a prevalent preference for trade secrets and non-disclosure agreements

The semiconductor and electronics industry of the Philippines and the respondent companies agree that IP awareness in the industry is low. They see the need to raise awareness to foster an IP culture in the industry. For this reason, IP is not discussed in the boardroom as it does not appear to create value for the company. As for the type of IP protection, most respondent companies are in patents, trademarks, and trade secrets. The local subsidiaries of multinational companies rely on direction from their parent companies abroad.

As for trade secrets, the biggest threats to misappropriation of a company's trade secrets are employees or third parties with access to those willing to share the information with competitors (Cahoy and Oswald 2016). When a company uses non-disclosure agreements or non-compete agreements to protect its trade secrets, there are still issues, such as monitoring for compliance with the agreement, understanding the trade secret portfolio within the company, measures to prevent trade secret leakages, etc.

6.5.2.4 Most companies do not have IP policies or a dedicated unit for IP management

While companies A and C both have IP policies and strategy, no dedicated department is in charge of IP management in all but one of the respondent companies. This shows that most respondent companies do not yet value IPR protection in the Philippines.

6.5.2.5 For companies to expand, there is a need to use the IP system and have an IP strategy

All respondent companies agree that in the ever-growing market, IPR protection and management are essential. Company C expressed its intention to rethink and revisit its strategies to include filing patent applications in the Philippines. Company C believes that 'the rate of innovation and disruption is now fast and now overtaken even the rigid system, such as IP, and I think it's time for us to revisit that'. Company B also gave an insight on how IP is valuable in a business by saying, 'It's very vital for most companies, especially if you are dealing with high technology.'

6.5.2.6 Perception that Philippine patents are not valuable

The majority of respondent companies does not file patent applications in the Philippines because they think Philippine patents do not create value. Most respondent companies are into exports; they do not see the Philippines as a primary market for their goods and services. Thus, they do not see value in protecting their IP in the Philippines. Since most respondents are multinational companies with parent companies abroad, patent filings are mostly done in the rich market regions of the US and Europe, and the Philippines is out of their radar. The Philippines' major contribution to the value chain is mostly in the manufacturing sector where they just assemble parts; thus, patenting in the Philippines is not a priority. However, one respondent company saw the urgency in revisiting this policy because of the need to expand its market.

6.5.2.7 Why should I invest in the Philippines?

While the Philippines is blessed with creative and innovative people, it is still finding its niche and core competency in the semiconductor and electronics industry. Company C shared that, in discussions with their foreign counterparts, it is still grappling with answers to what makes the Philippines more competitive and unique compared to other countries.

6.5.3 Theme 3: government support

6.5.3.1 Limited government patent incentive programs

While two respondent companies have patent incentive mechanisms to motivate their inventors to innovate, these mechanisms do not exist in most respondent companies. As a result, there is not much incentive to pursue IP protection activities. Unlike in the academe, where the Department of Science and Technology sponsors a large budget for research activities, there are very few government-sponsored programs for the industry. Thus, they have called on the government to give IPR protection incentives, especially in the semiconductor and electronics industry, similar to that of Israel, which offers a premium to innovative activities. One respondent company mentioned patenting as a requirement for registration in the economic zones before getting tax incentives for their company.

6.5.3.2 Barriers to patenting

All respondent companies agree that patenting technologies are important, but they do not find value in these because the Philippines is not their market. While cost is not a problem, some pointed out that lack of government support further hinders their patenting efforts. While there were trust issues in the past about the 'stealing of ideas' once those were disclosed, the confidence of the industry in the Philippine IPR protection system has markedly improved.

6.5.3.3 The Philippines is still on its way to becoming a major global player in the semiconductor and electronics industry

The Philippines shows great promise in contributing more to the semiconductor GVCs. Yet, a lot of work still needs to be done. The respondent companies admit that they need more government support and active collaboration with the academe to be a more active player in the global arena. An IP road map supported by legislation is needed towards this end.

6.5.4 Analysis and discussion

Economic data show that the Philippines is on its way to further growth in 2019 and beyond. This can be attributed partly to the semiconductor and electronics industry that has provided millions of dollars in exports and thousands of jobs. However, the Philippines still lags in trade and innovation compared to its ASEAN neighbours. This may be due to the lack of substantial contribution to the GVCs as the country is at the lower end of the value chain as a primary contributor in semiconductor assembly and testing activities. While Filipino workers have the skill and creativity to compete globally, limitations hamper them from reaching their full potential and moving Philippine companies up the value chain. This may be partly due to the lack of awareness, utilisation, and enforcement of IPR in the country in general and in the semiconductor and electronics industry in particular.

A survey of the legal and regulatory environment for IPR protection revealed that the Philippines has a well-structured legal and regulatory framework in protecting IPR. It has a comprehensive IP law (RA 8293) that is regularly amended to keep pace with the changes of the times. It also has other supporting laws that help protect IP, such as the Optical Media Act, the E-commerce Act, and the Technology Transfer Act, to name a few.

Moreover, IP protection is well supported by the government through the Intellectual Property Office of the Philippines; implementing agencies like the PNP and the NBI; and staunch supporters in the academe, non-government institutions, and cause-oriented groups.

However, even with sound economic fundamentals and sufficient laws, IP awareness, enforcement, and utilisation are still low in the semiconductor and electronics industry in the Philippines for the following reasons:

6.5.4.1 The semiconductor and electronics industry in the Philippines is a relatively small player in the GVCs

The economic data and the focus group discussion findings revealed that the Philippines contributes only a small part to the GVCs, and mainly in the manufacturing sector for export purposes. While the Philippine semiconductor and electronics industry is on its way to continued growth, its contribution remains at the lower end of the value chain. For this reason, IP protection is not the primary concern of Philippine companies. Nevertheless, the Philippines is home to major players in the industry, including Texas Instruments, Analog Devices, On Semiconductor, Maxim Integrated, Amkor Technology, STMicroelectronics, Microchip, ROHM, Toshiba, Ibiden, Western Digital, Continental-Temic, Integrated Micro-electronics, Ionics EMS, Epson, Canon, and Brother.

6.5.4.2 Lack of specialised talent to move up in the value chain

Being a minor player in the industry, most workers in the semiconductor and electronics industry are in the assembly line. For the Philippines to have an impact, there should be a contribution at the higher levels of the value chain, which includes product development and innovation, marketing and branding, and technology development. This requires investment in education and training to uplift the competence of industry workers.

6.5.4.3 IP protection is not a priority

The industry is mainly involved as a manufacturing hub to export products to the foreign market. This is expected since most members of the industry are subsidiaries of multinational corporations. The Philippines is not seen as a market but only as part of the production process. For these reasons, the industry, in general, does not find value in protecting IP in the Philippines since the market is abroad. Since patenting is not a priority, the company's resources are, hence, not geared towards IP portfolio development.

6.5.4.4 Lack of a vibrant IP culture

The current literature and focus group discussion revealed that awareness of IPR protection in the Philippine semiconductor and electronics industry is low. This is evidenced by the lack of IP policies, strategy and management, and a dedicated office for IP protection. There are efforts to spur IP activity, but most companies do not see value in it. Therefore, the goal is to increase IP awareness to achieve a vibrant IP culture in the company and the industry.

6.5.4.5 Lack of resources for innovation

Most companies in the Philippine semiconductor and electronics industry are in the manufacturing sector; not much support is given to R&D. This is one reason the country's contribution has not resulted in patented products and processes. To improve this situation, the government must support the industry by allocating more budget for IP awareness programs and commercialisation of innovative products.

6.5.4.6 Lack of government support

The Philippine Department of Trade and Industry supports the semiconductor and electronics industry. However, the industry needs more help for it to move up the value chain. Most government resources are given to the health, housing, and education sectors. While the government has funds for research, these do not trickle down much to the semiconductor and electronics industry.

6.5.4.7 Lack of communication among government, industry, and academe

For the industry to develop, more collaboration among the government, industry, and academe is needed. They need to talk. Efforts for activities to increase collaboration are few and far between. Each sector should reach out to each other and pool their resources to impact the economy and the GVCs more. Kong et al. (2014), in their study of China's semiconductor industry in GVCs, found that close linkages with public research institutions contributed to improving the technological capabilities of the Chinese integrated circuit industry. They argued for a greater role by universities in supplying human capital to develop local firms' innovation capabilities.

6.6 Policy recommendations

The findings and analysis of this paper, as discussed, have led us to make the following policy recommendations.

6.6.1 Provide programs and activities to increase IP awareness in the industry.

Admittedly, there is a low level of awareness about IPR protection and utilisation in the country's semiconductor and electronics industry. This is primarily due to the lack of knowledge about the IP system and how it can create value for a business. For this reason, there should be more IP awareness programs, like seminars, workshops, and conferences, specific to the industry to help spread information about the IP system and its impact on business and society. The IP system can only be appreciated and valued if there is enough knowledge about its importance in the industry and society.

6.6.2 Propose legislation to incentivise companies participating in the GVCs, particularly in the higher levels of the production chain

Currently, incentives for companies to innovate are not enough. While tax perks for investments exist in economic zones, there are no incentives for contributing to the value chain. Incentives can help attract and motivate Philippine companies to participate in more profitable GVC segments. Like the Technology Transfer Law for the academe (RA 10055), there should also be legislation for the industry to help support levelling up the GVC contribution in areas such as technology development and logistics. Each country must study how it can support local industries to keep them abreast with the GVCs (protect local technologies as value to the global chain). This involves studying how much IP is generated in the value chain in the form of patents, know-how, designs, and trade secrets, to name a few.

6.6.3 Implement policies to promote and incentivise the creation and protection of IP in the semiconductor and electronics industry

The focus group discussion revealed that while the government supports technology use, not enough support is given to the semiconductor and electronics industry. There is a need for financial and regulatory support for the industry to attain 'ease in doing business'. The withdrawal of some tax perks in the proposed TRAIN (Tax Reform for Acceleration and Inclusion) law has dampened companies' enthusiasm to invest in the Philippines further. Inventors, specifically in the semiconductor industry, should be given more incentives through education grants, skills training, and collaboration support to compensate for the negative impact of fewer tax breaks.

6.6.4 Give incentives to encourage utilisation of locally developed IP

Locally developed IP in the industry has been minimal. Giving out government incentives to invest locally will hopefully encourage more locally developed IP. In this aspect, Filipino-owned companies should lead as they are expected to use more locally developed products and services.

6.6.5 Provide incentives for government–academe–industry collaboration

Government, academe, and industry speak their language and do not usually agree. Each has its silos; and they do not usually talk to each other mainly because opportunities are few. By providing incentives for collaboration, these three stakeholders will start to communicate with each other. More incentives are needed for this collaboration to prosper. An example of this collaboration can be through faculty immersion in industry funded by the government.

6.6.6 Propose legislation on trade secrets

One finding in the focus group discussion is that semiconductor and electronics firms take the trade secret route to protect their IP. This may be due to cost considerations and trust concerns with the patent system. Ironically, the IP code does not have specific provisions on the protection of trade secrets. The proposal then is to explore the possibility of having a trade secret law to regulate protection since it is the most widely used form in the industry.

6.6.7 Emphasise the importance of IP protection through an IP strategy

Since IP protection is not deemed a priority and Filipino minds still do not see its value at the moment, the majority of respondent companies do not have an IP strategy or road map in creating, protecting, and commercialising their IP. Most IP protection activities are ad hoc and reactionary. Hence, there is a need to showcase the importance of having IP management and strategy. As a valuable business asset, IP should be properly managed to serve its purposes.

6.6.8 Mandate the government to identify the capabilities of its local industries and link them with their foreign counterparts

The government should lead in identifying key industries that can best contribute to the GVCs. By knowing their niche, companies can better contribute to making the Philippines a significant contributor to the GVCs.

6.7 Conclusion

The semiconductor and electronics industry in the Philippines shows excellent promise in contributing to national development. With the industry's continued growth and the increasing competition from other countries in the GVCs, the industry needs to level up and be at par with its competitors. One way of keeping pace with the competition is for companies to be more IP literate. Towards this end, local companies should realise that IP is the new currency of the 21st century – that they cannot successfully compete with others without engaging in the IPR protection system.

With sufficient laws and ample government support, the path is now paved for the industry to take the IP road towards being relevant in the

GVCs. Patenting should be seen as a form of protection and a way of building credibility to customers and letting them know that IP creates value and does make a difference.

The role of government cannot be overemphasised. The government should take the lead by creating, through legislation and regulation, an atmosphere to support innovative activities. The academe should also support the industry by educating its students to fulfil its needs.

The companies in the industry should get support from the government and collaborate with the academe. For the most part, the academe creates knowledge, and the government provides a mechanism to protect this knowledge. The industry must work hand-in-hand with the government and the academe to turn inventions into innovations. They cannot do it alone. These stakeholders should listen to each other and act together to advance economic growth and development. The road to success is narrow and arduous. But with the help of all sectors in the country, success is not far behind.

Notes

1 https://www.seipi.org.ph/homepage/
2 The semiconductor and electronics industry road map by SEIPI identified the niche products that the Philippines should focus on to gain a larger share in the global market.
3 http://bsp.dost.gov.ph/
4 *The Intellectual Property Code of the Philippines (Republic Act 8293 of 1997).* http://www.chanrobles.com/legal7ipcp.htm (accessed 25 July 2018).

Bibliography

Alikhan, S. (2000), 'Socio-Economic Benefits of Intellectual Property Protection in Developing Countries', *WIPO Publication* No. 454(E), Geneva, Switzerland: World Intellectual Property Organization.

Baldwin, R. (2006), 'Globalisation: The Great Unbundling(s)', *Economic Council of Finland*, 20(3), pp. 5–47.

Biolena, R.P. (2018), 'Philippines Joins Electronica, Looks beyond Manufacturing', *Rappler*, 26 November, https://www.rappler.com/business/217546-philippines-joins-electronica-2018 (accessed 26 January 2019).

Cahoy, D.R. and L.J. Oswald (2016), 'Are Trade Secrets a Weak Link in your Supply Chain?', *Industry Supply Management*, 27(1), pp. 10–11.

Carvalho, M., A. Dechezleprêtre and M. Glachant (2017), 'Understanding the Dynamics of Global Value Chains for Solar Photovoltaic Technologies', *Economic Research Working Paper* No. 40, Geneva, Switzerland: World Intellectual Property Organization – Economics and Statistics Division.

Chen, W., R. Gouma, B. Los and M.P. Timmer (2017), 'Measuring the Income to Intangibles in Goods Production: A Global Value Chain Approach', *Economic Research Working Paper* No. 36, Geneva, Switzerland: World Intellectual Property Organization – Economics and Statistics Division.

Clarivate Analytics (2016), 'ASEAN – The Emerging Research and Innovation Hub', https://clarivate.com/wp-content/uploads/2017/10/ASEAN-The-Emerging-Research-and-Innovation-Hub.pdf (accessed 27 January 2019).

Commission on Higher Education (2018), '2018 Higher Education Facts and Figures', https://ched.gov.ph/2018-qs-asia-university-rankings-of-philippine-heis/ (accessed 3 February 2019).

Concepcion, J. (2018), 'Digital Economy is Key to Inclusivity', *Philstar*, 8 February, https://www.philstar.com/business/2018/02/08/1785566/digital-economy-key-inclusivity (accessed 23 September 2020).

Cornell University, INSEAD, and WIPO (2018), *The Global Innovation Index 2018: Energizing the World with Innovation.* Ithaca, Fontainebleau, and Geneva.

Davis, R. (2011), *The Digital Dilemma.* Geneva: World Intellectual Property Organization (WIPO). http://193.5.93.81/edocs/mdocs/ecommerce/en/wipo_ec_conf_01/wipo_ec_conf_01_spk_2c.pdf (accessed 28 July 2018).

De Beer, J. (2016), 'Evidence-Based Intellectual Property Policymaking: An Integrated Review of Methods and Conclusion', *The Journal of World Intellectual Property*, 19(5–6), pp. 150–177, https://doi:10.111/jwip.12069.

Dedrick, J. and K.L. Kraemer (2017), 'Intangible Assets and Value Capture in Global Value Chains: The Smartphone Industry', *Economic Research Working Paper* No. 41, Geneva, Switzerland: World Intellectual Property Organization – Economics and Statistics Division.

Department of Trade and Industry (2017), 'The Philippines in the Electronics and Electrical Global Value Chain', *Policy Briefs Series* no. 2017-07, http://industry.gov.ph/wp-content/uploads/2017/11/DTI-Policy-Brief-2017-07-The-Philippines-in-the-Electronics-and-Electrical-Global-Value-Chain.pdf (accessed 27 January 2019).

Duke CGGC (2017a), *The Philippines in the Cocoa–Chocolate Global Value Chain.* Durham, NC: Center on Globalization, Governance & Competitiveness, Duke University.

Duke CGGC (2017b), *The Philippines in the Coffee Global Value Chain.* Durham, NC: Center on Globalization, Governance & Competitiveness, Duke University.

Duke CGGC (2016a), *The Philippines in Agribusiness Global Value Chains.* Durham, NC: Center on Globalization, Governance & Competitiveness, Duke University.

Duke CGGC (2016b), *The Philippines in Manufacturing Global Value Chains.* Durham, NC: Center on Globalization, Governance & Competitiveness, Duke University.

Duke CGGC (2016c), *The Philippines in the Electronics & Electrical Global Value Chain.* Durham, NC: Center on Globalization, Governance & Competitiveness, Duke University.

Ezell, S.J. and J.J. Wu (2017), *How Joining the Information Technology Agreement Spurs Growth in Developing Nations.* Washington, DC: Information Technology & Innovation Foundation. http://www2.itif.org/2017-ita-spurs-growth-developing-nations.pdf (accessed 28 January 2019).

Francisco, J.P., T. Canare, and J.R. Lablos (2018), 'Obstacles and Enablers of Internationalisation of Philippine SMEs through Participation in Global Value Chains', *Discussion Paper Series* no. 2018-07, July, Quezon City: Philippine Institute for Development Studies, https://pidswebs.pids.gov.ph/CDN/PUBLICATIONS/pidsdps1807.pdf (accessed 27 January 2019).

Frederick, S. (2016), *Global Value Chains – Concept & Tools.* Durham, NC: Duke University, https://globalvaluechains.org/concept-tools (accessed 26 July 2018).

Freeman, R.B. (2010), 'Globalization of Scientific and Engineering Talent: International Mobility of Students, Workers, and Ideas and the World Economy', *Economics of Innovation and New Technology*, 19(5), pp. 393–406.

Gada, K. (2016), 'The Digital Economy in 5 Minutes', *Forbes*, 16 June. https://www.forbes.com/sites/koshagada/2016/06/16/what-is-the-digital-economy/#5a20481e7628 (accessed26 July 2018).

Gereffi, G. and K. Fernandez-Stark (2016), *Global Value Chain Analysis: A Primer*, 2nd edition. Durham, NC: Center on Globalization, Governance & Competitiveness, Duke University.

Guan, J. and Z. Chen (2012), 'Patent Collaboration and International Knowledge Flow', *Information Processing & Management*, 48(1), pp. 170–181.

Hargreaves, I. (2011), 'Digital Opportunity: A Review of Intellectual Property and Growth', https://www.gov.uk/government/publications/digital-opportunity-review-of-intellectual-property-and-growth (accessed 27 July 2018).

Haslach, P.M. (2017), 'Intellectual Property is the Key to Innovation Economy', *US Embassy & Consulates in Turkey*, 26 April, https://tr.usembassy.gov/intellectual-property-key-innovation-economy (accessed 27 July 2018).

Hechanova, E.R. (2018), 'Chapter 19: Philippines', in D. Conde (ed.), *The Intellectual Property Review* (7th ed.). London: Law Business Research Ltd., pp. 230–234.

Hummels, D., J. Ishii and K.M. Yi (2001), 'The Nature and Growth of Vertical Specialization in World Trade', *Journal of International Economics*, 54(1), pp. 75–96.

ITU (2012), *Trends in Telecommunication Reforms 2012: Smart Regulation for a Broadband World*. Geneva: International Telecommunication Union.

Japan Patent Office, Asia-Pacific Industrial Property Center (APIC), and Japan Institute for Promoting Invention and Innovation (2016), 'Intellectual Property Management in Japanese Universities', https://www.jpo.go.jp/news/kokusai/developing/training/textbook/document/index/64_Intellectual_Property.pdf (accessed 23 September 2020).

Kappos, D., J. Villasenor and T. Misrhi (2013), 'Intellectual Property Rights in the Global Creative Economy', Geneva: World Economic Forum, http://www3.weforum.org/docs/GAC/2013/WEF_GAC_IntellectualPropertyRights_GlobalCreativeEconomy_Report_2013.pdf (accessed 28 July 2018).

Kim, Y.K., K. Lee, W.G. Park and K. Choo (2012), 'Appropriate Intellectual Property Protection and Economic Growth in Countries at Different Levels of Development', *Research Policy*, 41(2), pp. 358–375.

Kong, X.X., M. Zhang and S.C. Ramu (2014), 'China's Semiconductor Industry in Global Value Chains', *Asia Pacific Business Review*. doi: 10.1080/13602381.2014.990205.

Kowalski, P., J.L. Gonzalez and A. Ragoussis and C. Ugarte (2015), 'Participation of Developing Countries in Global Value Chains: Implications for Trade and Trade-Related Policies', *OECD Trade Policy Papers*, No. 179, Paris: Organisation for Economic Co-operation and Development.

Lachica, D. (2019), Intellectual Property (IP) Forum on the Semiconductor and Electronics Industry, Lecture presented at the IP Forum on Semiconductor and Electronics Industry, 15 January 2019 at Laguna, Philippines.

Lund, S., J. Manyika, J. Woetzel, J. Bughin, M. Krishnan, J. Seong and M. Muir (2019), 'Globalization in Transition: The Future of Trade and Value Chains', *McKinsey Global Institute Report*, 16 January, https://www.mckinsey.com/featured-insights/innovation-and-growth/

globalization-in-transition-the-future-of-trade-and-value-chains (accessed 3 February 2019).

Maskus, K.E. (2000), 'Intellectual Property Rights and Economic Development', *Case Western Reserve Journal of International Law*, 32(3), pp.471–506.

Nadia, C. (2011), 'Considerations about Intellectual Property Rights, Innovation and Economic Growth in the Digital Economy', *Economia Seria Management*, 14(2), pp. 310–323. https://core.ac.uk/download/pdf/6523348.pdf (accessed 28 July 2018).

Nathan Associates Inc. (2016), *Beyond Borders: The Global Semiconductor Value Chain*. Washington, DC: Semiconductor Industry Association. https://www.semiconductors.org/wp-content/uploads/2018/05/SIA-Beyond-Borders-Report-FINAL-May-6-1.pdf (accessed 27 January 2019).

NEDA (2017), *Philippine Development Plan 2017–2022*. Pasig: NEDA. http://pdp.neda.gov.ph/wp-content/uploads/2017/01/PDP-2017-2022-07-20-2017.pdf (accessed 28 January 2019).

OECD (n.d.), 'Global Value Chains (GVCs)', http://www.oecd.org/sti/ind/global-value-chains.htm (accessed 26 July 2018).

Palfrey, J. (2012), *Intellectual Property Strategy*. Cambridge, MA: The MIT Press.

Quimba, F.M.A., J.R.G. Albert and G.M. Llanto (2017), *Innovation Activity of Firms in the Philippines*. Quezon City: Philippine Institute for Development Studies. https://pidswebs.pids.gov.ph/CDN/PUBLICATIONS/pidsdps1744.pdf (accessed 27 January 2019).

Reyes-Macasaquit, M. (2010), 'Case Study of the Electronics Industry in the Philippines: Linkages and Innovation', in P. Intarakumnero and Y. Ueki (eds.). *Fostering Production and Science and Technology Linkages to Stimulate Innovation in ASEAN, ERIA Research Project Report* 2009 7-4. Jakarta: ERIA, pp. 145–229.

Rosales, E.F. (2019), 'PHL Lags in Protecting Intellectual Property', *Business Mirror*, 3 April, https://businessmirror.com.ph/2019/04/03/phl-lags-in-protecting-intellectual-property/ (accessed 9 April 2019).

RTI International (2014), *Science, Technology, Research and Innovation for Development: Philippines Innovation Ecosystem Assessment*. Research Triangle Park, NC: RTI International.

Samper, L.F., D. Giovannucci and L.M. Vieira (2017), 'The Powerful Role of Intangibles in the Coffee Value Chain', WIPO Economic Research Working Paper No. 39', Geneva: World Intellectual Property Organization – Economics and Statistics Division.

Schmoch, U. (2008), *Concept of a Technology Classification for Country Comparisons: Final Report to the World Intellectual Property Organization (WIPO)*. https://www.wipo.int/edocs/mdocs/classifications/en/ipc_ce_41/ipc_ce_41_5-annex1.pdf (accessed 24 September 2020).

Statista (2019a), 'Philippines: Growth Rate of the Real Gross Domestic Product (GDP) from 2012 to 2022 (compared to the previous year)', https://www.statista.com/statistics/578705/gross-domestic-product-gdp-growth-rate-in-philippines/ (accessed 27 January 2019).

Statista (2019b), 'Philippines: Gross Domestic Product (GDP) per Capita in Current Prices from 2012 to 2022 (in US dollars)', https://www.statista.com/statistics/578713/gross-domestic-product-gdp-per-capita-in-philippines/ (accessed 27 January 2019).

Sweet, C.M. and D.S.E. Maggio (2015), 'Do Stronger Intellectual Property Rights Increase Innovation?' *World Development*, 66, pp. 665–677.

Tantuico, D.S. and E.W. Zshornack (2006), 'Intellectual Property Rights: Talking Points for RP–US FTA Negotiations', *Discussion Paper Series* No. 2006-12, Quezon City: Philippine Institute for Development Studies. https://dirp4.pids.gov.ph/ris/dps/pidsdps0612.pdf (accessed 26 July 2018).

Tayao-Juego, A. (2018), 'Fight for Your IP Rights', *Inquirer.Net*, 10 August, https://business.inquirer.net/255389/fight-ip-rights (accessed 27 January 2019).

Tirole, J. (2017), *Economics for the Common Good*. Oxford: Princeton University Press.

Uriarte, F.A. Jr., J.P. Tabbada and A.B. Culaba (2013), *Promoting Innovation Enhancing Competitiveness*. Manila: De La Salle University Publishing House.

Valimaki, M. (2001), *Strategic Use of Intellectual Property Rights in Digital Economy – Case of Software Markets*. Helsinki, Finland: Helsinki Institute for Information Technology.

WEF (2018), 'The Global Competitiveness Report 2018', http://reports.weforum.org/global-competitiveness-report-2018/ (accessed 27 January 2019).

WIPO (n.d.), *WIPO IP Statistics Data Center*, https://www3.wipo.int/ipstats/ (accessed 22 January 2019 and 24 September 2020).

WIPO (2017), *World Intellectual Property Report 2017: Intangible Capital in Global Value Chains*. Geneva: WIPO.

WIPO (2015), *World Intellectual Property Report 2015: Breakthrough Innovation and Economic Growth*. Geneva: WIPO.

WIPO (2011), *2011 World Intellectual Property Report: The Changing Face of Innovation*. Geneva: WIPO.

Woo, S., P. Jang and Y. Kim (2015), 'Effects of Intellectual Property Rights and Patented Knowledge in Innovation and Industry Value Added: A Multinational Empirical Analysis of Different Industries', *Technovation*, 43, pp. 49–63.

World Bank (2017), *Global Value Chain Development Report 2017: Measuring and Analyzing the Impact of GVCs on Economic Development*, Washington DC: International Bank for Reconstruction and Development/The World Bank.

World Bank (2018), 'The World Bank in the Philippines', https://www.worldbank.org/en/country/philippines/overview (accessed 27 January 2019).

WTO (2017), *Global Value Chain Development Report 2017: Measuring and Analyzing the Impact of GVCs on Economic Development*. Washington, DC: The World Bank Group.

WTO (2019), 'Trade Profiles: Philippines', https://www.wto.org/english/res_e/statis_e/daily_update_e/trade_profiles/PH_e.pdf (accessed 27 January 2019).

Zitt, M. and E. Bassecoulard (2004), 'Internationalisation in Science in the Prism of Bibliometric Indicators', in H.F. Moed, W. Glanzel and U. Schmoch (eds.). *Handbook of Quantitative Science and Technology Research*. Dordrecht, Netherlands: Kluwer Academic Publishers, pp.408–436.

7 Enforcing IPR to leverage Viet Nam's benefits from the GVCs and the digital economy

Duong Anh Nguyen, Thanh Tri Vo and Hang Thu Dinh

7.1 Introduction

While Viet Nam enjoyed almost continuous and relatively rapid export growth since its accession to the World Trade Organization (WTO) in 2007, foreign-invested enterprises accounted for a major share in such exports. In 2018, exports amounted to approximately 108% of gross domestic product (GDP), but the foreign-invested enterprises accounted for almost 70.4% of gross exports. Various studies (Nguyen 2005, Nguyen 2015, Vo and Nguyen 2011) indicate that technology transfer from foreign direct investment (FDI) to domestic enterprises has been quite limited. International literature and studies on Viet Nam (Sitkoff 2018, Nguyen et al. 2007, Treutler and Duong 2011) show that the country has long encountered poor enforcement of intellectual property (IP) regulations. In that context, pushing technology transfer administratively may weaken the incentives for high-technology firms to establish a commercial presence. This, in turn, proves counterproductive in promoting the learning curve of domestic enterprises in the FDI-led export supply chain.

The rapid development of Industry 4.0 and the digital economy compels Viet Nam to rethink its approach to industrialisation and upgradation in the supply chain. The increasing application of digital services and technologies is becoming unavoidable. Yet despite increasing investment in digital infrastructures, Viet Nam still lacks adequate capacity to popularise digital services. This issue is also hampering Viet Nam's efforts to use non-equity modes of trade that have been used increasingly by large transnational corporations (especially in the information technology sector). More importantly, making it easier to use IP rights enables better access for firms, especially young ones, in the innovative sectors.

In various aspects, Viet Nam has adopted an IP policy according to international best practices. The main issue lies, however, in enforcing such a policy. Also, the IP policy is yet to be tailored to the needs of small and medium-sized enterprises. Specifically, strengthening IP enforcement is gaining more weight than simply ignoring IP infringements to enable the low-cost competitiveness of exports. Thus, Viet Nam needs to devise an IP strategy that is friendly to global value chains (GVCs) and the digital economy.

DOI: 10.4324/9781003147657-8

For that purpose, this study looks into the implications of intellectual property rights (IPR) to GVCs and the digital economy in Viet Nam.

This chapter serves several objectives. First, it reviews Viet Nam's IP policy and related progress (recent IP policy changes, number of IP applications and the share of foreign holders, number of IPs granted and the share of foreign holders, etc.). Second, it looks into IPR enforcement issues in Viet Nam that restrain domestic firms' net benefits from arising opportunities in the GVCs and the digital economy (especially in such areas as protection of trade secret, geographical indicators, etc.). Third, it identifies approaches and solutions to enforce IPR more effectively to realise opportunities from the GVCs and the digital economy. Finally, this study showcases the need for harmonising IPR enforcement in line with international best practices.

The authors employed a combination of qualitative methodologies to realise the above objectives. First, the authors reviewed the existing literature on IP-related aspects in Viet Nam. Specifically, they summarised the key changes in Viet Nam's IP policy in the past decades. The authors also reviewed the studies on FDI impacts in Viet Nam, focusing on technology transfer from FDI and factors (including IP policy) that restrain such technology transfer. Second, they compared Viet Nam's IP policy and international standards and/or suggestions by foreign chambers of commerce to identify the regulatory gaps and need for improvement. The authors emphasised aspects that may weaken or strengthen the enforcement of IP regulations in Viet Nam. Finally, they interviewed selected experts and firms for a case study focusing on IP protection in electronics to elaborate on implications for firms' participation in the GVCs.

7.2 Overview of Viet Nam's IP policy

7.2.1 Legal framework on intellectual property

In Viet Nam, IP is regulated by the Law on Intellectual Property and the Civil Code and other relevant laws, such as the Customs Law, the Law on Handling of Administrative Violations, the Competition Law, the Criminal Code, and the Law on Technological Transfer. Furthermore, many governmental decrees and ministerial circulars have concretised and guided the implementation of the Law on Intellectual Property and other related IP provisions under relevant laws. These laws and guiding documents were amended, supplemented, or issued anew over time to meet the emerging requirements on IP protection in specific domestic and international socio-economic development. During the process of reviewing, amending, and supplementing existing legal documents, and formulating new regulations on IP, coordination among competent authorities is essential to ensure the consistency and quality of regulations, and avoid conflicts and overlaps in the national IP legal system.

Before Viet Nam acceded to the WTO, the country's IP regulatory system was based on 'sub-law' legal documents. Ordinance No. 13-LCT/HDNN8 of the State Council on the protection of industrial property rights in 1989[1] and Ordinance No. 38/L-CTN1 of the Standing Committee of the National Assembly on the protection of copyrights in 1994[2] were the initial bases for the legal framework of IP in Viet Nam. The first significant improvement was the promulgation of the Civil Code in 1995, dedicating one section with 61 articles on IP.[3] This was the first time in Viet Nam's history that IPR was recognised as a type of civil right, similar to the ownership rights over a property. These rights are recognised by the highest legislative authority, the National Assembly. However, the 1995 Civil Code still excludes in its provisions several subject matters like trade secrets, geographical indications, trade names, protection against unfair competition, plant varieties, layout designs of integrated circuits, and putting these instead under 'other subject matters' for subsequent under-law clarifications.

The Law on Intellectual Property was promulgated in 2005, amended in 2009,[4] and its guiding implementing legislations, such as decrees or circulars, were issued accordingly. Some provisions of the 2005 IP Law were amended to meet international standards (on copyright and related rights, inventions, IPR enforcement). These were supplemented by necessary provisions on the protection of inventions financed by the state budget regarding the law's implementation, such as time for handing IP application, right to practice IP representative services, IP assessment, IP protection by administrative measures, etc. The 2009 IP Law further amended and supplemented many provisions of the 2005 IP Law. In June 2019, the National Assembly of Viet Nam approved the law amending some articles of the IP Law and the Insurance Law to implement the Comprehensive Progressive Agreement for Trans-Pacific Partnership (CPTPP). The 2019 law only focuses on some provisions related to patents, geographical indications, trademarks, IP protection enforcement, and validity regarding IP regulation. However, some provisions under this amended law were claimed to be higher than the required level of commitment under the CPTPP.[5]

The government of Viet Nam introduced and implemented a series of five-year national programs to support IP development: Decision No. 68/2005/QD-TTg for 2005–2010,[6] Decision No. 2204/QD-TTg for 2011–2015,[7] and Decision No. 1062/QD-TTg for 2016–2020.[8] The program for 2016–2020 focuses on (i) improving awareness and capacity to create and develop IP assets; (ii) supporting registration, management, and protection of intellectual assets; (iii) supporting the commercialisation and development of intellectual assets; (iv) supporting the application of intellectual assets which are the results of individuals' creativity (Government of Viet Nam 2016).

On 12 June 2018, the amended Competition Law was issued to come into force on 1 July 2019. Accordingly, this Competition Law eliminated the discrepancies between the previous Competition Law (issued in 2004) and the Law on IP in dealing with IP-related unfair competition. Previously, both the 2004 Competition Law and the Law on IP have provisions on cybersquatting, the use of misleading trade indications, and the unauthorised use of a trademark by an agent. Both laws also consider the infringement of trade secrets as an act of unfair competition. These provisions confused law enforcement agencies and rights holders as to which enforcement mechanism should be employed against unfair competition relating to IP. The amended Competition Law explicitly states that the sectoral law (i.e. the Law on IP) shall prevail in case of such discrepancies. However, this is a major step backward, as experiences in other advanced countries suggest that the Competition Law is more effective in handling IP-related unfair competition cases.

Viet Nam also participates in IPR conventions or agreements under bilateral and multilateral frameworks and/or international integration. The first milestone of its international cooperation on IP was the participation in the ASEAN Framework on Intellectual Property Cooperation in 1995. Upon accession to the WTO, Viet Nam also joined the Agreement on Trade-Related Aspects of Intellectual Property Rights (henceforth TRIPS Agreement). Viet Nam also contracted with IP-related agreements under the World Intellectual Property Organization (WIPO), such as the Paris Convention for the Protection of Industrial Property, the Berne Convention for the Protection of Literary and Artistic Works, the Rome Convention, and the Madrid Protocol.[9] As the country joined more ambitious free trade agreements (FTAs), such as the Comprehensive and Progressive Agreement for Trans-Pacific Partnership (CPTPP) and the European–Viet Nam FTA (EVFTA), it exerted efforts to fulfil its commitments and fully comply with regional and international standards and practices on IP. Consequently, the design of Viet Nam's legislation and protection level of IP follows the protection standards under the TRIPS Agreement and other related conventions to which Viet Nam is a member.

7.2.2 Compatibility of IP commitments under major FTAs with domestic regulations

The Viet Nam Chamber of Commerce and Industry (VCCI) reviewed the country's legal framework against EVFTA's commitments on IP. The review concluded that Viet Nam's legal framework is compatible with many EVFTA commitments on IP under Chapter 12. Meanwhile, the proportion of commitments incompatible with Viet Nam's legal framework or which do not fall within its scope is insignificant. In principle, with the first group of obligations, Viet Nam's legal framework does not need to be amended, supplemented, or adjusted to implement EVFTA's commitment on this issue. However, by recognising the most-favoured-nation principle under Chapter 12 of EVFTA, Viet Nam commits to accord nationals of the European Union (EU) no less favourable treatment than under other treaties, including the CPTPP. On the other hand, CPTPP commitments on similar EVFTA issues with which Viet Nam's legal framework is compatible provide many TRIPS-plus provisions. Examples are commitments on the term of protection, exceptions of copyright and related rights, protected subject and conditions to safeguard patent, security of information and unpublished data, responsibilities of intermediary service providers, and so on. Therefore, CPTPP commitments on

IP should be reviewed before revising Viet Nam's legal framework to meet EVFTA commitments. From VCCI's review in 2017, the Trans-Pacific Partnership (TPP) and CPTPP generally require higher IP protection (with more TRIPS-plus regulations) than EVFTA (except issues relating to geographical indication) (WTO Center–VCCI 2017a, WTO Center–VCCI 2017b). In particular, several areas are committed under the TPP and CPTPP but not the EVFTA, including pharmaceutical exceptions (relating to public health),[10] protection of trademarks and industrial designs. Meanwhile, many issues are committed under both the CPTPP and the EVFTA. However, these have different requirement levels, such as non-discrimination principles, cooperation on IP, cooperation on patents and work-sharing, trademark, geographical indication, and so on. Compared with Viet Nam's existing laws and regulations on IP protection, various commitments under the IP chapter of the CPTPP are relatively consistent and applicable (WTO Center–VCCI 2017b). Most of the incompatible commitments are those exhibiting TRIPS-plus protection level relating to (i) subject matter (expanding the group of subject matters protected by IPR); (ii) protection conditions (reduction, expansion, or flexibility of protection conditions); (iii) term of protection (expanding or revising to broaden the actual validation term of protection certificates) (iv) improving the rights of rights holders (e.g. more transparent exclusive rights, right of receiving information on free sale registration of related products, right of implementation requirement, right of choosing damage compensation requirement); and (v) increasing infringement controlling structures (structures for easier implementation, more crimes of infringement on IP). The VCCI review showed that Viet Nam's legal framework is compatible with 55 out of 82 articles on IP under the TPP. As an explanation, the TPP and CPTPP commitments on IP are consistent with the TRIPS principles and/or already included in the United States (US)–Viet Nam Bilateral Trade Agreement (BTA). Upon the BTA implementation and WTO accession, Viet Nam's legal framework was revised to fulfil its commitments under the WTO (including those under TRIPS) and the BTA.

Besides, Viet Nam's legal framework is incompatible with a group of CPTPP commitments. This is mainly related to transparency and facilitation requirements (published information of form, certificate, reconfirming vocabulary, maintaining electronic system) or protection of rights holders from infringement (protecting secret information, announcing when counterfeiting goods is detected and seized). These requirements are consistent with administrative reforms to improve Viet Nam's legal framework and IP-related legislation.

7.2.3 IP implementation and enforcement

7.2.3.1 Copyright

Copyright refers to the exclusive rights granted to authors, artists, and other creators for their creations. The kinds of works protected by copyright laws in Viet Nam are defined as literary, artistic, and scientific works. These principally include (i) literary works, scientific works, textbooks, teaching courses; (ii) lectures, speeches, and press work; (iii) musical, stage, photographic, and cinematographic works; (iv) plastic and applied artwork; (v) sketches, plans, maps, and architectural works; and (vi) computer programs and data collections.

Viet Nam is a member of the Berne Convention; thus, any copyright conferred in other state parties to the convention are automatically granted in Viet Nam without the need for official registration. A copyright owner's moral rights (except for the moral right to publish or authorise others to publish the work) are protected for an indefinite term. The Berne Convention protects the economic rights and the exclusive right to publish the work and authorise somebody else to do so for the author's lifetime plus 50 years. Exceptions are cinematographic works, photographs, plays, applied artworks, and anonymous works. These are protected for 50 years from the date of first publication, with no possibilities for extension.

7.2.3.2 Patents

Two types of patents are available under Vietnamese law: invention patents and utility solution patents (known as utility model patents in China and several EU countries, such as Austria, Belgium, Denmark, Finland, France, Germany, Italy, and the Netherlands, among others). Invention patents are granted for novel inventions, involve an inventive step, and have an industrial application. Utility solution patents do not require an inventive step (novelty and industrial application are enough). However, the law still requires the utility solution to be something more than common general knowledge. To distinguish: utility solution patents are not necessary to have the same level of 'inventiveness' as the invention patents; thus, the different registration process.

Viet Nam employs the 'first-to-file' system, meaning the first person to file a patent in the country's jurisdiction will own that right once the application is granted, regardless of whether another party invented or first used the patented creation. Viet Nam is also a party to the Paris Convention for the Protection of Industrial Property. Thus, applicants for invention patents and utility solution patents are entitled to a 'right of priority' if the same filing is made within the last 12 months in any other country that is also a party to the convention. Viet Nam has also been a member of the Patent Cooperation Treaty (PCT) since 1993. Thus, if a patent is granted in another PCT-contracting state, the application requirements and approval time may be reduced for an invention patent or utility solution patent application in Viet Nam. The application should be done via the National Office of Intellectual Property. Invention patents registered in Viet Nam last for 20 years from the filing date, with no possibilities for extension or renewal. Utility solution patent protection in Viet Nam lasts for ten years from the filing date, with no extension or renewal possibilities. The registration process typically takes up to 18 months.

7.2.3.3 Industrial designs

For an industrial design to be granted, the design must be new, creative, and have an industrial application. An industrial design is 'new' if it differs substantially from industrial designs that are already disclosed to the public inside or outside Viet Nam. Industrial designs cover products with a distinctive shape, pattern, or colour, and maintain novelty and industrial applicability.

Viet Nam again employs the 'first-to-file' system on industrial designs. Due to Viet Nam's membership in the Paris Convention for the Protection of Industrial Property, applicants for industrial designs are entitled to a 'right of priority' if filed within the previous six months in any country that also belongs to the convention. Industrial designs last five years from the filing date in Viet Nam, with the option to extend two more times for consecutive five-year periods (15 years maximum protection). The registration process typically takes up to 15 months.

7.2.3.4 Trademarks

Vietnamese law provides that trademarks are visible signs in the form of letters, words, drawings, or images, including holograms, or a combination of these, represented in one or more colours. A mark is distinctive if it consists of one or more easily noticeable and memorable elements or of many elements forming an easily noticeable and memorable combination. In Viet Nam, three-dimensional signs (shapes) can be registered as trademarks; however, so-called 'unconventional trademarks' based on sound and smell are not yet recognised. The law provides several circumstances under which a mark is not eligible for protection. Examples are when the mark is identical or confusingly similar to national flags, names of political organisations, and real names, or would cause misunderstanding or confusion about the origin, properties, quality, or other characteristics of the goods or services.

As Viet Nam is a contracting party to the Madrid Protocol and the Paris Convention for the Protection of Industrial Property, trademark applications are entitled to the provisions of the two conventions. Viet Nam operates under a 'first-to-file' system for trademark registration. Trademark protection lasts for ten years from the filing date in Viet Nam, with the option to extend for consecutive ten-year periods for an unlimited number of times. The registration process typically takes between 12 up to 15 months. Trademark registrations should be filed at the National Office of Intellectual Property, and the preliminary examination of applications will be completed within three months upon receiving the applications. Further evaluations will follow in the next nine to 12 months.

7.2.3.5 Geographical indications

Since the 2005 IP laws took effect in 2006 (as amended in 2009), geographical indications are recognised and can be registered in Viet Nam. Paragraph 22, Article 4 of the IP Law defines geographical indication as 'a sign which identifies a product as originating from a specific region, locality, territory or country'. Following the definition, geographical indications include geographical names, signs, symbols, and images.

The following subject matters are not protected as geographical indications:

i. Names or indications that have become generic names of goods in Viet Nam;
ii. Geographical indications of foreign countries where they are not or no longer protected or no longer used;
iii. Geographical indications identical or similar to a protected mark, where the use of such geographical indications is likely to confuse as to the origin of products;
iv. Geographical indications that mislead consumers as to the true geographical origin of products bearing such geographical indications.

Geographical indications can be protected in Viet Nam by a 'sui generis system' under the registration procedures to acquire rights and alternative legal tools of certification or collective mark and anti-unfair competition (Article 87 of the IP Law; Southeast Asia SME IPR Helpdesk 2016). Also, the IP Law of Viet Nam sets out that any commercial indications (including marks, trade names, business symbols, business slogans, geographical indications, package designs, label designs) that cause confusion as to the business entities, business activities, commercial source of goods or services, the origin, production method, feature, quality, or other characteristics of goods or services will be considered an act of unfair competition.

Protection of geographical indications is offered on an unlimited term basis without any need to renew the registration. The application for a geographical indication registration must be filed on site or by mail at the National Office of Intellectual Property.

7.2.3.6 IP-related applications and grants

In general, IPR protection has been gradually strengthened since 2000 – after the signing of the Viet Nam–US BTA. In parallel, guidance on the establishment and protection of IPR was enhanced. Also, the government implemented measures to encourage and promote innovative and creative activities all over the country with diversified activities. For instance, the Ministry of Science and Technology (MOST) organised training courses and workshops for businesses on creating, acquiring, protecting, exploiting, and managing IP rights. Also, a new initiative funded by WIPO in 2018–2022 (which already began in 2017) includes an advanced training course on technology transfer for universities and research institutes. Decision No. 1062/QD-TTg on the national program supporting the development of IP assets in 2016–2020 targets raising awareness and supporting leveraging of IP. Inter-government coordination of IP rights enforcement has been promoted. Action Program No. 168, first introduced in 2006 for 2006–2010 and reinstated in subsequent years, involves several entities – nine ministries and agencies involved in IP enforcement, including the Ministry of Science and Technology; the Ministry of Culture, Sports, and Tourism; the Ministry of Agriculture and Rural Development; the Ministry of Finance; the Ministry of Industry and Trade; the Ministry of Public Security; the Ministry of Information and Communication; and the Supreme People's Court.

In 2011–2017, 282,717 IP-related applications were submitted to the National Office of Intellectual Property (1.8 times higher than the figure for 2006–2010). These included 31,906 applications for inventions; 2,671 for utility solutions; 16,301 for industrial designs; 231,791 for trademarks; and 43 for geographic indicators (Table 7.1). All IP-related applications also witnessed a significant jump in 2011–2017 compared to 2006–2010. The majority of IP-related applications comprised trademarks (82% of all applications in 2011–2017), followed by inventions (11%), and industrial designs (6%). Geographic indications were very modest and slightly increased (43 applications in 2011–2017 relative to 30 in 2006–2010).

Foreigners filed most applications for invention, accounting for 90% of all invention applications in 2011–2017 (28,558 by foreign residents and only 3,348 by Vietnamese). Meanwhile, applications by Vietnamese in the field of utility solutions, industrial designs, and trademarks were overwhelming (66%, 65%, and 85% of total applications for each type, respectively). Viet Nam also witnessed a steep rise in both resident and non-resident registration of all types of IP-related assets in 2011–2017, with an average growth rate of more than 100% per year in the studied period. This indicates that awareness of IP protection has gradually improved.

Grants of IP-related assets, however, were relatively modest compared with the total number of applications. Accordingly, in 2006–2017, 537,673 applications for inventions, utility solutions, industrial designs, and trademarks were filed in the National Office of Intellectual Property, but only 299,320 grants (55.7%) were issued. In particular, only 29.0% of applications for utility solutions were approved, while the figures for industrial designs and trademarks were more significant (63.6% and 58.4%, respectively) (Table 7.2).

By technological classification, patent applications for invention and utility solutions are in technology, chemistry, pharmaceuticals, and machines and equipment (17%, 16%, 14%, and 14% of the total, respectively). More broadly, IP applicants are mostly concentrated in the sub-sectors of communications and engineering (Figure 7.1).

International applications of new-to-the-world technological innovations in Viet Nam are low. This is reflected in its performance in treaties administered by WIPO, including the Patent Cooperation Treaty patent

Table 7.1 Viet Nam's IP-Related Applications 2006–2017

Period	*Origin*	*Inventions*	*Utility Solution*	*Industrial Designs*	*Trademarks*	*Geographic Indication*	*Total*
2006–2010	*Total*	*14,697*	*1,292*	*8,865*	*134,481*	*30*	*159,365*
	Vietnamese	1,183	744	6,168	100,137	27	108,259
	Foreigners	13,514	548	2,697	34,344	3	51,106
2011–2017	*Total*	*31,906*	*2,671*	*16,301*	*231,791*	*43*	*282,712*
	Vietnamese	3,348	1,773	10,560	197,447	36	213,164
	Foreigners	28,558	898	5,741	34,344	7	69,548

Source: NOIP (2018).

Table 7.2 Viet Nam's Intellectual Property-Related Applications and Grants, 2006–2017

	Inventions	*Utility Solution*	*Industrial Designs*	*Trademarks*	*Total*
Applications	54,867	4,809	31,238	446,759	537,673
Grants	17,080	1,396	19,878	260,966	299,320
Share of grants in total applications	31.1	29.0	63.6	58.4	55.7

Source: NOIP (2018).

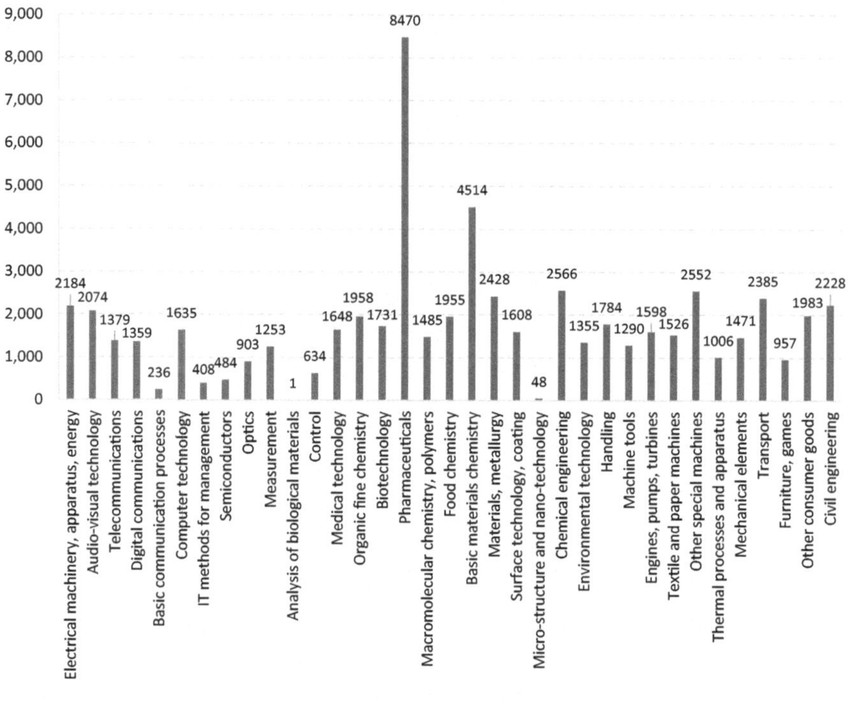

Figure 7.1 Patent Applications of Invention and Utility Solution in Viet Nam, by Technological Classification, 2006–2017.

applications, the Madrid System, and the Hague System (Table 7.3). Viet Nam's international applications via the three systems were 1,289 in 2011–2020, significantly up compared to that of 2001 - 2010 periods. The numbers outpaced those of Indonesia (334) and the Philippines (637). However, they are similar to those of Thailand (1,595) but much lower than Malaysia (2,563) and Singapore (13,738).

Viet Nam's performance in the Global Innovation Index (GII) by WIPO also witnessed a significant improvement; it ranked 45th out of 126

Table 7.3 IP Application by Viet Nam via WIPO-Administered Treaties, 2001–2020

	PCT System	*Madrid System*	*Hague System*
2001–2010	49	317	0
2011–2020	190	1092	7
2011	18	65	0
2012	13	82	0
2013	18	72	1
2014	7	80	1
2015	21	83	0
2016	10	105	1
2017	23	91	0
2018	22	159	0
2019	34	189	2
2020	24	166	2

Note: Madrid System = applications by office of origin (by filing date); PCT (Patent Cooperation Treaty) System = applications by filing date; Hague System = applications by origin.

Source: WIPO (2021).

economies in 2018. In particular, knowledge and technology outputs and creative outputs jumped by 14 and 12 positions, respectively. Further disaggregation for 2018 revealed that the IP-related sub-indices were relatively good, including trademarks (18th out of 126 ranked economies), industrial designs (37/126), utility models (35/126) (Table 7.4).

According to the International IP Index by the US Chamber of Commerce Global Innovation Policy Center,[11] Viet Nam ranked 42nd out of 50 economies with an overall score of 36.6% (18.31 out of 50) in 2020, compared to 30.6% (13.81 out of 45) in the previous edition. This result reflects the improvement of Viet Nam's performance in trade secrets, market assets, and commercialisation while other categories' scores did not change, including (i) patents, related rights, and limitations; (ii) copyrights, related rights, and limitations; (iii) trademarks, related rights, and limitations; and (iv) international treaties. The 2020 index also reveals that Viet Nam has taken steps towards aligning its IP framework more closely with its Southeast Asian peers, particularly regarding trade secrets, trademarks, systemic efficiency, and commercialisation of IP assets (Figure 7.2).

7.2.4 Discussions

Although Viet Nam's legal framework on IP is relatively sound, enforcing these laws is the main issue. Specifically, the country's IPR enforcement system offers three measures to deal with IP infringements: civil, administrative, and criminal. Administrative measures are the most frequently used method

Table 7.4 Viet Nam's Performance in 2018 GII Output Indices

S/N	*Indicators*	*Score in 2018*	*Rank in 2018*	*Rank Improvement in 2018 vs 2014*
6	**Knowledge and technology outputs**	**32.4**	**35**	**14**
6.1	***Knowledge creation***	***8.1***	***76***	***18***
6.1.1	Patents by origin/billion PPP$ GDP	0.9	67	-3
6.1.2	PCT patents by origin/billion PPP$ GDP	0.0	88	8
6.1.3	Utility models by origin/billion PPP$ GDP	0.5	35	3
6.1.4	Scientific & technical articles/ billion PPP$ GDP	4.9	79	23
6.1.5	Citable documents H index	11.3	57	2
6.2	***Knowledge impact***	***49.9***	***19***	***14***
6.3	***Knowledge diffusion***	***39.1***	***21***	***9***
6.3.1	Intellectual property receipts, % total trade	-	-	-
6.3.2	High-tech net exports, % total trade	29.9	1	5
6.3.3	ICT services exports, % total trade	0.1	120	11
6.3.4	FDI net outflows, % GDP	0.6	64	5
7	**Creative outputs**	**35.0**	**46**	**12**
7.1	***Intangible assets***	***46.5***	***49***	***8***
7.1.1	Trademarks by origin/billion PPP$ GDP	92.3	18	-4
7.1.2	Industrial designs by origin/billion PPP$ GDP	3.5	37	17
7.1.3	ICTs & business model creation	56.6	80	-42
7.1.4	ICTs & organisational model creation	53.3	66	-9
7.2	***Creative goods and services***	***35.1***	***29***	***17***
7.3	***Online creativity***	***12.1***	***54***	***7***
	Overall GII ranking		***45***	***26***

FDI = foreign direct investment, GDP = gross domestic product, GII = Global Innovation Index, ICT = information and communications technology, PCT = Patent Cooperation Treaty.

Source: Cornell University, INSEAD, and WIPO (2014, 2018).

because they are less expensive and quicker. However, the fine is not high enough to deter violators (American Chamber of Commerce in Viet Nam 2013, 2018). Relatively few IP cases are brought to court because the award may not often be worth the litigation costs. With criminal measures, it is

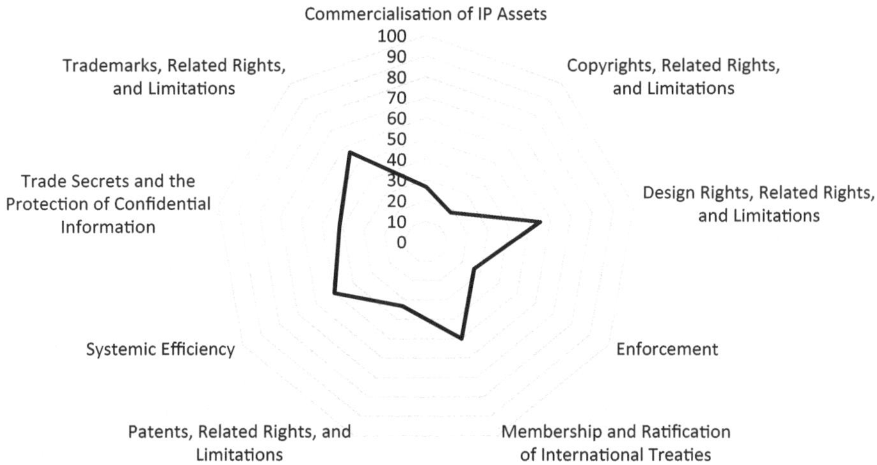

Figure 7.2 Viet Nam's Performance in International IP Index 2020.

tough to prove intentional acts of trading counterfeit goods even with prior knowledge of counterfeit goods. Meanwhile, the success of administrative action largely depends on the choice of enforcement authority (Inspectorate Department under the Ministry of Science and Technology, or competent ministries, or market control department, etc.), which in turn depends on the scale and complexity of infringement.

Difficulties and challenges in handling counterfeit goods and IP infringement also come from the hesitation and non-cooperation of enterprises. Some IP rights owners are afraid of dealing with fake goods since naming counterfeit goods may negatively affect their firms' reputation. Notably, in many cases, after a company cooperated with the authorities in identifying real goods from counterfeit ones, the counterfeit goods are then produced with more sophistication.

The protection of copyrighted movies and sound recordings is another issue of concern. Additionally, online piracy has become an even bigger problem; more robust mechanisms to combat piracy need to be put into effect and enforced to deter infringement. For example, the criminal provisions on copyright piracy have rarely, if ever, been implemented. Civil remedies can also be an effective deterrent. However, there are many barriers to effective civil actions in Viet Nam, such as lack of preliminary injunctions, lack of statutory damages awards, and difficult judgement enforcement procedures, as mentioned earlier.

The capacity of IPR enforcement agencies remains weak, both in terms of technical infrastructure and staff (American Chamber of Commerce in Vietnam 2018; EU Southeast Asia IPR SME Helpdesk 2017). Some enforcement agencies do not even have any IP specialised officials. Meanwhile, Viet Nam's court system cannot resolve quickly, nor effectively, complex IP cases, as judicial experience and professional knowledge of judges in the IP field are limited. This has prolonged the processing time and lowered the quality of IP infringement case settlement. As a result, a special focus on improving the self-determination of administrative enforcement agencies should be considered, including establishing IP specialised courts at the local level, to improve the justice available to IP rights holders.

7.3 Impacts of IP policy on trade

7.3.1 Trade pattern by technology level

Viet Nam's exports increased almost 44-fold between 1995 and 2018, with an average annual growth rate of 18%. After the accession to the WTO, exports continued to grow from US$39.8 billion in 2006 to US$62.7 billion in 2008 and US$243.5 billion in 2018 (Figure 7.3). Overall, during 2006–2018, exports increased by 6.11 times and attained an average annual growth rate of 16.3%, a bit slower than the 2001–2006 period (18.4%). Viet Nam also expanded its exports relative to GDP. The ratio of exports to GDP increased from 46.2% in 2001 to 64.3% in 2008 and 99.4% in 2018 (General Department of Customs 2017).

Nguyen et al. (2018) analyses the shares of Viet Nam's merchandise exports from 2004 to 2015 by commodity at the two-digit HS classification. Accordingly, the share of processed agricultural, forestry, and fishery products decreased as their exports grew more slowly than overall exports. For instance, food products (HS16-24) only saw their modest share improved gradually from 2.27% in 2004 to a peak of 3.15% in 2013, after which it started to go down. Meanwhile, the proportions of assembling products or natural resources and raw materials are relatively high. Machinery and

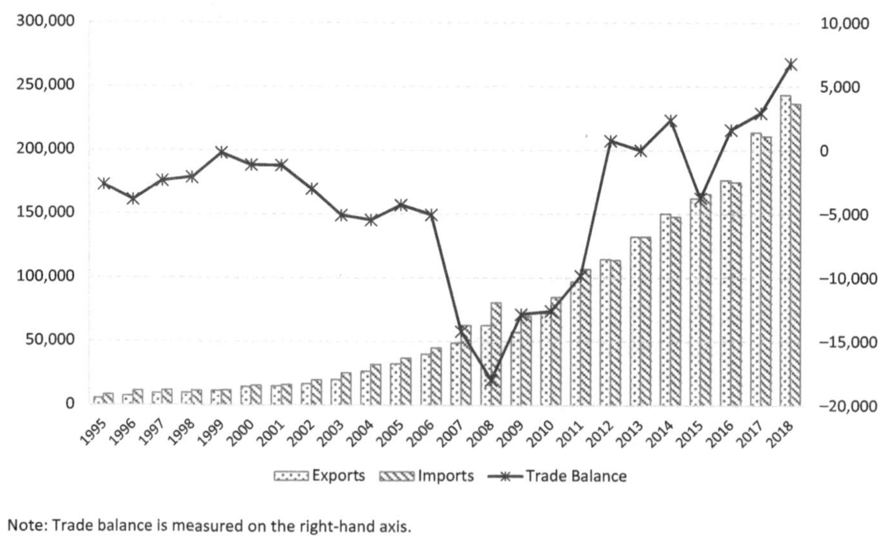

Figure 7.3 Viet Nam's Trade, 1995–2018 (in million US$).

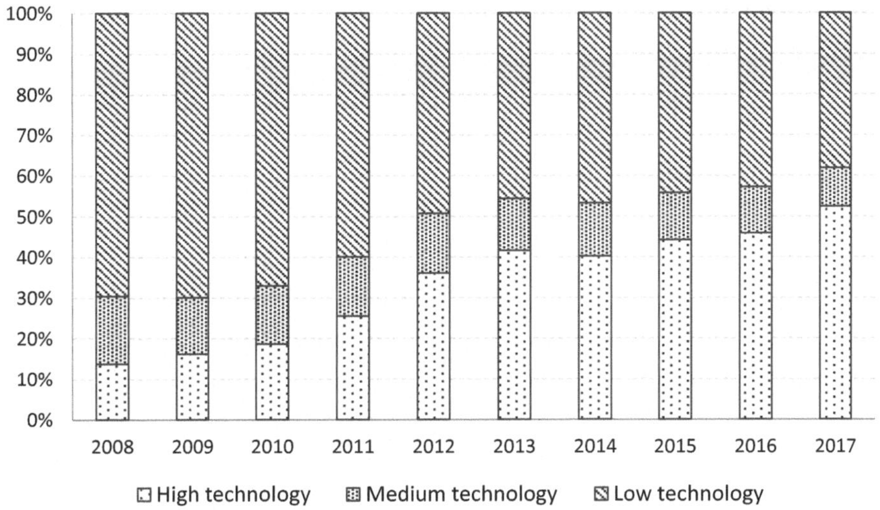

Figure 7.4 Viet Nam's Export by Technology Level (%), 2008–2017.

electricity witnessed the biggest jump in export share, from only about 8.24% in 2004 to 17.56% in 2011 and 35.46% in 2015.

In the 2017 export structure, high-tech products accounted for half, followed by low-tech products (accounting for 38.2%) and qualified products. Average technology accounted for 9.4%. The shift of high-tech export products increased rapidly in proportion, from 13.8% in 2008 to 52.4% in 2017. Meanwhile, exports with low technology decreased sharply from 69.6% in 2008 to 38.2% in 2017 (Figure 7.4).

However, most of Viet Nam's key export products, such as phones and components, computers, electronic products and parts, machinery and equipment, spare parts, cameras, and camcorders (belonging to high-tech products) in recent years, are from FDI enterprises. Domestic enterprises mainly engaged in products with low technology content such as textiles, garments, wood, and products from wood, fisheries, and footwear (Ministry of Planning and Investment 2018). This fact shows Viet Nam's technology dependence on the FDI sector, while the domestic technology capacity is still low. There are several possible implications from this. First, the transfer of technology from FDI enterprises to domestic counterparts has been relatively modest. Second, the better attitude to IP protection of FDI enterprises has not been transmitted to domestic counterparts, which deters the latter from participating in FDI-led technology-reliant value chains.

7.3.2 Trade in value added

Figure 7.5 shows that Viet Nam's domestic share in value added of exports decreased from over 63.9% in 2005 to almost 55.5% in 2015. However, its exports increased by about five times in the same period. The domestic value

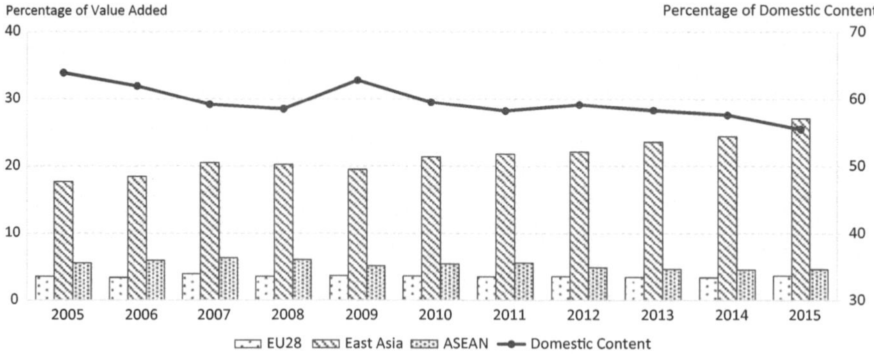

Figure 7.5 Share of Value Added Embodied in Gross Exports, by Country (%), 2005–2015.

added in Viet Nam's exports, measured in US dollars, therefore, increased by over 4.3-fold. This showcases Viet Nam's benefit from participating in the GVCs, which was already documented in Vo et al. (2017a) using data for 1995–2011. As previously noted, the first Law on IP was issued in 2005. At the aggregate level, it appears that the formalisation of the IP legal framework contributed to enhancing Viet Nam's participation in the GVCs.

The share of ASEAN in Viet Nam's value added from exports was relatively stable if excluding the country itself (Figure 7.5). East Asia's figure tended to increase, reflecting the outcomes of integration efforts with East Asian countries that induced more import flows of intermediate products from these countries. Among the East Asian countries, China stood out as the primary source of intermediate goods exported to Viet Nam. China's share of value added in Viet Nam's exports is estimated to increase from 4.9% in 2005 to 7.4% in 2008 and 14.1% in 2015.[12] Consistent with this finding, Truong et al. (2011) showed that intermediate inputs accounted for an increasing share in Viet Nam's imports from China. The figures reached 41.3%, 59.4%, and 50.2% in 2000, 2008, and 2009, respectively. Meanwhile, the EU played a stable but very modest role in Viet Nam's exports, from the perspective of value added. The share of Japan in Viet Nam's value added from exports decreased from 4.0% in 2005 to 3.3% in 2015. To this extent, it seems that Viet Nam was yet to leverage benefits from more technologically advanced partners such as the EU and Japan to upgrade value-added export contents.

Table 7.5 shows the pattern of value added in gross exports by source industry. The largest sources of value added in gross exports are (i) agriculture, forestry, and fishing; (ii) mining and quarrying; (iii) textiles, wearing apparel, leather, and related products; (iv) chemicals and non-metallic mineral products; and (v) wholesale, retail trade, hotels, and restaurants. However, the shares of mining and quarrying, and textiles, wearing apparel, leather, and related products went down significantly during 2005–2015. While Viet Nam aggressively promoted the development of the manufacturing

Table 7.5 Share of Value Added Embodied in Gross Exports (%), by Source Industry, 2005–2015

	2005	*2007*	*2010*	*2015*
D01T03: Agriculture, forestry, and fishing	8.78	8.74	8.94	8.90
D05T09: Mining and quarrying	17.64	16.87	14.09	9.69
D10T12: Food products, beverages, and tobacco	4.16	3.78	4.01	3.64
D13T15: Textiles, wearing apparel, leather, and related products	14.31	12.85	13.73	13.53
D16T18: Wood and paper products; printing	1.44	1.46	1.54	1.55
D19T23: Chemicals and non-metallic mineral products	9.54	10.15	10.04	9.85
D24T25: Basic metals and fabricated metal products	4.60	5.34	5.44	5.82
D26T27: Computers, electronic, and electrical equipment	3.39	4.12	5.10	8.10
D28: Machinery and equipment (nec.)*	1.32	1.08	1.20	2.00
D29T30: Transport equipment	0.71	0.90	1.02	1.68
D31T33: Other manufacturing; repair and installation of machinery and equipment	2.38	2.44	3.08	2.78
D35T39: Electricity, gas, water supply, sewerage, waste and remediation services	2.85	2.87	2.84	2.80
D41T43: Construction	0.15	0.17	0.18	0.38
D45T56: Distributive trade, transport, accommodation, and food services	19.89	19.83	19.66	18.93
D58T63: Information and communication	1.10	1.11	1.05	1.26
D64T66: Financial and insurance activities	3.38	3.64	3.65	3.95
D68: Real estate activities	0.78	0.80	0.91	1.04
D69T82: Other business sector services	2.52	2.70	2.44	2.92
D84T88: Public administrative, defence; education and health	0.61	0.67	0.62	0.71
D90T98: Other social and personal services	0.47	0.49	0.46	0.47

* not elsewhere classified

Source: OECD TiVA database (2018) (accessed January 2019).

sector, which generally accounted for around 20% of GDP, the sector had only limited contributions to the value added of exports. The manufacturing sub-sector with a notable increase in contribution to the value added of exports is computers, electronics, and electrical equipment. As discussed widely in the literature (Truong et al. 2011; Nguyen et al. 2018), the above industries saw their exports largely dominated by FDI enterprises. In this regard, IP policy only worked to the extent that it enhances the confidence of large foreign firms in Viet Nam's environment. Meanwhile, IP policy is yet to contribute to promoting technology transfer between FDI enterprises and domestic counterparts.

7.3.3 IP protection in the electronics sector

Since 1994, after the US lifted the trade embargo, Viet Nam's electronics sector became more open to foreign investors. The country received more investment into electronics by Japanese producers such as Canon, Panasonic, Sony, and Mitsubishi. Exports of the electronics industry started to increase over time. However, it was only in 2012, with the shift of world-leading mobile phone brands, including Nokia, Apple, LG, and most notably Samsung from China to Viet Nam, that Viet Nam's electronics industry became the export champion of Viet Nam.

In 2017, electronics and household electrical products accounted for 28.9% of Viet Nam's exports. Specifically, the export turnover of this category of exports (including mobile phones and components, cameras and other spare parts, and machinery and equipment) reached US$61.8 billion, up by US$14.45 billion, equal to 130% of the figure for 2016. Meanwhile, electronics and household electrical products accounted for 25.5% (about US$53.9 billion) of Viet Nam's imports. Specifically, imports of this product category increased by US$11.93 billion or 28.4% compared to 2016. These imports mainly came from such markets as Japan, China, the Republic of Korea (henceforth Korea), Hong Kong, and Chinese Taipei.

The World Integrated Trade Solution GVCs database shows that Viet Nam's top electronic exports at the six-digit level are printers (844331 and 844332), automatic data processing machines (847130 and 847190), line telephone sets (851711), telephones for cellular networks (851712), and headphones and earphones (851830). In particular, cellular phones attained large export values, high average export growth, and a relatively high share in the global market (Table 7.6). In exporting cellular phones, Viet Nam faces competition from China, Hong Kong, Korea, and the US (Table 7.7).

Table 7.6 Electronic Exports of Viet Nam

HS Code	*Export Value (thousand US$)*		*Global Market Share (%)*		*Average Growth*
	2012	*2016*	*2012*	*2016*	
844331	889,681	1,088,598	3.83	5.79	5.17
844332	1,235,520	1,156,814	7.46	9.06	-1.63
847130	1,128,561	2,996,363	0.72	2.58	27.65
847190	254,313	467,446	4.42	7.85	16.44
851711	251,909	125,854	9.44	8.12	-15.93
851712	10,093,132	27,155,262	5.74	12.08	28.07
851830	478,825	1,275,233	5.42	13.05	27.75

Source: WITS database (2018) (accessed January 2019).

Table 7.7 Market Shares of Main Competitors of Viet Nam in Electronics Exports

HS	*Viet Nam*		*China*		*Hong Kong*		*Korea*		*Malaysia*		*Netherlands*		*Mexico*		*Germany*		*Thailand*		*United States*	
Code	*2012*	*2016*	*2012*	*2016*	*2012*	*2016*	*2012*	*2016*	*2012*	*2016*	*2012*	*2016*	*2012*	*2016*	*2012*	*2016*	*2012*	*2016*	*2012*	*2016*
844331	3.83	5.79	50.39	40.96							7.93	11.80			7.66	6.54	4.56	8.88		
844332	7.46	9.06	29.82	26.95							12.08	10.83							6.72	7.20
847130	0.72	2.58	72.65	68.55	2.22	5.13									2.79	4.10			4.30	4.39
847190	4.42	7.85	8.48	10.40											11.98	11.49			17.42	16.28
851711	9.44	8.12	35.95	33.51	17.88	14.24				5.84					10.34	11.50				
851712	5.74	12.08	46.34	51.63	6.27	10.56	6.88	3.63											4.19	4.40
851830	5.42	13.05	47.62	36.33	19.02	15.90							3.51	4.18					5.31	4.85

Source: WITS database (2018) (accessed January 2019).

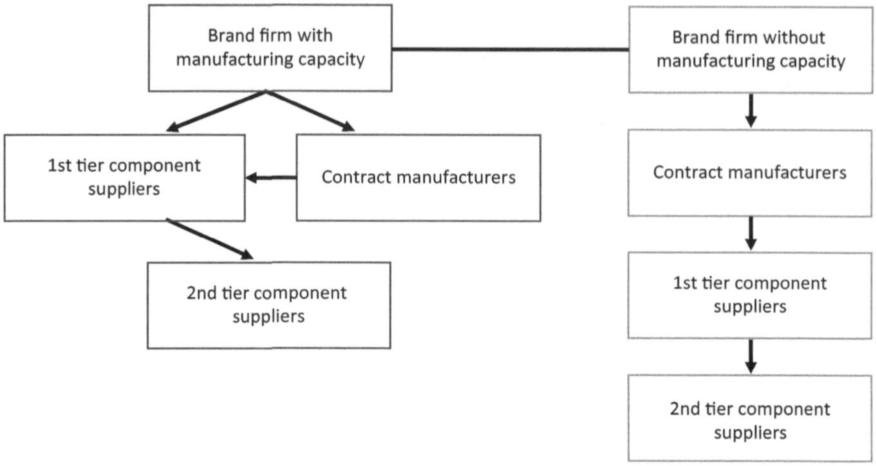

Figure 7.6 Electronics Supply Chain in Viet Nam.

The main destinations for Viet Nam's cellular exports are the EU (31%), Saudi Arabia (13%), US (12%), and Korea (8%).

Viet Nam has 1,088 electronics companies employing 325,583 workers, with female workers accounting for 70% of the labour force in 2015 (Do 2017). Viet Nam's electronics industry generally comprises brand firms, contract manufacturers, and component suppliers (Figure 7.6). The first-class suppliers for the electronics industry are mostly foreign-invested enterprises. Domestic enterprises primarily supply at the second and third tiers and are even modest in number. Domestic enterprises mainly provide some low-value rubber and mechanical components and components (for example, plastic pieces, glossy glass, metal covers, metal frames, etc.), and 'Other' parts and supplies (including packaging, guidebooks, tools, moulds, and fixtures for production). According to the Industrial Development Enterprise Center, Vietnamese enterprises can meet 22.5% of the demand for mechanical components in the electronics industry, 19.2% of the plastic–rubber components, and only 9.5% of dedicated electronic components. More importantly, while Viet Nam has seen a rapid increase in the number of software and services firms, its share in employment and revenues is only a fraction of that in electronic hardware manufacturing (Sturgeon and Zylberberg 2017).

According to the OECD TiVA database, Viet Nam's exports of computer, electronics, and optical products increased continuously from US$633.4 million in 2005 to almost US$1.3 billion in 2007 and over US$8.6 billion in 2015. (Figure 7.7) However, the share of domestic value added increased until 2011 and went down continuously during 2012–2015. The figure reached 42.4% in 2015, significantly lower than that in 2005 (61.5%) and 2008 (66.1%). Still, the domestic value added rose from US$418.7 million in 2005 to US$3,646.4 million in 2015, that is, by 24.2% per year on average. More importantly, as previously noted, the decrease since 2012 was

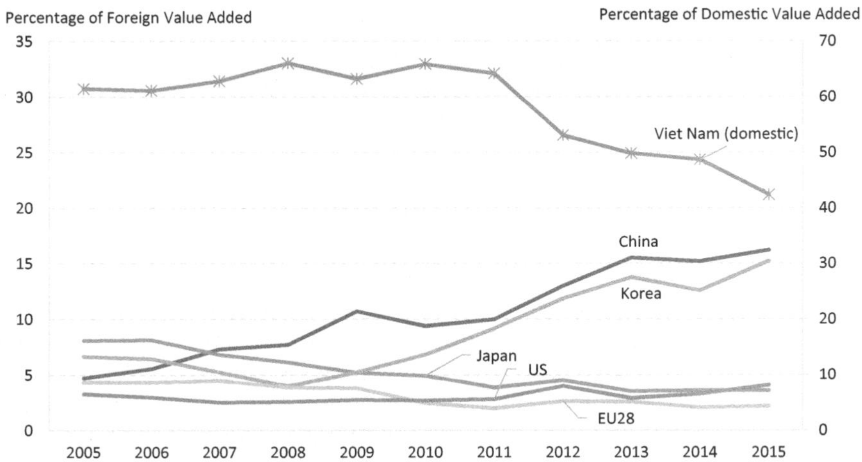

Figure 7.7 Value Added of Viet Nam's Electronics Exports, by Source Country, 2005–2015.

associated mainly with large foreign-invested firms such as Canon and Nokia, which boosted import-reliant electronic exports. Meanwhile, the shares of China and Korea increased continuously. The number of enterprises using modern machinery and technology imported from the EU or the US is somewhat limited.

Various studies (Ministry of Planning and Investment 2018; Vietnam Academy of Social Sciences et al. 2019) have looked into the weak linkages between domestic firms and foreign firms in the electronics industry. Such a weak link may include the inadequate access to finance by domestic firms, business strategies of domestic firms that are unfriendly to GVCs, and international commitments that prevent Viet Nam from forcing technology transfer. However, low technology transfer was also due to poor enforcement of IPR regulations that fail to deter violations. In the first instance, large foreign firms had to develop routines to prevent theft of electronics products by their local workers. In our visit to a foreign firm in the electronics industry, we noted its management supervise local workers' entry and exit in the production premises. This prevention was deemed necessary since any IP theft will imply a cost that can hardly be recovered, given the perceived poor enforcement of IP regulations. This imposed a cost to foreign firms, making them more sceptical of providing training on technological advances to local workers. While technology transfer from FDI can be via movement of labour (Nguyen 2005), this possibility seems to be smaller as electronics firms have to avoid thefts by their workers.

Another area of IP infringement in the electronics sector is fake or counterfeit products. Fake or counterfeit peripherals for smartphones such as batteries, chargers, ear pods, and so on, are rather popular. In 2017, the General Department of Customs identified 13,562 counterfeit products using Apple and Samsung trademarks. Without compliance with IP regulations, such peripherals can be sold at a relatively low price than authentic ones. The increasing popularity of e-commerce channels also helps such fake peripherals reach consumers easier. Nevertheless, they also expose users to several risks and incidents, such as explosion, electric shocks, damage to mobile devices, and so on. From the policy perspective regarding digital economy development, poor enforcement of IP in electronics hardware may also weaken consumers' confidence in e-commerce, given the high perceived risk of buying a fake or counterfeit one.

Customs authorities are facing some obstacles regarding the process of controlling goods infringing IP rights. Specifically, Decree 45/2017/ND-CP stipulates that, if imported goods fail to comply fully with the required contents, they must be allowed to write additional Vietnamese labels first when circulated. The customs authorities detected many electronics sub-labels showing signs of counterfeit origin, trademarks, or instructions forging goods origin. But there is no basis for handling at the import stage.

The handling of goods in transit that infringe IP rights is also inadequate. The Customs Law stipulates that the transit of goods will not be temporarily stopped for customs procedures, but Decree 99/2013/ND-CP provides that there must be handling with this infringement. Therefore, customs authorities do not know which rules to enforce when electronics products in transit infringe IP regulations. As a result, in 2017, the subjects took full advantage of the Customs Law provisions. They transited counterfeit and fake goods and those infringing IP rights from China to Viet Nam, then the Lao PDR and Cambodia.

Finally, for exported goods infringing on IP rights, the Law on IP stipulates that customs must inspect, supervise, and suspend customs procedures. Still, handling counterfeit goods of this type have no sanctions. The induced extra time and cost turn out to be a burden to many businesses and individuals, making it even more difficult for them to protect their brands and products. This has further weakened the enforcement of IP regulations in the country.

7.4 Policy recommendations

To further engage local enterprises into the GVCs and the digital economy, Viet Nam should undertake measures in various areas. These areas include reforms in the business environment and state-owned enterprises, developing a more focused industrial policy, access to finance, and human resources development. From the analysis, this chapter yields insights to support the following policy recommendations.

First, Viet Nam should increase the adoption of international best practices in enforcing IP regulations. In this process, FTAs can be an essential means of delivery, but not enough. While the FTAs, such as the CPTPP and the European–Viet Nam FTA, may often allow a road map to phase in IP commitments, Viet Nam should implement the road map on time. More frequent and effective dialogues with partners on IP policy may also be helpful. In this regard, Viet Nam needs to acquire more confidence from such partners as the EU and the US on its IP policy.

Second, IP support to small and medium-sized enterprises (SMEs) joining the GVCs may be essential. Such support includes lower or zero costs of IP advice for SMEs and an upgraded patent system to avoid overloads due to heavy demands that can deter market entry. In this regard, Viet Nam may learn from the IPR helpdesk model of partners such as the EU).

Third, leveraging IP compliance and protection seems necessary for Vietnamese SMEs to upgrade their position in the GVCs. While building awareness is essential, being patient in enforcement – to develop a culture of IP compliance – should be important.

Fourth, Viet Nam should harmonise the IP regulations in line with international norms, balancing the needs to foster creativity and innovation and enabling competition. The IP framework itself should be adaptive to technology changes. Thus, reforms in the IP office are required.

Finally, Viet Nam should improve the availability and quality of IP-related statistics (e.g. the cost to apply for and maintain patents added in annual enterprise censuses). This will help the administration calibrate the policies and measures based on feedback from the market. More importantly, it will increase the transparency and credibility of the system.

Notes

1 Ordinance No. 13-LCT/HDNN8 dated 28 January 1989.
2 Ordinance No. 38/L-CTN1 dated 2 December 1994.
3 Part VI, 'Intellectual Property Rights and Technology Transfer'.
4 Law No. 50/2005/QH11 dated 29 November 2005 on IP; Law No. 36/2009/QH12 dated 19 June 2009, amending and supplementing several articles of the IP law.
5 For instance, in opposing geographical indication protection due to customary name, Article 18.33 of the IP chapter in the CPTPP states '*...in determining whether a term is the term customary in common language as the common name for the relevant good in the territory of a Party, that Party's authorities shall have the authority to take into account how consumers understand the term in the territory of that Party*'. However, the amended provisions of the 2019 IP Law only specifies that '*...name, geographical products have been customary in understanding of related customers in Viet Nam*'. The Viet Nam Chamber of Commerce and Industry (VCCI 2019) claims that the definition in Viet Nam covers a smaller group of customers and, thus, increases the possibility of geographical indication being opposed. This in turn adversely affects the people and the community in Viet Nam who actually own the geographical indication.
6 Decision No. 68/2005/QD-TTg dated 4 April 2005 on approving the program in support of development of enterprises IP.
7 Decision No. 2204/QD-TTg dated 6 December 2010 on approving the program to support intellectual asset development during 2011–2015.
8 Decision No. 1062/QĐ-TTg dated 14 June 2016 on approving the National Program for Supporting the Development of IP Assets in the period of 2016–2020.
9 For more details, see Nguyen (2019).

10 Patent term adjustment for unreasonable curtailment, and protection of undisclosed test and other data were suspended under the CPTPP.
11 This index analyses intellectual protection in 50 economies based on 40 indicators that benchmark activities surrounding patent, trademark, copyright, and trade secrets protection, released annually by the US Chamber of Commerce's Global Innovation Center.
12 From OECD TiVA database (2018).

Bibliography

American Chamber of Commerce in Vietnam (2018), 'Position Paper on Intellectual Property Issues', http://www.amchamhanoi.com/wp-content/uploads/2018/03/AmCham-Position-Paper-on-IP-issues.pdf (accessed 18 May 2019).

American Chamber of Commerce in Vietnam (2013), 'Intellectual Property Rights in the Socialist Republic of Vietnam', http://www.amchamhanoi.com/wp-content/uploads/2014/01/special301old.pdf (accessed 6 June 2017).

Cornell University, INSEAD, and WIPO (2018), *Global Innovation Index 2018: Energizing the World with Innovation*. Ithaca, Fontainbleau, and Geneva: WIPO.

Cornell University, INSEAD, and WIPO (2014), *Global Innovation Index 2014: The Human Factor in Innovation*, second printing. Fontainebleau, Ithaca, and Geneva: WIPO.

Dinh, H.P. (2019), 'Promoting Effectiveness of IPR to Meet the Requirements of Development and International Integration' ('*Nâng cao hiệu quả của hoạt động sở hữu trí tuệ ở nước ta để đáp ứng yêu cầu của phát triển và hội nhập quốc tế*') (In Vietnamese), *Communist Review Online.*

Do, Q.C. (2017), 'The Missing Link in the Chain? Trade Regimes and Labour Standards in the Garments, Footwear and Electronics Supply Chains in Vietnam', in *Country Study for Viet Nam.* Core Labour Standards Plus.

EU Southeast Asia IPR SME Helpdesk (2017), 'IP Factsheet: Vietnam', online, https://www.southeastasia-iprhelpdesk.eu/sites/default/files/publications/Vietnam%20Factsheet.pdf (accessed 18 May 2019).

General Department of Customs (2017), 'Statistical Data', https://www.customs.gov.vn/Lists/ThongKeHaiQuan/Default.aspx (in Vietnamese) (accessed 12 July 2017).

General Statistics Office of Vietnam (2019), 'Annual Flows of Exports and Imports.' https://www.gso.gov.vn (accessed 31 January 2019)

Government of Viet Nam (2016), Decision 1062/QD-TTg of the Prime Minister Approving Program to Develop Intellectual Property in 2016–2020 ('*Quyết định 1062/QD-TTg năm 2016 phê duyệt Chương trình phát triển tài sản trí tuệ giai đoạn 2016–2020 do Thủ tướng Chính phủ ban hành*') (in Vietnamese).

Mai, D.L. and T.J. Treutler (2018), *Viet Nam: New Law on Competition Impacts IP.* http://www.managingip.com/Article/3830115/VietNam-New-Law-on-Competition-impacts-IP.html (accessed 2 February 2019).

Ministry of Planning and Investment (2018), An Assessment of Suppliers of Inputs for Foreign-Invested Firms in Cities, Provinces Directly under the Central Government ('*Đánh giá tình hình các doanh nghiệp sản xuất sản phẩm phụ kiện đầu vào cung cấp cho các doanh nghiệp đầu tư nước ngoài tại các tỉnh/thành phố trực thuộc Trung ương*'], Report to the Government of Vietnam (in Vietnamese), Ha Noi: Ministry of Planning and Investment, Viet Nam.

Ministry of Science and Technology (2003), *Accession to the WTO and the Intellectual Property System in Viet Nam*. Ha Noi.

National Office of Intellectual Property (NOIP) (2018), *Annual Report on Intellectual Property Activity*. Various years from 2005 to 2017. Ha Noi: Ministry of Planning and Investment, Viet Nam.

Nguyen, D.A. (2019), 'Intellectual Property Rights in TPP Agreement: Commitments and Implications for Viet Nam', in L. Chen, S. Urata, J. Nakagawa, and M. Ambashi (eds), *Emerging Global Trade Governance: Mega Free Trade Agreements and Implications for ASEAN*. Routledge, pp. 134–150.

Nguyen, D.A., T.T. Vo and T.N.T. Do (2018), 'Vietnam's Exports after Joining the WTO', Manuscript for Economic Research Institute for ASEAN and East Asia.

Nguyen, P.M., V.H. Nguyen, N.C. Tran and T.H. Nguyen (2007), 'Country Report – Vietnam', *WIPO-UNU Joint Research Project on Impact of the Intellectual Property System on Economic Growth*, online. https://www.wipo.int/export/sites/www/about-ip/en/studies/pdf/wipo_unu_07_vietnam.pdf (accessed 3 May 2019).

Nguyen, T.T.A. (2015), 'A Study of the Adjustment of Foreign Direct Investment Policy in Viet Nam until 2020' ('*Nghiên cứu điều chỉnh chính sách đầu tư trực tiếp nước ngoài ở Việt Nam đến năm 2020*') (In Vietnamese), *State-Level Research Project KX.01.03/11-15.*

Nguyen, T.T.A. (2005), *Impact of FDI on Economic Growth in Vietnam*. Ha Noi: Science and Techniques Publishing House (in Vietnamese and English).

OECD (2019), Trade in Value Added (TiVA) database 2018. https://www.oecd.org/sti/ind/measuring-trade-in-value-added.htm#access (accessed 3 February 2019).

Sitkoff, A. (2018), 'IPR Protection and Enforcement in Vietnam Is Not As Strong As It Should Be', *Vietnam Law and Legal Forum*, http://vietnamlawmagazine.vn/ipr-protection-and-enforcement-in-vietnam-is-not-as-strong-as-it-should-be-6217.html (accessed 4 May 2019).

Southeast Asia SME IPR Helpdesk (2016), 'IP Factsheet: Vietnam', https://www.southeastasia-iprhelpdesk.eu/sites/default/files/publications/Vietnam%20Factsheet.pdf (accessed 6 February 2019).

Sturgeon, T. and E. Zylberberg (2017), 'Vietnam's Evolving Role in ICT Global Value Chains', Chapter 9, in C.H. Hollweg, T. Smith, and D. Taglioni (eds), *Vietnam at a Crossroads: Engaging in the Next Generation of Global Value Chains*. Washington, DC: World Bank Group, pp. 133–157.

Tran, M.H. (2017), 'The Intellectual Property Review – Edition 6: Viet Nam', *The Law Reviews Online*. https://thelawreviews.co.uk/chapter/1144678/Viet-Nam (accessed 2 February 2019).

Treutler, T.J. and A.M. Duong (2011), 'Vietnam', https://www.tilleke.com/sites/default/files/2011Dec_Pat_Lit_Vietnam.pdf (accessed 3 May 2019).

Truong, D.T., T.T. Vo, T.G. Bui, V.C. Phan, T.D. Le, A.D. Nguyen and S.A. Pham (2011), 'Impacts of Commitments on Opening the Market under WTO and other Free Trade Agreements on Vietnam's Production and Trade Activities and Mechanism to Improve Import and Export Management Scheme of the Ministry of Industry and Trade in 2011–2015' ('*Tác động của cam kết mở cửa thị trường trong WTO và các hiệp định thương mại tự do đến hoạt động sản xuất, thương mại của Việt Nam và các cơ chế hoàn thiện cơ chế điều hành xuất nhập khẩu của Bộ Công Thương giai đoạn 2011–2015'*) (In Vietnamese). Report for Multilateral Trade Assistance Project (MUTRAP).

US Chamber of Commerce (2020), *Art of the Possible – US Chamber International IP Index*. Washington, DC: US Chamber of Commerce.
Viet Nam Academy of Social Sciences, Ministry of Planning and Investment, and United Nations Development Program (2019), *Productivity and Competitiveness of Viet Nam's Enterprises – Volume 1: Manufacturing*. Ha Noi: Vietnam Academy of Social Sciences (VASS).
Viet Nam Chamber of Commerce and Industry (2019), 'Draft Revision of Law on IP "Higher" than CPTPP Commitment' ('*Dự thảo sửa đổi Luật Sở hữu trí tuệ "vượt trần" cam kết CPTPP*'), online, http://www.trungtamwto.vn/chuyen-de/13135-du-thao-sua-doi-luat-so-huu-tri-tue-vuot-tran-cam-ket-cptpp (accessed 16 June 2019).
Viet Nam Legal Library database (n.d.), www.thuvienphapluat.vn (accessed 30 January 2019).
Vo, T.T. and D.A. Nguyen (2011), 'Revisiting Exports and Foreign Direct Investment in Vietnam', *Asian Economic Policy Review*, 6(1), pp. 112–131.
Vo, T.T., D.A. Nguyen and T. Bui (2017a), 'Trade in Value Added: The Case of Viet Nam' in L.Y. Ing and F. Kimura (eds), *Production Networks in Southeast Asia*. New York, NY: Routledge Publishing House, pp. 183–201.
Vo, T.T., D.A. Nguyen and H.T. Dinh (2017b), 'Innovation Policy in Viet Nam', Chapter 9 in H. Ambashi (ed.), *Innovation Policy in ASEAN, ERIA Research Report 2018*. Jakarta: Economic Research Institute for ASEAN and East Asia.
WIPO (2019), 'Statistiscal Country Profiles: Viet Nam', https://www.wipo.int/ipstats/en/statistics/country_profile/profile.jsp?code=VN (accessed 11 July 2021).
WTO Center–VCCI (2017a), *The Review of Viet Nam Legal Framework against Commitments under EVFTA on Intellectual Property*. Ha Noi: WTO Center-VCCI.
WTO Center–VCCI (2017b), *The Review of Viet Nam Legal Framework against Commitments under TPP on Intellectual Property*. Ha Noi: WTO Center-VCCI.

8 Korea's intellectual property protection strategy and its implications for ASEAN

Keon-Hyung Ahn

8.1 Introduction

Intellectual property (IP) is an essential element to secure and achieve a successful business and to strengthen national competitiveness in the digital economy. An IP system protects new ideas and innovations with economic value or business growth potential to thrive in the business world. IP rights holders' ability to enforce their rights from infringement has become a major economic policy trend in this knowledge-based economy so that major leading countries strive to implement various policies to respond to these changes arising from technology innovation.

The Republic of Korea (henceforth Korea) is no exception to this trend. It sought to establish and develop fundamental IP and information technology infrastructure to catch up with other leading countries to date. According to the World Intellectual Property Office (WIPO), Korea has topped the number of resident patent applications per gross domestic product (GDP) and population for ten consecutive years since 2007 (WIPO 2017). Korea continued to have the second highest research and development intensities[1] (4.24%) after Israel (4.25%) in 2016 (OECD 2018a). Korea is also the fifth largest country in terms of the number of Patent Cooperation Treaty applications (KIPO 2017). A report of the Korea Intellectual Property Office (KIPO) stated that the employment inducement coefficient of Korea's IP service industry was 21.1% as of 31 January 2018. This is much higher than the 14% all-industry average, including the manufacturing industry (KIPO 2018a).

Thanks to its substantial efforts to revolutionise its economy, including IP industry development, Korea became the first country to transform itself from a recipient country – it was the second poorest country in the 1950s after the Korean War – into a donor country of global donations.

With the strong standing of Korea in the IP sector, since 2004, KIPO has contributed around 11.2 million Swiss francs for the continued operation of the WIPO Korea Funds-in-Trust (KIPO 2017). It applies this fund to KIPO–WIPO projects that support developing countries, including those of the Association of Southeast Asian Nations (ASEAN) (OECD 2018b).

DOI: 10.4324/9781003147657-9

Fourteen states designated Korea (usually KIPO) as an International Searching Authority (ISA) concerning the Patent Cooperation Treaty. ISA includes six ASEAN member states – Indonesia, Malaysia, the Philippines, Singapore, Thailand, and Viet Nam. Korea was ASEAN's fifth largest trading partner and fifth largest source of foreign direct investment (FDI) in 2016. On the other hand, ASEAN is Korea's second largest trading partner and second largest investment destination (ASEAN 2017). The fact that Korea has achieved economic development in such a short period should inspire most ASEAN member states, particularly in establishing and implementing policies to create, use, and protect IP in ASEAN effectively and efficiently.

With these in mind, this chapter introduces Korea's Intellectual Property Protection Strategy and draws implications for ASEAN. Specifically, this chapter first discusses the recent domestic reforms for IPR protection in Korea in Section 8.2. This includes Korea's (i) legal IP framework, (ii) administrative structure for IP, and (iii) recent trends on domestic reforms for IPR protection. Section 8.3 examines Korea's policies to enhance IP protection enforcement at home and abroad. These include (i) the Special Judicial Police for Trademark, (ii) the Counterfeit Goods Reporting Center and Anti-Counterfeit Council, (iii) overseas IP protection, and (iv) the Industrial Property Right Dispute Mediation Committee. Section 8.4 discusses Korea's experience of free trade agreements (FTAs) on IP, including major issues in the Korea–US FTA and Korea–European Union (EU) FTA on IP. Lastly, while ASEAN encounters common policy challenges, there are considerable differences in the digital economy's development among ASEAN member states. This means that each member state needs unique strategies and sets of priorities for effective and efficient implementation, respectively (OECD 2018b). Therefore, Section 8.5 summarises the above discussion and draws on how effectively and efficiently ASEAN may facilitate IPR protection strategies to achieve business success and strengthen regional competitiveness in the future.

8.2 Recent trends on domestic reforms for IPR protection in Korea

8.2.1 Korea's legal framework for IP

The most basic and essential law regarding IP in Korea is the Framework Act on IP).[2] This Act is composed of 40 articles under five chapters and addenda. Chapter 1 comprises the general provisions, such as goals, principles, and definitions. Chapter 2 sets forth the formulation of IP policies and IP promotion system.[3] Chapter 3 provides for the creation, protection, dispute resolution, and use of IP. Chapter 4 deals with infrastructure, including fostering an IP-friendly environment, IP education and training of IP experts, and global cooperation and aid to developing countries. Lastly, Chapter 5 contains a couple of supplementary provisions.

The IP Framework Act aims to contribute to the economic, social, and cultural development and improvement of people's quality of life by reinforcing the foundation for creating, protecting, and utilising IP (Article 1). The Act defines IP as

> knowledge, information, technology, the expression of thoughts or feelings, the indication of business or goods, varieties of organism or genetic resources and other intangibles created or discovered by creative activities, experience, etc. of human beings, the value of property of which may be realized.
>
> (Article 3[1])

'New intellectual property' means 'intellectual property that appears in new fields in line with economic, social, or cultural changes or the development of science and technology' (Article 3[2]). 'Intellectual property right' is 'any right relating to intellectual property recognized or protected according to Acts and subordinate statutes, treaties, etc.' (Article 3[3]).[4] In Korea, IPR is divided into three types: industrial property right, copyright, and new IPR.

The major IP laws in Korea include the (i) Patent Act, Utility Model Act, Design Protection Act, and Trademark Act regarding Industrial Property Laws; (ii) the Copyright Act; and (ii) the Act on the Protection of New Varieties of Plants, Act on Quality Control of Agricultural and Fishery Products, Act on Prevention of Unfair Competition and Protection of Trade Secrets, Act on the Layout-Designs of Semiconductor Integrated Circuits regarding new types of IP laws. Also, there are the Content Industry Promotion Act,

Table 8.1 Types of Intellectual Property Right in Korea

Industrial Property Right	*Copyright*	*New Intellectual Property Right*
• Patent (lasts for 20 years from the filing date of the patent application) • Utility model (10 years) • Design (20 years) • Trademark (10 years, may be renewed for another 10 years)	• Literary works/Musical works • Theatrical works • Paintings, sculptures, crafts, works of applied art, and other works of art • Architectural works • Photographic works • Cinematographic works • Maps, charts, design drawings, etc. • Computer program works • Protects for 70 years after the author's death	• New Intellectual Property means 'intellectual property that appears in new fields in line with economic, social, or cultural changes or the development of science and technology' (Art. 3[2] IP Framework Act). • Industrial copyright, high-tech industrial property, information property, trade dress, tangible material assets, etc.

Source: Author, referring to Patent Act, Utility Model Act, Trademark Act, Design Protection Act, Copyright Act, Framework Act of Intellectual Property of Korea.

the Act on Prevention of Divulgence and Protection of Industrial Technology, and the Invention Promotion Act that covers employees' invention, utility model, or design.

8.2.2 Korea's administrative structure for IP

The IP administrative system is classified into four types: (i) the pluralist system, (ii) the coordination system, (iii) the concerted action system, and (iv) the centralist system. In the pluralist system,[5] each ministry administers its respective related IP matters. Korea and China fall within this category.

Even though the Presidential Council on Intellectual Property (hereinafter PCIP) was established on 28 July 2011 under the IP Framework Act, the PCIP merely coordinates and advises each ministry on IP-related policies. More specifically, the PCIP and its administrative body, the Office of IP Strategy and Planning, was established under the Prime Minister's Office in 2011. Then the Office of IP Strategy and Planning moved and was located in the Ministry of Science and ICT in 2013. The PCIP's most important function is to formulate a master plan for national IP. The PCIP comprises two co-chairs – the Prime Minister and a civilian expert appointed by the President – 12 government members and 18 civilian members.

The PCIP and its Secretariat, however, have been criticised for their inefficient and ineffective role. This is because the PCIP is just an advisory body that cannot be a control tower in planning, coordinating, and evaluating IP-related policies. Continuity and expertise are lacking, as the Secretariat, comprising officials from each ministry, serve only for one year. Another criticism is the lack of communication and coordination with the President of Korea, as no Senior Secretary in charge of IP is in the Office of the President.

Other IP-related tasks are distributed to ministries, such as KIPO; the Ministry of Trade, Industry, and Energy; the Ministry of Culture, Sports, and Tourism (MCST); the Ministry of Agriculture, Food, and Rural Affairs; the Ministry of Environment; and the Ministry of Health and Welfare. For IP protection and enforcement, the Ministry of Foreign Affairs, the National Intelligence Service, the Ministry of Justice, the Fair Trade Commission, Korea Customs Service, MCST, and KIPO are involved (Figure 8.1).

In the case of China, a huge government restructuring was implemented in 2018. As Figure 8.2 illustrates, among other things, the super State Market Regulatory Administration (SMRA) was established combining the (i) State Administration for Industry and Commerce; (ii) the General Administration of Quality Supervision, Inspection, and Quarantine; and (iii) the China Food and Drug Administration. The antitrust divisions of the National Development and Reform Commission and the Ministry of Commerce were also merged into the SMRA. Furthermore, the National Intellectual Property Administration of the People's Republic of China (CNIPA), formerly known as the State Intellectual Property Office (SIPO), was established by merging the trademark offices under one roof – the SMRA (Jing and Zhixing 2018).

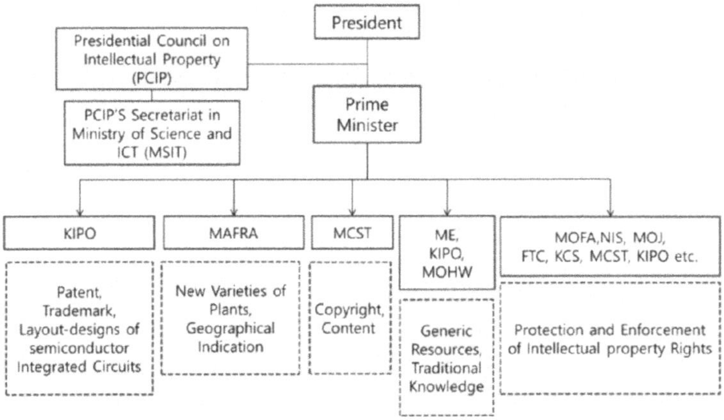

FTC = Fair Trade Commission; KCS = Korea Customs Service; KIPO = Korea Intellectual Property Office; MAFRA = Ministry of Agriculture, Food, and Rural Affairs; MCST = Ministry of Culture, Sports, and Tourism; MOHW = Ministry of Health and Welfare; MOJ = Ministry of Justice.

Figure 8.1 Intellectual Property Administrative Structure of Korea.

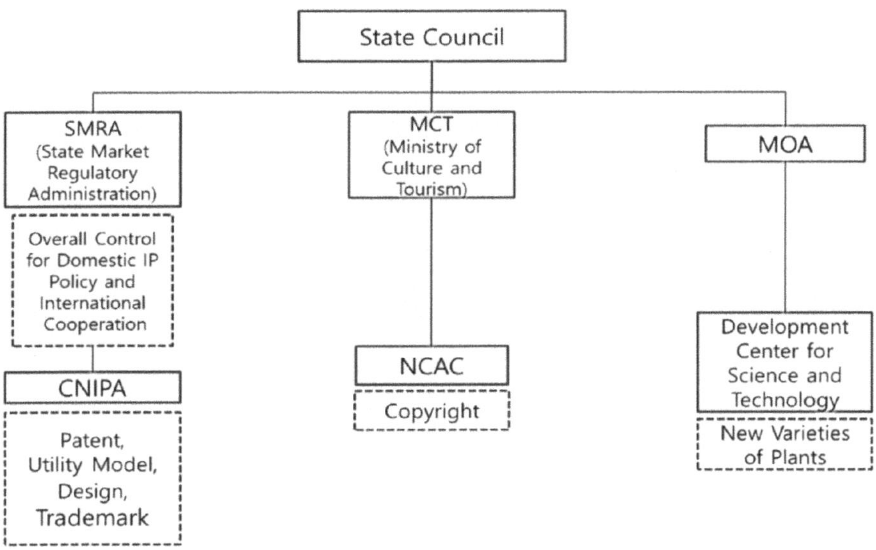

Figure 8.2 Intellectual Property Administrative Structure of China.

SIPO reported all IP-related matters directly to the State Council, but the CNIPA is under the supervision of the SMRA at the moment. Each ministry is still responsible for its relevant IP tasks separately. For example, the CNIPA is the authority for patents, utility models, designs, trademarks, and geographical indications. The National Copyright Administration of China is responsible for copyright, while the Ministry of Agriculture and Rural Affairs is for new plant varieties, and so on.

Regarding other types of IP administrative systems, the second category, coordination system, establishes a higher level of strong coordinating body over each ministry that deals with its respective IP-related matters without designating a sole competent authority in charge of IP matters and policies. Japan and China[6] fall within this classification.

Japan's IP administrative structure is similar to that of Korea. Several ministries are in charge of the execution and enforcement of their related IP policies (see Figure 8.3). For example, the Japan Patent Office is responsible for industrial property; the Agency for Cultural Affairs for copyright; the Ministry of Agriculture, Forestry, and Fisheries for new plant varieties, and so on. However, unlike Korea, Japan established the Intellectual Property Strategy Headquarters directly under the Prime Minister. The headquarters plans, controls, and coordinates all IP policies at the national level.

The third type is the centralist system,[7] where a sole ministry is in charge of all IP-related administrative tasks, including the creation, utilisation, protection, and overall planning and coordination of IP. The United Kingdom (UK) is the best example of this category. Its Intellectual Property Office is in charge of overall control of all related policies regarding industrial property and copyright.

The fourth category, considered the most desirable system, is the concerted action system where a sole competent authority leads all IP-related matters and policies as well as a higher coordinating body at the national level. The US is one of the best examples in this category (see Figure 8.4). The IP Enforcement Coordination (IPEC) is the leading authority that

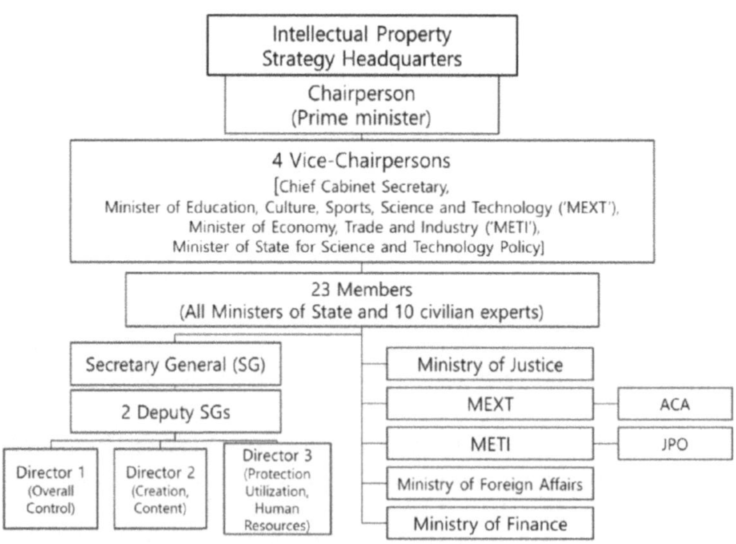

ACA = Agency for Cultural Affairs, JPO = Japan Patent Office.

Figure 8.3 Intellectual Property Administrative Structure of Japan.

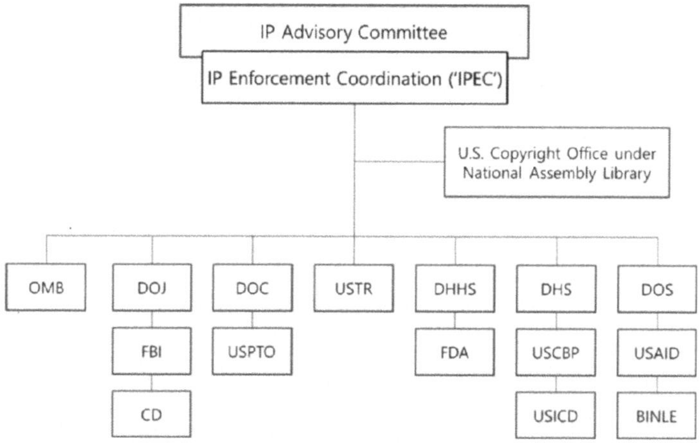

BINLE = Bureau of International Narcotics and Law Enforcement Affairs, CD = Criminal Division, DHHS = Department of Health and Human Service, DHS = Department of Homeland Security, DOC = Department of Commerce, DOJ = Department of Justice, DOS = Department of State, FBI = Federal Bureau of Investigation, FDA = Food and Drug Administration, OMB = Office of Management and Budget, USCBP = US Customs and Border Protection, USICD = US International Council on Disabilities, USPTO = US Patent and Trademark Office, USTR = US Trade Representative, USAID = US Agency for International Development.

Figure 8.4 Intellectual Property Administrative Structure of the United States.

formulates policies on IPR protection and infringement response at the federal level and disseminates its policies to all the relevant ministries. The IPEC is in charge of the IP Advisory Committee. The committee is responsible for combining and coordinating IP policies from a strategic perspective over the relevant ministries. Meanwhile, the US Patent and Trademark Office handles internal and external IP policies, including industrial property, trademark and even copyright, international cooperation, and trade negotiation (Lee and Park 2018).

8.2.3 Recent trends in Korea's domestic reforms for IPR protection

To enhance IPR protection, the Korean government sought the amendment of some major IP-related laws. The Unfair Competition Prevention and Trade Secret Protection Act was revised in January 2017 and entered into force in July 2017. Under the revised Act, anyone who imitates products developed by others and wrongfully gains from it may be criminally charged. In particular, criminal charges may be filed when any person imitates someone's product within the first three years of its launch and where it was leased, transformed, or exhibited for gains (Article 18[3]). Also, relevant government agencies can start an investigation and recommend corrections for the infringement (Article 8) (KIPO 2017). Furthermore, as of 18 July 2018, the Act also adopted punitive damages against infringement of trade secrets to the effect that the court can decide the amount of damage within the limit of three times the damage caused where the infringement was intentional (Article 14[2][6] and Article 14[2][7]). The Act came into force on 9 July 2019.

Similarly, as of 8 January 2019, the Patent Act also adopted punitive damages against patent infringement or exclusive licence. It provided that the court can decide the amount of damage within the limit of three times the damage caused where the court considers the infringement intentional (Article 128[8]). This provision of the Patent Act entered into force on 9 July 2019.

Meanwhile, a significant change was correspondingly made to the judicial system over IP disputes in Korea. To resolve IP disputes in a more specialised, effective, and expeditious manner, the jurisdiction over IP-related litigations was concentrated in the Patent Court by the amendments of the Civil Procedure Act (Law No. 13521) and the Court Organization Act (Law No. 13522), both enacted on 1 December 2015. As a result, the Patent Court located in Daejeon, Korea has had exclusive appellate jurisdiction over civil actions relating to IPR since 1 January 2016 (Patent Court of Korea 2017). The Patent Court has jurisdiction over trial cases provided in Article 186(1) of the Patent Act, Article 33 of the Utility Model Act, Article 166(1) of the Design Act, and Article 162 of the Trademark Act. The Patent Court also has jurisdiction over appellate cases provided in Article 24(2)(3) of the Civil Procedure Act and other cases under the jurisdiction of the Patent Court under the law, such as Article 103(1) of the Act on the Protection of New Varieties of Plants. This court has authority over actions requesting revocations of contested decisions by the Intellectual Property Trial and Appeal Board (IPTAB) on a patent, utility model, design, and trademark. Since 1 January 2016, the Patent Court also has exclusive appellate jurisdiction over civil actions relating to IP rights. The court presides over the first instance proceedings of actions requesting revocation of IPTAB decisions. Its fact-finding is final since the Supreme Court takes over the next instance only on questions of law when the Patent Court's decisions are contested.

In this regard, it is necessary to know the relationship between the Patent Court and KIPO. The Patent Court was established as a 'court' under the Court Organization Act. The Patent Court has jurisdiction over special cases such as cancellation proceedings on decisions of the Intellectual Property Tribunal, headed by the KIPO commissioner. On the contrary, KIPO is an executive agency established by the Ministry of Trade, Industry, and Energy to manage general affairs regarding patent, utility model, design, trademark examinations, and related decisions. As such, the Patent Court is organisationally unrelated to KIPO, even if it reviews cancellation appeals from diverse decisions rendered by the Intellectual Property Tribunal.

Last among the recent domestic IPR reforms initiated by Korea is the Court Organization Act's amendment through the International Litigation Chamber Legislation passed on 24 November 2017 and entered into force in May 2018. The amendment now allows Korea's district courts and Patent

Court's IP cases to be heard entirely in English and other foreign languages. The Korean National Assembly's amendment to the Court Organization Act creates an exception for foreign languages in the chamber. Previously, all cases had to be heard in Korean to have legal effect (Asia IP 2018).

8.3 Korea's policies to enhance IPR protection

KIPO is the most crucial force in planning and performing IPR protection policies and strategies in Korea. In this regard, KIPO established a promotional strategy (2018–2022) in 2017 with a vision of 'Leading the Fourth Industrial Revolution with IP' as follows (see Table 8.2).

Our discussion here focuses on the 'reinforcement of IP protection backing fair economy' among KIPO's four strategies (2018–2022), among other things, industrial property rights such as patents and trademarks in Korea's perspective.

8.3.1 Special Judicial Police for Trademarks

In September 2010, KIPO launched the Special Judicial Police for Trademark (SJP) to improve law enforcement on counterfeits and established offices in Seoul, Busan, and Daejeon. In 2017, the SJP criminally arraigned 362 suspects found producing and/or selling counterfeit goods and seized

Table 8.2 KIPO's Vision Structure (2018–2022)

To create strong IP that will lead to innovative growth	*To strengthen IP protection to support fair economy*
1. Renovating patent examination quality 2. Securing core patent in the Fourth Industrial Revolution fields. 3. Managing full cycle patent creation 4. Establishing a fast and fair patent trial	1. IP protection of small and medium-sized enterprises (SMEs) and ventures 2. Expanding support for exporting enterprises and leading international cooperation 3. Settlement of economic, social digital divide
To lay the groundwork of IP to prepare for the future	**To facilitate IP commercialisation for high-quality jobs creation**
1. Reforming the law system in preparation for the Fourth Industrial Revolution 2. Ensuring the efficiency of patent administration using future technology 3. Expanding infrastructure for inventors' development 4. Encouraging invention and creating a culture of respect for IP	1. Fostering the IP service industry focusing on the private sector 2. Strengthening SMEs and ventures' IP capacity 3. Vitalising IP finance and trade

Source: Author, referring to KIPO (2018b).

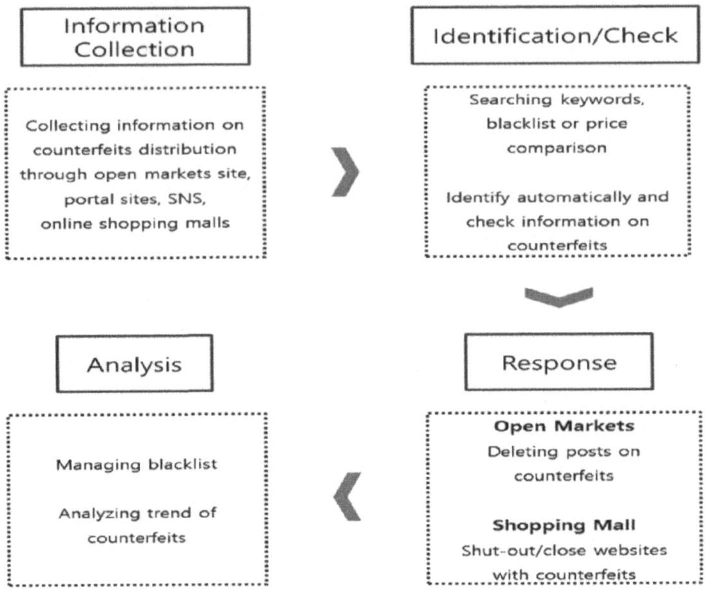

Figure 8.5 Task Flow of IPOMS.

a total of 691,630 counterfeit goods (KIPO 2017). As e-commerce grows, online transactions of counterfeit goods have been rapidly increasing. In November 2011, KIPO established an online law enforcement task force equipped with digital forensic equipment to regulate this matter to address this issue. Online sellers' counterfeit goods were seized and illegal websites were blocked or shut down.

KIPO also established the Intellectual Property Online Monitoring System (IPOMS), the 24-hour online monitoring system against the distribution of counterfeits through open markets, online shopping malls, portal sites, and Social Network Service. Figure 8.5 shows the task flow of IPOMS.

Furthermore, KIPO has been strengthening the enforcement cooperation system to prevent mass production and distribution of counterfeits domestically and internationally (Figure 8.6).

8.3.2 Counterfeit goods reporting centre and Anti-Counterfeit Council

KIPO operates a reward system to facilitate the reporting of counterfeit goods and raise public awareness of the illegality of counterfeit goods (see Table 8.3).

The Anti-Counterfeit Council, a public–private cooperation system, also contributes to enforcement activities to prevent the distribution of counterfeit goods. This council consists of 62 organisations, including KIPO, Korea Intellectual Property Protection Agency established under KIPO, well-known trademark holders, and online market operators.

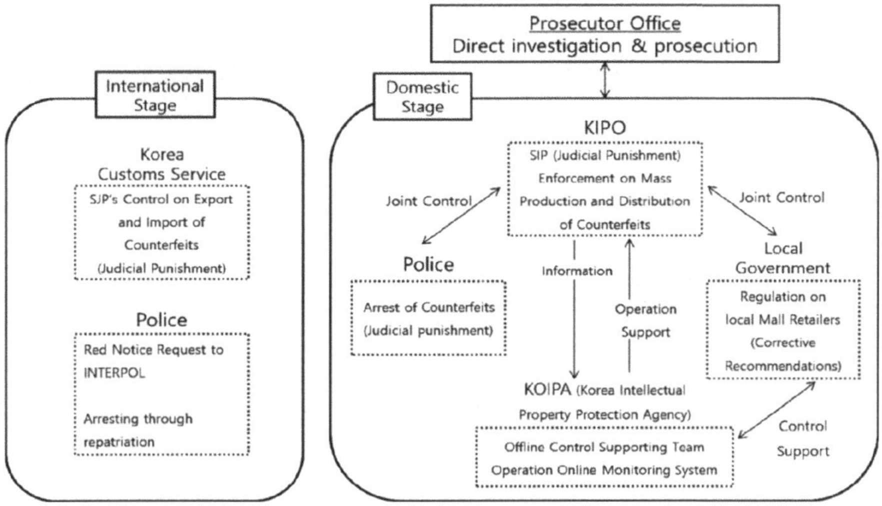

Figure 8.6 KIPO's Enforcement Cooperation System.

Table 8.3 Counterfeit Goods Reporting Reward in Online Sales (unit: cases, thousand US$)

2013		*2014*		*2015*		*2016*		*2017*	
Cases	*Amount*	*Cases*	*Amount*	*Cases*	*Amount*	*Cases*	*Amount*	*Cases*	*Amount*
2	0.9	5	3.3	7	5.7	23	19.2	25	39.4

Source: Author, referring to KIPO (2018b).

8.3.3 Overseas IP protection

8.3.3.1 Cooperation with overseas online market

In 2014, the Korea Intellectual Property Protection Agency and a global e-commerce enterprise, Alibaba Group, signed a bilateral memorandum to curb counterfeit goods. In 2017, KIPO monitored 53 trademark trolls in China and shared the information with Korean companies to determine the appropriate countermeasures. In cooperation with the Alibaba Group, KIPO prosecuted around 20,302 counterfeit goods on Alibaba.com and blocked related sites (KIPO 2017).

8.3.3.2 Korea IP-DESKs

KIPO, in cooperation with the Korea Intellectual Property Protection Agency and Korea Trade-Investment Promotion Agency (KOTRA), operates 14 IP-DESKs in eight countries (including Indonesia, Thailand, and Viet Nam) to protect and further promote IPR belonging to Korean companies with businesses overseas. These IP-DESKs provide Korean companies

Figure 8.7 Current Status of Korea's Overseas IP-DESKs.

with consultations on registering, protecting, and resolving IPR, whether currently active or preparing to enter foreign markets. Recently, additional IP-DESKs were added in areas where Korean companies are frequently embroiled in IPR disputes. KIPO set up an IP-DESK in Tokyo in 2015; in Xi'an, China in 2016; and in New Delhi, India and Jakarta, Indonesia in 2017. KIPO planned to open the 15th IP-DESK in Hong Kong in 2019 (Seo 2019). In this regard, KIPO established its IP-DESKs in KOTRA's overseas offices in 126 cities globally to save tax and enhance efficiency in IPR protection (Figure 8.7).

KIPO also held various seminars to help IPR-related government officials of China, Thailand, and Viet Nam enhance their enforcement protection against counterfeit goods. Furthermore, KIPO is making efforts to develop cooperative channels with foreign IPR-related organisations to protect the IPR of Korean companies' overseas.

8.3.4 IPR Dispute Mediation Committee

The Industrial Property Right Dispute Mediation Committee was established pursuant to Articles 41 and 49 of the Invention Promotion Act in 1995. It is the only dispute mediation organisation on industrial property right in Korea. The committee, composed of 40 experts appointed by the KIPO commissioner, helps the parties settle their dispute over industrial property rights, employees' inventions, or trade secrets. Recording matters on which parties agree in a protocol shall form mediation, and the protocol shall be effective as judicial conciliation. The committee's mediation service provides prompt dispute resolution (within three months) free of charge and guarantees private procedure, namely, confidentiality.

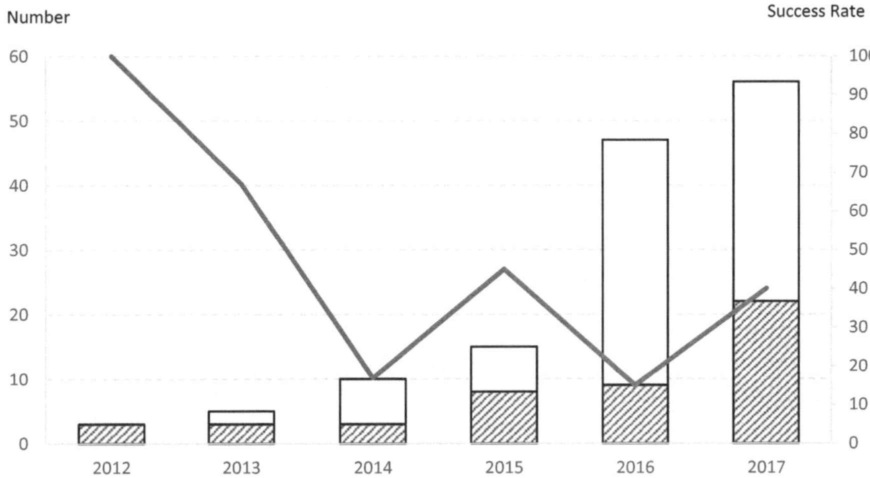

Figure 8.8 Industrial Property Right Dispute Mediation Cases.

To save time and cost in resolving industrial property rights disputes, KIPO has been actively promoting the mediation committee's role and function. The author expects that requests for mediation regarding IPR will increase, and the committee's role will be continuously strengthened (Figure 8.8).

8.4 Korea's experience of FTA on IP

This section examines some major issues regarding the Korea–US FTA (hereinafter KORUS FTA) and the Korea–EU FTA that resulted in Korea's most significant ripple effect regarding IPs, and draws implications for ASEAN.

8.4.1 Major IP issues in the Korea–US FTA

Korea signed an FTA with the US, which came into force on 15 March 2012. The KORUS FTA has many TRIPS-plus provisions reflecting the interests of the US. The US has been using the IP chapter of FTAs as international rule-making efforts to take advantage of FTAs (Kim 2016).

8.4.1.1 Major patent issues in the KORUS FTA

First, the KORUS FTA extended the grace period for a patent application from six months to 12 months. Specifically, each party to the FTA shall disregard the information in public disclosure used to determine if an invention is novel or has an inventive step if the public disclosure occurred within 12 months before the date of filing of the application in the territory of the party (KORUS FTA, Article 18.8[7][b]). Korea amended the Patent Act by extending the grace period from six months to 12 months on 2 December 2011, reflecting this provision of the KORUS FTA (Patent Act, Article

30[1]). In this regard, it is worth noting that US businesses' use of the grace period increased from 35 times in 2007–2011 before the KORUS FTA's effectivity to 103 times for the next five years after its effectivity (Huh 2017).

Second, the KORUS FTA clarifies the definition of 'unreasonable delays' and adopted the provisions that require the FTA party's duty to provide compensation in case of such delays that occur in granting the patent. Article 18.8(6)(a) of the KORUS FTA provides that:

> an unreasonable delay shall at least include a delay in the issuance of the patent of more than four years from the date of filing of the application in the territory of the party, or three years after a request for examination of the application, whichever is later. Periods attributable to actions of the patent applicant need not be included in the determination of such delays.

For patents covering a new pharmaceutical product and methods of making or using a new pharmaceutical product approved for marketing in the territory of the party, the KORUS FTA adjusted the patent term (KORUS FTA, Article 18.8[6][b]). Korea also amended the Patent Act on 2 December 2011 by inserting Articles 92.2 to 92.5 reflecting the said provisions of the KORUS FTA.

Third, the KORUS FTA abolished a patent revocation system except for grounds of fraud, misrepresentation, or inequitable conduct (KORUS FTA, Article 18.8[4]). Before the Patent Act was amended on 2 December 2011, Article 107(1)(1) of the old Act (Law No. 9381, 20 January 2009, partial amendment) provided that where the patented invention has not been worked for more than three consecutive years in Korea – except in cases of natural disasters, unavoidable circumstances, or other justifiable reasons prescribed by the presidential decree – the patent could be revoked. Furthermore, Article 116(1) of the old Act set forth that where a patented invention has not been continuously worked in Korea for two years or more from the date of adjudication under Article 107(1)(1), the KIPO commissioner might cancel the patent right ex officio or upon the request of any interested party. However, Korea deleted Article 116 of the Patent Act to reflect the KORUS FTA provision (Park 2014).

8.4.1.2 Major trademark issues in the KORUS FTA

The KORUS FTA adopted sound and scent marks, providing that neither party may require, as a condition of registration, that signs be visually perceptible, nor may either party deny registration of a trademark solely because the sign comprises a sound or scent (KORUS FTA, Article 18.2[1]). In this regard, the application of 21 sound marks and 25 scent marks of US businesses were registered with KIPO as of February 2017 (Huh 2017). Korea incorporated these new concepts in the Trademark Act on 2 December 2011. It provided that trademark right shall be extended to a trademark with shapes or colours, the combination of colours, sound, or odour essential to secure the functions of the designated goods of a registered trademark or their packaging (Trademark Act, Article 51[1][4]).

Second, Article 18.2(2) of the KORUS FTA also adopted the certification marks system that 'each party shall provide trademarks, along with certification marks, and that geographical indications are eligible for protection as trademarks'. US businesses applied for registration of 25 certification marks as of February 2017 (Huh 2017). To incorporate Article 18.2(2) of the KORUS FTA, Korea amended the Trademark Act, providing the definition of certification mark in Article 2(1)(7) and setting forth the provision of PERSONS entitled registration of a trademark in Article 3 of the Act.

Third, Article 18.10(6) of the KORUS FTA adopted pre-established damages in civil judicial proceedings concerning works, phonograms, and performances protected by copyright or related rights and in cases of trademark counterfeiting. Korea already concluded the measure of execution in this regard by incorporating the concept of pre-established damages in the Trademark Act. Article 111 of the Act provides that a trademark rights holder or an exclusive licensee may claim compensation for a reasonable amount to the extent not exceeding 50 million won (₩) instead of claiming damages under Article 109 against any person's intentional or negligent infringement.

Lastly, Article 18.2(13) of the KORUS FTA provides that neither party may require recordation of trademark licences to establish the validity of the licence, to assert any rights in a trademark, or for other purposes. Under this provision, Korea abolished the requirement for effects of registration by deleting Article 56(2) of the old Trademark Act (Act No. 10358, 9 January 2010, partial amendment). This article provided the establishment, transfer (excluding transfer by inheritance or other general succession), modification, or extinguishment (excluding cases caused by confusion of any right) or restriction on exclusive licence disposal.

8.4.1.3 Major issues on IPR enforcement in the KORUS FTA

The KORUS FTA adopted a provision on judicial orders concerning the protection of confidential information produced or exchanged in a judicial proceeding (KORUS FTA, Article 18.10[11][b]). Under this provision, judicial authorities can impose sanctions on parties to a civil judicial proceeding, their counsel, experts, or other persons, subject to the court's jurisdiction, for violating said judicial orders. This provision commonly applies to Korea's major IP-related laws. The country adopted the confidentiality obligation by amending Article 129(3) of the Copyright Act, Article 224.3 of the Patent Act, and Article 92.7 of the Trademark Act (Kim 2016).

Second, the KORUS FTA adopted specific border measures regarding IPR infringement (KORUS FTA, Article 18.10[19]). This provision states that each state shall ensure that any rights holder can commence procedures for its competent authorities to suspend the release of suspected counterfeit or confusingly similar trademarked goods, or pirated copyright goods into free circulation. However, the rights holder must provide adequate evidence and sufficient information to prove that the rights holder's IPR is infringed, and sufficient information is supplied. To reflect the said provision, Korea amended Article 235(1) of the Customs Act on 30 December 2010. The amendment provided that goods infringing on trademark rights, copyrights and neighbouring rights, variety protection rights, geographical rights, patent rights, and design rights may not be imported or exported. If goods obviously infringed any IPR, the head of a customs office may withhold customs clearance for such goods or keep them in custody ex officio (Customs Act, Article 235[7]). Also, Korea amended the Act on the Investigation of Unfair International Trade Practices and Remedy against Injury to Industry to Protect IPR against Distribution of Counterfeits. Article 4(1) of the Act prohibits importing or exporting goods that violate all kinds of IPR under the relevant Acts or Treaties signed by Korea. Article 5(1) also provides that any person may apply for the investigation in writing to the Trade Commission, where he or she considers that unfair international trade practices have occurred. According to Article 6 of the Act, the Trade Commission may also undertake an *ex officio* investigation if it deems such is necessary due to a reasonable suspicion of unfair international trade practices. Furthermore, Article 10 of the Act sets forth that where the Trade Commission judges decide that unfair global trade practices exist, they may order the relevant actor to do corrective measures.

Furthermore, Article 18.10(23) of the KORUS FTA provides that:

> Each Party *shall* provide that goods that have been suspended from release by its customs authorities, and that have been forfeited as pirated or counterfeit, shall be destroyed, except in exceptional circumstances. In regard to counterfeit trademark goods, the simple removal of the trademark unlawfully affixed shall not be sufficient to permit the release of the goods into the channels of commerce. In no event shall the competent authorities be authorized, except in exceptional circumstances, to permit the exportation of counterfeit or pirated goods or to permit such goods to be subject to other customs procedures.
>
> (emphasis added)

On the contrary, Article 15.26(5) of the Korea–China FTA sets forth that:

> each Party *may* provide that goods that have been suspended from release by its customs authorities, and that have been confiscated under infringement of an intellectual property right *stipulated in paragraph 1* shall be destroyed, except in exceptional circumstances. In regard to counterfeit trademark goods, the simple removal of the trademark unlawfully affixed shall not be sufficient to permit the release of the goods into the channels of commerce.
>
> (emphasis added)

Under Article 15.26(1), 'each state shall adopt procedures concerning border measures *subject to the provisions of domestic legislation*' (emphasis added). In this case, Article 27 of the Regulations of the People's Republic of China on Customs Protection of IPR[8] provides that 'the confiscated goods infringing an IPR *can be used for public welfare undertakings*' (emphasis added). The provision further sets forth that the customs office shall hand such goods over to the relevant public welfare institutions for use in public welfare undertakings (Kim 2016). It is a pity that Korea lost a chance to enhance IPR protection in China through the Korea–China FTA. Unlike the KORUS FTA, the Korea–China FTA stipulates more relaxed provisions by (i) using 'may' instead of 'shall' and (ii) empowering each party's government to refer to its laws in enforcing this FTA, as discussed above.

8.4.2 Major issues on IP in the Korea–EU FTA

The Korea–EU FTA came into force on 1 July 2011 and became fully effective on 13 December 2015. As Korea already made an extremely comprehensive agreement to enhance IPR protection through the KORUS FTA, only a few major issues remained, among other things, geographical indication in the Korea–EU FTA negotiation.

The Korea–European Union (EU) FTA defines geographical indications (GIs) as:

> (a) geographical indications, designations of origin, quality wines produced in a specified region and table wines with geographical indication as referred to in Council Regulation (EC) No. 510/2006 of 20 March 2006; Regulation (EC) No. 110/2008 of the European Parliament and of the Council of 15 January 2008; Council Regulation (EEC) No. 1601/1991 of 10 June 1991; Council Regulation (EC) No. 1493/1999 of 17 May 1999; and Council Regulation (EC) No. 1234/2007 of 22 October 2007, or provisions replacing these regulations; and (b) geographical indications as covered by the Agricultural Products Quality Control Act (Act No. 9759, 9 June 2009) and the Liquor Tax Act (Act No. 8852, 29 February 2008) of Korea.
>
> (Korea–EU FTA, subsection C, footnote 2)

In this FTA, both parties undertook to protect 162 GIs of the EU and 64 GIs of Korea listed in Annex 10-A [Korea–EU FTA, Article 10.18(3)]. Korea and the EU also agreed to add GIs listed in Annexes 10-A and 10-B (Korea–EU FTA, Article 10.18[3]) by recommendation and decision of the Working Group on GIs under Article 10.25 of the Korea–EU FTA. These provisions show the EU's strategy to strengthen the GIs' level of protection by exchanging a simple list of GIs in each party's annex to the bilateral agreement and then expanding the number of GIs subsequently.

To reflect the provision on GIs in the Korea–EU FTA, Korea amended the Trademark Act on 27 January 2016 (effective on 28 April 2016),[9] the

Act on Quality Control of Agricultural and Fishery Products on 27 March 2015 (effective on 28 March 2016),[10] the Unfair Competition Prevention and Trade Secret Protection Act on 27 January 2016 (effective on the same date).[11]

The GIs of the Korea–EU FTA mainly relate to agricultural products and foodstuffs. The Korea–EU FTA is considered the most comprehensive and significant FTA concerning GI protection for Korea. However, there is a criticism that Korea should have included fishery products to the GIs' scope as it recognises GIs for fishery products under Article 2(1)(8) of the Act on Quality Control of Agricultural and Fishery Products (Lee 2016).

8.5 Conclusion

The Organisation for Economic Co-operation and Development (2016) reported that total trade in counterfeit and pirated products to the EU amounted to as much as US$116 billion (€85 billion) in 2013, implying that as much as 5.1% of EU imports in 2013 were counterfeit and pirated. Korea's counterfeit and pirated products market was estimated to amount to as much as ₩5.2 billion (inflow: ₩2.3 trillion, domestic production: ₩2.9 trillion) based on actual distribution price, amounting to 1.8% of Korea's nominal GDP in 2013 (Hyundai Research Institute (HRI), 2014). Counterfeit and pirated products (i) bring about loss of tax, (ii) deprive the related industry's development opportunity, (iii) result in loss of social capital, and (iv) damage national prestige, among others.

Having recognised these problems, most developed and developing countries strive to make a better environment to create, use, and protect IP in the knowledge-based economy era. To this end, major leading countries seek to establish an optimal administrative structure for IP.

Thus, this chapter first recommends that ASEAN member states precisely check out the administrative system regarding the IP policy and adopt a concerted action system, such as that of the US or, at least, the coordination system like that of Japan. Specifically, it seems desirable to assign a sole competent authority to lead all IP-related matters and policies like the IPEC, as well as a higher coordinating body at the national level, such as the IP Advisory Committee in the US or the IP Strategy Headquarters in Japan. ASEAN member states should also unify the planning and enforcement on industrial property and copyright under a sole authority, such as US Patent and Trademark Office.

Meanwhile, the TRIPS Agreement has effectively required member states of the World Trade Organization to adopt a minimum IP protection standard. However, some states did not adopt stronger TRIPS standards when it was not optimal to do so. In other words, some states chose not to enforce the IP standards they have legally adopted, thereby creating a divide between statutory levels and enforced levels of IP protection (Briggs and Brown 2012). To address this matter, the US and the EU have been aggressively utilising bilateral agreements with other developing countries that are eager to access the largest markets to enhance the level of IPR protection in those developing countries. Korea is the best example. Korea signed FTAs with the US, the EU, and China. The GDP of Korea's FTA bloc amounts to 77% of the world economy, placing third in the world in 2017.

Furthermore, Korea is the only country among the world's top ten foreign trade countries, which have FTAs with both the US and China (Ministry of Trade, Industry and Energy of Korea 2018). After the KORUS FTA, Korea's IPR protection level dramatically rose. With the confidence gained from extensive experience in the FTAs with the US and the EU, Korea has been more actively promoting IPR protection policies and activities at home and abroad these days.

It is likely that leading countries in the IP industry will continuously enhance the IP protection level at the multilateral or regional FTA negotiations or renegotiations, such as the Regional Comprehensive Economic Partnership (RCEP), to that achieved in their previous bilateral FTAs with non-ASEAN member states. ASEAN needs to create an IP-friendly atmosphere and strengthen the IPR protection at its respective domestic level. In this regard, it will be desirable for ASEAN member states to pay more attention to GIs, among others. In recent years, many Asian countries realised that their IP owners could benefit from stronger protection of GIs (Lee 2016). Also, ASEAN member states can get support from other international IP-related institutions and non-governmental organisations. For instance, KIPO supported developing a local coffee produced in Flores Bajawa, Indonesia as a brand, and it obtained a GI in 2015. The findings also suggest that ASEAN collaborates with Korea to include fishery products as GIs because ASEAN member states and Korea, having plenty of rivers and seas, can succeed.

Finally, Korea experienced several troubles in implanting the concept of GIs in the Korean legal system, particularly the level, duration, and scope of protection required for GIs and whether GIs should be a public or private right. Accordingly, considering what ASEAN member states encounter, ASEAN should consider these factors in the RCEP negotiations and the effective enforcement and dispute resolution scheme concerning GIs in the future.

Notes

1 Research and development (R&D) intensity means expenditure on R&D as a percentage of GDP.
2 Framework Act on Intellectual Property (Act No. 10629, enacted on 19 May 2011 and effective since 20 July 2011), available at http://www.ipkorea.go.kr/uploads/FullText.pdf (accessed 2 January 2019).
3 Chapter 2 covers basic and execution plans, the Presidential Council on Intellectual Property, and financial allocation and assessment.
4 In this regard, it is notable that trade secrets fall within the scope of intellectual property (IP), not intellectual property right (IPR) pursuant to the Act.
5 It includes Australia, Denmark, Finland, Germany, Greece, Iceland, Mexico, Norway, Poland, Portugal, Spain, Sweden, Turkey, etc.

6 China may be categorised as a mixture of two systems – the pluralist and the coordination systems.
7 The centralist system includes Canada, Russia, Singapore, Switzerland, Chinese Taipei, the United Kingdom.
8 Available at http://english.customs.gov.cn/Statics/d95ecac5-4be9-4d69-b71f-c77169e73360.html (accessed 10 January 2019).
9 The Trademark Act defines 'GI', 'homonymous GI', 'collective GI', respectively, in Articles 2(1)(4), 2(1)(5), and 2(1)(6). Articles 6(1)(3) and 6(1)(4) also set forth a trademark consisting solely of mark indication in a common way the origin, and a trademark consisting solely of a conspicuous geographical name may not be granted, respectively.
10 The Act on Quality Control of Agricultural and Fishery Products defines 'GI', 'homonymous GI', 'collective GI', respectively, in Articles 2(1)(8), 2(1)(9), and 2(1)(10). The Act also added Chapter III (Articles 32–55) to register, adjudicate, reexamine, and litigate on GIs.
11 The Unfair Competition Prevention and Trade Secret Protection Act uses the term 'geographic mark' instead of 'geographical indication'. Article 3(2) prohibits the use of geographic mark protected under the FTA.

Bibliography

ASEAN (2017), 'Chairman's Statement of the 19th ASEAN–Republic of Korea Summit', 13 November, Manila, Philippines, http://asean.org/storage/2017/11/19th-ASEAN-ROK-Summit-Chairs-Statement-FINAL.pdf (accessed 30 May 2018).

Asia IP (2018), 'International Litigation Chamber to Hear English Trials', 19 April, http://www.asiaiplaw.com/article/35/3031/ (accessed 5 January 2019).

Briggs, K. and S. Brown (2012), 'The Impact of Institutional Enforcement Mechanisms on Perceived Intellectual Property Protection', *Journal of Applied Economics & Policy*, 31(1), 1–24.

Government Accountability Office (GAO) (2006), 'Report to the Chairman, Committee on Government Reform, House of Representatives: Intellectual Property: Strategy for Targeting Organised Piracy (STOP) Requires Changes for Long-Term Success', https://www.gao.gov/new.items/d0774.pdf (accessed 2 January 2019).

Huh, W.S. (2017), *Current Status of FTA and Major Content of FTAs regarding IP*, presented at *KIPO's FTA General Briefing Session on IP*, 28 November 2017, Seoul, Korea.

Hwang, G.C. (2018), *Introduction of Industrial Property Right Dispute Mediation System*, presented at the *KIPO–WIPO Joint Workshop*, 4 May 2018, Seoul, Korea.

Hyundai Research Institute (HRI) (2014), *Estimation of Size and Loss due to Underground Economy of Counterfeit and Pirated Products.* Seoul: HRI, pp. 1–11.

Jing, H. and C. Zhixing (2018), 'China Patents: How Will China's Government Reform Affect IP in the Country?', *Managing Intellectual Property*, 1 May, http://www.managingip.com/Article/3804321/China-patents-How-will-Chinas-government-reform-affect-IP-in-the-country.html (accessed 31 January 2019).

Kim, Y.J. (2016), 'IP Enforcement Provisions Intersected in Korea's FTAs with the EU and the US', *BUP JO Korean Lawyers Association Journal*, 715, 125–173.

KIPO (2017), *Annual Report 2017.* Daejeon: Korea Intellectual Property Office (KIPO). http://www.kipo.go.kr/kpo/user.tdf?a=user.english.html.HtmlApp&c=60114&catmenu=ek07_01_01_15 (accessed 29 May 2018).

KIPO (2018a), *Intellectual Property Administration Major Statistical Data*. Daejeon: Korea Intellectual Property Office (KIPO).

KIPO (2018b), *2017 Intellectual Property White Paper*. Daejeon: Korea Intellectual Property Office (KIPO).

Lee, G.H. (2016), 'A Comparative Study on Geographical Indications', *Science, Technology and Law*, 7(1).

Lee, S.M. and Y.S. Park (2018), 'The Fourth Industrial Revolution and Intellectual Property Administration', *Korean Society and Public Administration*, 29(3).

Lim, J.Y. (2017), 'Institutional Arrangements Put in Place in the Republic of Korea to Address the Proliferation of Counterfeit Goods Online', 5 September, Daejeon: KIPO.

Ministry of Trade, Industry and Energy of Korea (2018), *Recent Driving Trend on FTA*, presented at the *2018 International Commerce and Trade Seminar*, 16 November 2018, Seoul, Korea.

OECD (2016), *Trade in Counterfeit and Pirated Goods: Mapping the Economic Impact*. Paris: OECD/EU Intellectual Property Office, pp. 1–133.

OECD (2018a), *OECD Main Science and Technology Indicators 2018*. http://www.oecd.org/sti/DataBrief_MSTI_2018.pdf (accessed 29 May 2018).

OECD (2018b), *Economic Outlook for Southeast Asia, China, and India 2018: Fostering Growth through Digitalization*. Paris: OECD Publishing.

Park, J.S. (2014), 'The Study on Intellectual Property Chapter in TPP', *International Trade Law, 2014–2*.

Patent Court of Korea (2017), *Patent Court Guidebook*, Daejeon: Patent Court of Korea, http://patent.scourt.go.kr/dcboard/new/EngDcNewsViewAction.work?seqnum=5&gubun=547&cbub_code=&scode_kname=특허영문-Announcements&searchWord=&pageIndex=1 (accessed 30 May 2018).

Ryu, T.G., J.S. Choi and S.W. Lee (2017), 'Reorganization Plan on National IP Administrative System', *Issue Paper* (Issue 2017-1), Seoul: Korea Institute of Intellectual Property.

Seo, M.W. (2019), 'Mr. Park Won-Joo, Commissioner of KIPO's New Year's Address', *Sedaily*, 3 January, https://www.sedaily.com/NewsView/1VDW6BA8ZN (accessed 5 January 2019).

WIPO (2017), *World Intellectual Property Indicators 2017*. Geneva: WIPO.

9 Patent regulatory framework in ASEAN in the light of new generation FTAs

A comparative analysis with the Andean Community and the Pacific Alliance

Liliana Lizarazo-Rodríguez

9.1 Research design and background

This chapter addresses the role of patents in innovation and technology transfer as key conditions for technological upgrading in value chains. As the topic is vast and complex, this chapter focuses on whether a regulatory framework of patent protection is crucial for developing patents in a developing country context and reaching innovation and technology transfer. It also assesses whether intellectual property rights (IPR) clauses in new generation free trade agreements (FTAs) of the European Union (EU) and the United States (US) interact with regional and national rules in this respect. For this purpose, it assesses and compares paths of countries belonging to the Association of Southeast Asian Nations (ASEAN) (Viet Nam and Singapore) and of the Andean Community (CAN) and the Pacific Alliance (PA) that have concluded FTAs with the EU and the US (Peru and Colombia). Patent protection in Peru and Colombia is more complex because the subregional schemes overlap with IPR clauses in FTAs that in many aspects go beyond the Agreement on Trade-Related Aspects of Intellectual Property Rights (henceforth TRIPS Agreement) of the World Trade Organization (WTO). The PA lacks an institutional IPR protection, but it has influenced the CAN system by actively supporting trade with and investment in the Asia-Pacific Rim and innovation through technology transfer and IPR protection. In contrast, no formal regional IPR regulatory framework exists in ASEAN. The member states only signed the ASEAN Framework Agreement on Intellectual Property Cooperation in 1995, which refers to the intention to create common mechanisms such as an ASEAN patent or trademark system. However, these mechanisms have not materialised.

This chapter addresses the following research questions: (i) How does patent regulation correlate with innovation levels and technology transfer in countries belonging to ASEAN, CAN, and PA? (ii) What is the role of the (regional) institutional framework of patent protection for innovation and technology transfer? (iii) What is the role of IPR clauses (particularly on patents) of the FTAs concluded by ASEAN, CAN, and PA member states with

DOI: 10.4324/9781003147657-10

the US and/or the EU in promoting innovation and technology transfer beyond the TRIPS Agreement? (iv) Can other mechanisms, such as soft law or corporate social responsibility, impact patent protection?

The economic development literature argues, theoretically and empirically, that innovation and technology transfer are key factors linked to long-term productivity and income growth. In turn, innovation is the main goal of research and development (R&D) and/or technology transfer. The success of innovation policies depends on many factors, such as development level, education level, public funding, public–private partnerships among research centres and industries, and venture capital to adapt technologies to local markets (Dhar and Joseph 2016). Many developing countries struggle with these factors and seek technology transfer to reach innovation, with mixed results. Technology transfer, in turn, is 'the process by which one party gains access to the knowledge of another party and becomes able to adopt successfully the knowledge in the production processes' (Maskus 2004, quoted by Dhar and Joseph 2016, p. 5; Watson et al. 2009). Therefore, developing countries expect that by having access to international technology transfer (ITT),[1] they will achieve technological upgrading in value chains and sustainable economic growth.

Developing countries have used various policies implemented with varied pace and diverse levels of effectiveness to promote ITT. At the international level, the coordination of ITT policies has sought to increase its effectiveness and avoid distortionary competition effects. Global value chains (GVCs) are also shaping technology transfer towards developing countries, mainly under investment facilitation (Kowalski et al. 2017). However, besides implementing ITT policies, developing countries also need to strengthen their diffusion and absorptive capacity. Absorptive capacity is the availability to 'assimilate and replicate knowledge gained from external sources', which depends on the educational level of the workforce (that applies the transferred technology), access to finance, and infrastructure (Kowalski et al. 2017, p. 21). Then, IPR protection and the promotion of foreign direct investment (FDI) would improve the business climate (Kowalski et al. 2017, pp. 6, 9, 23).

IPR protection, particularly patent protection, is a central instrument for innovation and technology transfer. States and regional organisations facilitate the transfer of technology by disclosing the invention in exchange for the recognition of an exclusive temporary right of exploitation (patent rights) recognised by international agreements[2] in line with national or regional industrial policies and FDI (WIPO 2010, quoted by Kowalski et al. 2017, p. 25). Other instruments oriented towards innovation are license contracts[3] to commercialise goods without necessarily transferring technology, or joint ventures to adapt products to local conditions and/or benefit from lower-cost skilled workers (Maskus 2004, quoted by Dhar and Joseph 2016, p. 12). All these mechanisms are complemented by the prohibition of unfair competition practices to avoid license or patent holders' abuse. The TRIPS Agreement, for instance, allows compulsory licensing to prevent patent holders from obstructing the use of technology (Dhar and Joseph 2016).

Trade and investment level correlates with patent protection. This correlation between trade and patent flows and patent applications is measured to identify levels of technology transfer among countries where the application was first filed and any other country with subsequent filings (Watson et al. 2009), or used as a proxy for technological innovation (Dhar and Joseph 2016:12). Several empirical studies have attempted to find correlations among innovation, FDI, ITT, and IPR protection. The results are nuanced, though. A study on FDI conducted in Latin America found that 'imports and FDI are sensitive to patent index only for the higher income countries and insensitive to patents in poorer countries' (Blyde and Acea 2002, quoted by Dhar and Joseph 2016, p. 12). Another empirical study conducted for 94 countries from 1965 to 2005 inquired whether stronger IPRs increase innovation using an index of economic complexity. The findings showed that more robust IPRs might engender higher levels of economic complexity, which benefit countries that initiated an above-average level of development and complexity (Sweet and Maggio 2015).

The United Nations Industrial Development Organization (UNIDO) tested whether stronger IPR protection can benefit countries and how this relates to R&D. The findings showed several interesting aspects: first, that implementing more robust IPR protection produces weaker advantages when an increasing number of countries strengthen their IPR regimes because less extra market is covered and less extra innovation is to be expected. Second, IPR holders may abuse their monopoly, which obstructs this protection's expected benefits, particularly when there is no or very low R&D. Third, when stronger IPR protection is combined with licensing in the host country, home countries (of the licensor) may increase innovation, but not necessarily the host country because innovators increase their incomes due to lower production costs and more robust IPR protection. This explains why home countries promote this combination to increase their resources to innovate and reinforce the innovators' IPR. This also means better expectations of economic growth in the long run. Fourth, stronger IPR protection may foster innovation in countries with high domestic potential for innovation but not necessarily in countries with low innovative potential (Falvey et al. 2006). This means that IPR-strengthening policies depend on the income and development level of the country. In most high-income countries, these policies benefit growth because innovation and technology diffusion increase. In middle-income countries, these policies do not necessarily help growth (because they lose the growth benefits obtained from imitation) but encourage domestic innovation and technology diffusion, which may upgrade their position in the value chains in the long term.[4] In low-income countries, these policies encourage growth but do not increase innovation, and the impact on international trade is negative, although the latter nexus cannot be well explained (Falvey et al. 2006). Fifth, technology diffusion and patent protection benefit relatively open economies, developed (high GDP per capita) countries, and countries with larger markets where foreign firms lack strong market power (Falvey et al. 2006).[5] The reason is that stronger IPR protection mainly benefits FDI in manufactures, particularly in chemicals and pharmaceuticals, and less in 'high-tech industries' due to the difficulties to imitate the latter (Falvey et al. 2006).

Countries owning advanced technologies are usually net investors and promote trade and investment liberalisation in R&D with IPR protection as conditions to contribute to ITT and diffusion. Less technologically advanced countries prefer policies promoting ITT and diffusion (Gehl Sampath and Roffe 2012, Kowalski et al. 2017). However, FDI can be a better option over licensing to get access to ITT and reduce costs if the host country has enough capacity to absorb the technology (Yang and Maskus 2009, Falvey et al. 2006).

As national capabilities correlate with the success of national IPR protection in terms of innovation, TRIPS standards should be adapted to the national context. However, in practice, IPR protection has been systematically implemented by enforcing the TRIPS Agreement and concluding FTAs with TRIPS-plus clauses that reduce the policy space of national IPR systems (Maskus 2015, quoted by Kowalski et al. 2017, p. 14). In many cases, the current regulatory framework of patent protection does not necessarily foster ITT and innovation because host countries' economic climate is not adequate.[6] Other empirical studies corroborate that a generalised recommendation of stringent IPR protection without considering the development level will not always have positive results in terms of innovation (Hudson and Minea 2013).

Therefore, developing countries that seek innovation through ITT and IPR protection should consider various interconnected aspects: (i) complementary educational and labour market policies oriented towards improving the diffusion and absorptive capacity (training of high-skilled workforce, adequate financing and infrastructure); (ii) a strategic ITT regulatory framework and its channels – international trade, FDI, and relevant commercial contracts (franchising, licensing, joint ventures, etc.) (Watson et al. 2009); (iii) investment in R&D, as just relying on ITT and IPR protection would not guarantee innovation in the long run or effective upgrading in GVCs (Kowalski et al. 2017).

This chapter is an attempt to compare paths and differences in terms of patent protection and innovation among member states from ASEAN, on the one hand, and CAN and PA, on the other. It also assesses whether the conclusion of FTAs with the EU and the US can be a valid option to strengthen innovation. It combines four interconnected perspectives that shape the chapter's structure: first, it conducts a statistical assessment of data patterns on innovation and technology transfer in South America and ASEAN. This descriptive statistical assessment aims to contextualise the comparative legal analysis and to explore possible correlations between patent regulation, on the one hand, and innovation and technology transfer, on the other. Second, it assesses the regulatory framework at the regional level in CAN, PA, and ASEAN, with emphasis on CAN, as pioneer regional integration group in structuring a system of IPR protection (older than the

TRIPS Agreement) enforceable before the Andean Tribunal of Justice (ATJ) (Alter and Helfer 2017). Third, the regulatory framework of patent protection at the multilateral level (TRIPS Agreement) is contrasted with the IPR (patent) clauses in new generation FTAs concluded with the EU and the US by Colombia, Peru, Singapore, and Viet Nam. This is because FTAs have deeply transformed the IPR system, mainly by adopting TRIPS-plus regulations[7] (Lizarazo-Rodríguez and De Lombaerde 2015, Helfer and Alter 2014, Degelsegger et al. 2016). Fourth, this chapter concludes with policy recommendations related to (i) the link between patent regulation, innovation, and technology transfer from a developing country perspective; (ii) the role of regional integration groupings such as CAN, PA, and ASEAN in the global regulation of patent protection, particularly concerning compliance with the TRIPS Agreement; (iii) the influence of other factors, such as soft law mechanisms on patent protection, innovation, and technology transfer; and (iv) the translation of institutional developments regarding patent protection into results in terms of innovation.

9.2 Research context and empirical evidence for ASEAN and South America

This section aims at contrasting the literature review with selected descriptive statistics on IPR in South America and ASEAN to contextualise patent legal regimes of countries involved in the new generation FTAs: Colombia–Peru–Ecuador–EU, Colombia–US, Peru–US, Viet Nam–EU, and Singapore–US. The sources of this section are (i) the Global Innovation Index, (ii) the indicators of the World Intellectual Property Organization (WIPO) regarding patents and plant varieties, (iii) the FDI Regulatory Restrictiveness Index of the Organisation for Economic Cooperation and Development (OECD), and (iv) the International Property Rights Index of the Property Rights Alliance.

9.2.1 The Global Innovation Index (GII)

The GII reflects the multidimensional facets of countries' innovation performance and is published by Cornell University, INSEAD, and WIPO. The GII is composed of an Innovation Input Sub-index (based on five pillars related to innovative activities enabled by the national economies – performance of institutions, human capital and research, infrastructure, market sophistication, and business sophistication) and an Innovation Output Sub-index measuring the performance of innovative economic activities (and based on the following pillars: knowledge and technology outputs and creative outputs).

The available figures for ASEAN and South America (Figure 9.1) suggest that the most active FTA signatory countries can be associated with relatively higher index values. However, most countries showed a declining innovation performance in 2018 compared to 2013, except for Singapore

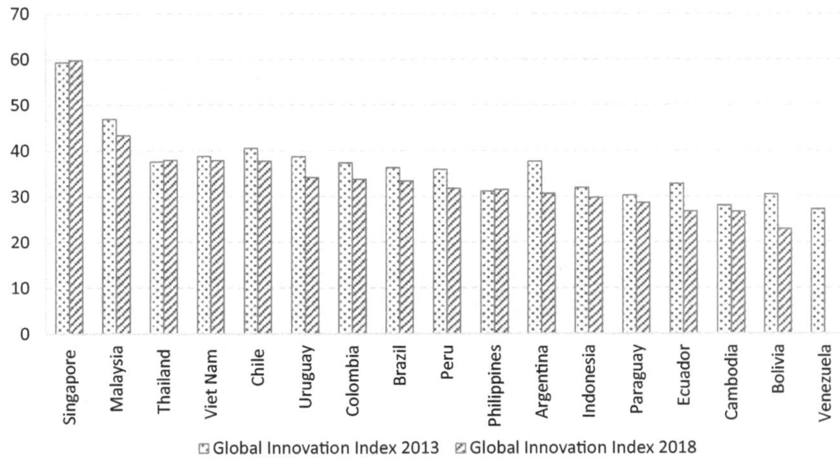

Figure 9.1 Global Innovation Indices in ASEAN and South America, 2013 and 2018.

Source: www.globalinnovationindex.org/analysis-indicator.

and Thailand. In general, most countries in both regions have similar scores in 2018, except for Singapore's notorious superiority, followed by Malaysia, Thailand, and Viet Nam. In contrast, Ecuador, Bolivia, and Cambodia performed notoriously below the average of the group.

On the output side, ASEAN countries performed better than South American countries from 2013 to 2018. The values of the index of Innovation Output reveal that all ASEAN countries also showed clear progress in their rankings on knowledge creation and knowledge diffusion over the last five years. In South America, Chile, Uruguay, and Colombia showed progress in knowledge creation in 2018 but far below most ASEAN countries. Regarding knowledge diffusion, only Chile and Uruguay showed a sharp improvement compared to 2013 but, again, performing well below ASEAN countries.

On the input side, as revealed by the index of Innovation Input, Singapore is the only country with exceptional rankings. In contrast, the other countries in both regions showed medium or low rankings. The ranking on political environment showed better results for South America as only Malaysia ranked as Chile, Uruguay, Peru, Colombia, or Brazil. On regulatory environment, South American countries also performed better than ASEAN countries (excluding Singapore). The data for business sophistication showed that Thailand and Peru most progressed since 2013. Regarding the figures on R&D, all the observed ASEAN countries but Indonesia showed clear progress over the same period. In South America, Argentina and Brazil had the best scores, and they did not have FTAs with IPR clauses.

Several issues of the GII are interesting for this analysis. Regarding royalty and licensee fee payments as a percentage of the import service (IP payments), Singapore ranked highest in both years, followed by Argentina,

Brazil, and Chile. The country also ranked first in royalty and licensee fee payments as a percentage of the export service (IP revenues), followed by the same countries. Singapore is again the positive outlier in terms of patent activity: national resident office patent applications (2013), patent applications by origin (2018), Patent Cooperation Treaty (PCT) resident applications (2013), PCT international applications by origin (2018), and patent families filed in at least three offices (2013) or patent families filed in at least two countries (2018). The other selected countries were ranked at an intermediate level (Malaysia, Thailand, Brazil, Argentina, Colombia, Chile, and Uruguay) or lower levels, but without a clear regional trend. From a more macro perspective, IP offices in Asia received the highest number of applications for patents, utility models, trademarks, and industrial designs in 2017. Notably, these represented 65.1% of all patent applications worldwide, of which only three countries represented 60% of these figures (China 43.6%, Japan 10%, and the Republic of Korea [henceforth Korea] 6%). These strongly contrast with Latin American figures that represent only 1.8% of all patent applications worldwide.[8]

9.2.2 Patent grant statistics of the WIPO

From the panel data of patent grants by filing office and applicants´ origin (Figure 9.2), we cannot conclude a clear regional trend. Countries' growth paths varied. In South America, Brazil is by far the country that granted most patents, followed by Argentina, Chile, and Colombia. Colombia and Peru that concluded FTAs with the US and the EU show diverging figures. In 2012 and 2013, Colombia increased the figures of patents granted, but Peru did not show a growing trend. In ASEAN, the number of patents filed in Singapore is by far the highest, with Malaysia showing a similar peak in 2007 and 2008 followed by a drop over the next ten years until 2017 when it showed a significant increase of granted patents, together with the Philippines and Thailand. None of these three countries had concluded any FTA with the US or the EU. Viet Nam, which signed an FTA with the EU (in force since 2020), shows a sustained increase from 2011 onwards.

9.2.3 FDI Regulatory Restrictiveness Index of the OECD

The FDI Regulatory Restrictiveness Index seeks to capture and measure statutory restrictions on FDI across 22 economic sectors. It concentrates on the following restrictions: (i) foreign equity limitations, (ii) discriminatory screening or approval mechanisms, (iii) restrictions on the employment of foreigners as key personnel, and (iv) other operational restrictions that are not specified. Figure 9.3 shows the overall restrictiveness index, which is an average of sectoral scores. The restriction is counted if it discriminates against foreign investors only. This index does not reflect the national investment climate nor regulations such as state ownership in key sectors. This is obviously not the only variable affecting FDI. Many other variables intervene,

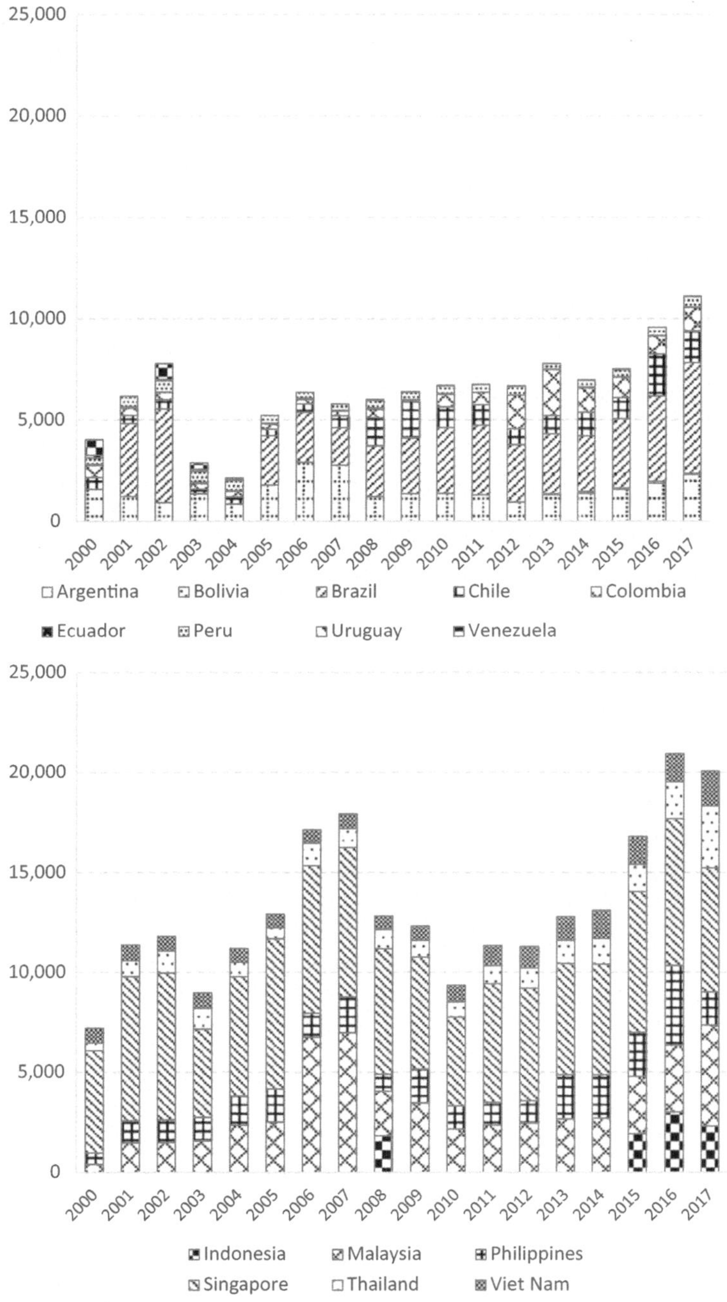

Figure 9.2 Evolution of Total Patent Grants (Direct and PCT National Phase Entries) for ASEAN and South American Countries, 2000-2017.

Source: www.internationalpropertyrightsindex.org/countries

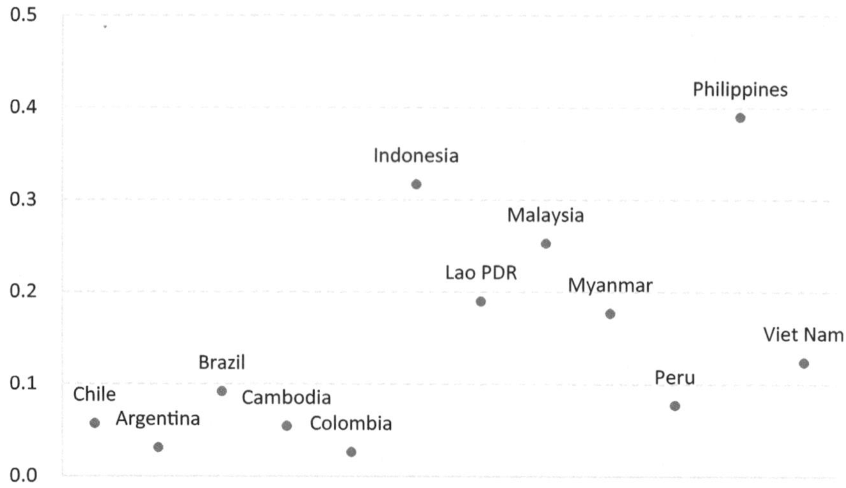

Figure 9.3 OECD FDI Regulatory Restrictiveness Index for ASEAN and South American Countries, 2017.

Source: Data extracted on 02 Feb 2019 10:45 UTC (GMT) from OECD.Stat

including geo-economic and geopolitical variables, but these restrictions may play a role in the FDI decision.

FDI promotion is related to a good business environment, and the level of investment restrictions can affect ITT. First, the most common restrictions are the share of equity that foreigners can own, which seeks to force local partners' participation or prefer licence contracts. Second, screening and permit requirements to invest may restrict technology transfer as investors are discouraged from investing. Also, these controls and restrictions may be discretionary vis-à-vis the investment and are defended as a way to orient technology transfer per local policies (Kowalski et al. 2017). Figure 9.3 is based on the OECD FDI Regulatory Restrictiveness Index (Kalinova et al. 2010) that measures the level of regulatory FDI restrictiveness that includes the two mentioned restrictions and restrictions on key foreign personnel, among others.

9.2.4 The International Property Rights Index (IPRI)

The Property Rights Alliance produced the IPRI (PRA 2018) based on ten factors and organised in three components: legal and political environment, physical property rights, and IPR. Figure 9.4 shows selected country IPRI scores for the two regions for 2007–2020. Again, Singapore is the 'positive' outlier with a property rights system that offered the highest protection to economic actors and citizens. Malaysia and Chile followed Singapore. Remarkably, countries actively participating in FTAs, such as Singapore, Malaysia, Chile, Uruguay, Colombia, and Peru, have more or less maintained

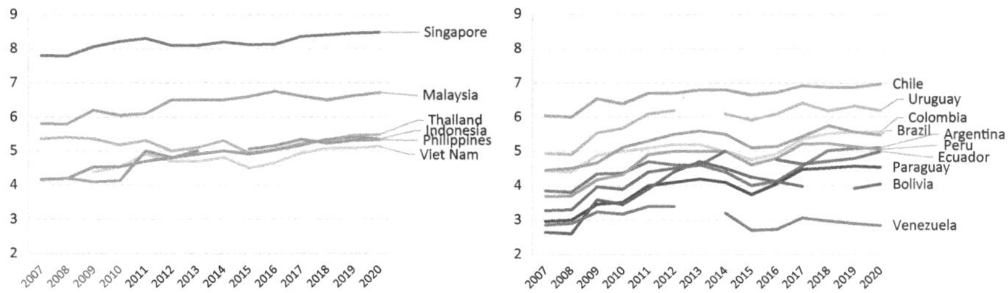

Figure 9.4 IPRI for ASEAN and South American Countries, 2007-2020.

Source: www.internationalpropertyrightsindex.org/countries

their positions in the horizontal comparison. However, in both regions, a subset of countries seemed to lag behind in IPR protection when compared to the others' pace of progress. These countries saw their global rankings worsen. In Southeast Asia, these were notably Thailand, Indonesia, and the Philippines, while in South America, the rankings were even more outspoken in Argentina, Bolivia, Eduador, Paraguay, and Venezuela.

9.3 Regulatory framework: the WTO and regional arrangements

The World Bank analysed a database of 279 agreements signed by 189 countries between 1958 and 2015, representing the entire set of preferential trade agreements (PTAs) in force notified to the WTO until 2015. It found that PTAs have increasingly detailed provisions with an increasing binding character in several policy areas of WTO competence. The four leading areas outside the WTO mandate are competition policy, investment, movement of capital, and IPR protection (Hofmann et al. 2017).

From a legal perspective, the relation between ITT, innovation, and IPR (patent) protection are regulated by the Trade-Related Investment Measures established by a multi-level regulatory framework. The main binding regulations are included in the WTO and WIPO rules, FTAs, regional and subregional integration arrangements, and national rules. Therefore, the creation and diffusion of innovation, ITT, and IPR protection have a transnational character with increasing relevance for emerging markets in areas such as digital trade, climate change, food safety, and public health (Peng et al. 2018).

The WTO has actively promoted trade liberalisation aimed at fostering scientific and technological development. More particularly, the TRIPS protects IPR but it also prevents the abuse of patent holders. Article 7 stipulates that IPR protection and enforcement should foster technological innovation and the transfer and dissemination of technology to benefit producers and users from technological knowledge and positively influence social and economic welfare. Also, Article 8(2) allows states to prevent abusive practices of patent holders that restrain trade or affect ITT (Grosse Ruse-Khan 2018, Kowalski et al. 2017). The Doha Declaration (which became a binding rule in 2018) further sought to promote public health and access to medicines, which means that TRIPS should not obstruct the national policy space in this respect (Grosse Ruse-Khan 2018).

In Latin America, CAN, Mercosur,[9] and PA are trade-oriented regional integration organisations that contrast with the Union of South American Nations. The PA actively promotes the conclusion of FTAs, whereas Mercosur and some members of CAN have been reluctant to negotiate such agreements. The PA also seeks to strengthen its member states' IPR regimes (Lizarazo-Rodríguez and De Lombaerde 2015). In contrast, CAN and Mercosur protect the regional and national policy space in this respect. In Asia, ASEAN is also trade-oriented but with no clear supranational structure and no common IPR regime. In contrast, the Comprehensive and Progressive Agreement for Trans-Pacific Partnership (CPTPP) contains IP institutional designs (Peng et al. 2018, Yu 2018). The CPTPP is currently in force in Singapore and Viet Nam but not yet in South American participatory states or other ASEAN countries.

CAN has a common regime for industrial property, including patents, since 1969,[10] being a pioneer regional integration group regulating IPR[11] to promote innovation and science and technological development. Decision 24/1974 is the first regional regulation on industrial property.[12] The Commission of the Cartagena Agreement legislates on industrial property, and the ATJ has exclusive jurisdiction to interpret CAN IPR rules. Also, Decision 154/1980 created the Andean System of Technological Information to promote ITT, FDI, and industrial property, but it disappeared in the 1990s (Mamani 2013). The current CAN IP regulatory framework (Decision 486/2000) is a supranational rule that prevails on national laws from member states.[13] It harmonises the CAN IP regime with the TRIPS regime regarding patent claim procedure and terms. Moreover, Decision 486/2000 (49) requires member states to apply the International Classification of Invention Patents established by the Strasbourg Agreement Concerning the International Classification of Patents (1971)[14] to classify patents. However, no PA member state but Mexico is a party to this treaty. Decision 486/2000 requires that this IP regime be compatible with competition rules, such as regulating restrictive commercial practices. Most administrative IPR offices of the Andean countries are also competent in supervising industrial policy and competition (Mamani 2013).

The negotiation and implementation of EU and US FTAs by Colombia and Peru partially dismantled this subregional IPR regime. As the ATJ held that some TRIPS-plus provisions were contrary to CAN law, these two countries promoted the CAN patent regime's reform to conclude these FTAs (Helfer and Alter 2014). The ATJ had ruled that patent registration of proof data for medicines would threaten free competition and access to medicines because it may be a way to extend patents (Ruling 114-AI-2004). Thus, Decision 632/06, interpreting Decision 486/00 (266, second paragraph), allowed member states to decide on whether to protect proof data or not. The FTAs concluded by Colombia and Peru with the US

(16) and the EU (231) incorporated the protection of proof data (Lizarazo-Rodríguez and De Lombaerde 2015, Lizarazo-Rodríguez et al. 2015). Decision 689/2008[15] authorised member states to develop some IPR issues through national legislation, considering the socio-economic asymmetries and multilateral standards. Peru proposed this reform to allow the negotiation of the FTA with the US, against the will of Bolivia, which challenged the new decision before the ATJ.[16] These reforms were catalogued as an obstacle for technological progress because they extended the patent protection period beyond the TRIPS and Decision 486 (Mamani 2013, pp. 106–7). The reforms also affect the competence of the ATJ and the uniform application of CAN IPR regulations, as member states can legislate in some cases on the subject and the tribunal would lack jurisdiction to interpret domestic legislation using prejudicial decisions (Mamani 2013).[17] However, CAN IPR regulations are still binding for member states (Table 9.1).

Besides this regulatory framework, in 2013, the Andean Development Corporation, the former financial corporation of CAN and now a development bank for Latin America, launched the Regional Initiative of Technological Patents for Development. This initiative aims at improving the level of education to foster the capacity for patentable technological innovation and increase exports of high technology.

In contrast, the PA subregional integration model is based on a network of bilateral FTAs (instead of being one preferential trade agreement) and does not follow the European institutional model. The PA also involves sectoral cooperation agendas on trade and investment-related issues. The model is also based on a (market-friendly) ideological convergence rather than geographical proximity (Chaves García 2018, Gardini 2013). The PA is also the first Latin American group that seeks political coordination and economic projection towards Asia-Pacific, particularly with Southeast Asia, and with China as an observer country (Chaves García 2018, Herreros 2016). This policy is coherent with the CPTPP to which all PA members but Colombia are signatories, although none of them have ratified it, even if China is not a member state.

However, contrary to CAN and the CPTPP, neither the PA nor its additional protocol regulates IPR. However, PA member states have developed soft law mechanisms oriented towards innovation and ITT. The memorandum of understanding on the Pacific Cooperation Platform seeks to tackle environment and climate change, innovation, science and technology, small and medium-sized enterprises support, and social development (Chaves García 2018). Moreover, the Joint Declaration of the IP offices of PA member states (2015)[18] sought to facilitate IPR mutual recognition to foster innovation and regional economic growth. PA members also agreed on the Patent Prosecution Highway (PPH) Program[19] to streamline and harmonise the patent application procedure. The procedure authorises patent applicants who have filed a patent application in one of the PA countries to request another member state's IP office to consider the study conducted in the patentability examination performed in the member state where the

Table 9.1 US FTAs Signed with Colombia, Peru, and Singapore

Provision	*Colombia PTA*	*Peru PTA*	*Singapore FTA*
Government procurement			
Exceptions: A party is not prevented from adopting or maintaining measures necessary to protect public morals, order, or safety; human, animal, or plant life or health; IP	X	X	X
Investment			
IPR is defined as a form of investment and related conflicts shall be solved by a state dispute settlement mechanism	X	X	X
IPR			
Ratifications or accession by the date of entry into force of this Agreement	X	X	X
Convention Relating to the Distribution of Programme-Carrying Signals Transmitted by Satellite (1974)	X	X	X
Budapest Treaty (1977), as amended in 1980	X	X	
WIPO Copyright Treaty (1996)	X	X	X
WIPO Performances and Phonograms Treaty (1996)	X	X	X
Patent Cooperation Treaty (1970), as amended in 1979	X	X	X
Trademark Law Treaty (1994)	X	X	X
International Convention for the Protection of New Varieties of Plants (UPOV) (1991)	X	X	X
Articles 1-6 of the Joint Recommendation on the Protection of Well-Known Marks (1999), adopted by the Paris Union for the Protection of Industrial Property and the WIPO			X
Trademark Law Treaty[a]			X
Recommendation to ratify or accede to the following agreements:			
Patent Law Treaty (2000)	X	X	
Hague Agreement Concerning the International Registration of Industrial Designs (1999)	X	X	X
Protocol Relating to the Madrid Agreement Concerning the International Registration of Marks (1989)	X	X	X
General rules			
The parties affirm their existing rights and obligations under the TRIPS Agreement and WIPO IP agreements		X	
The parties may prevent anticompetitive practices that may result from the abuse of the IPR if such measures are consistent with this chapter	X	X	
Optional more extensive IPR protection and enforcement	X	X	
National treatment	X	X	X
Transparency	X	X	

(*Continued*)

Table 9.1 (Continued)

Provision	*Colombia PTA*	*Peru PTA*	*Singapore FTA*
Patents			
Patents available for any invention (product or process) in all fields of technology if the invention is new, involves an inventive step, and is capable of industrial application	X	X	X
Patent owners have the right to assign, or transfer by succession, a patent and to conclude licensing contracts with specific provisions for protecting licensing of pharmaceutical products			X
A party can exclude inventions from patentability as set out in the TRIPS Agreement (27.2 and 27.3) but the party should protect plant patent by the date of entry into force of the FTA	X	X	
Limited exceptions to the exclusive rights of patent holders, but respecting their legitimate interests and the ones of third parties	X	X	X
A patent may be revoked or nullified only when it would have justified a legal refusal to grant the patent. A patent can be revoked, nullified, or held unenforceable in case of fraud, misrepresentation, or inequitable conduct. This is according to the Paris Convention (5.A[3])	X	X	X[b]
A third person may use the subject matter of a patent to support an application for marketing approval of a pharmaceutical product or agricultural chemical product, but respecting the rights of the patent holder	X	X	X
A party may permit the use of the subject matter of a patent without the authorisation of the right holder in accordance with TRIPS (31): (a) to remedy a judicially or administratively declared anticompetitive practice under the competition national laws (b) for public non-commercial use or in case of national emergency or extreme urgency, if it is only used by the government or third parties authorised by the government, the patent owner is duly compensated, the patent owner must not transfer undisclosed information or technical 'know how' for use without his/her consent The parties recognise that an IPR does not necessarily confer market power upon its owner			X
Each party shall provide the means to compensate for unreasonable delays in the issuance of a patent, other than a patent for a pharmaceutical product, by restoring patent term or patent rights. For pharmaceutical products, this also includes compensation to the patent owner for unreasonable curtailment of the effective patent term resulting from the marketing approval process	X	X	X[c]

(*Continued*)

Table 9.1 (Continued)

Provision	*Colombia PTA*	*Peru PTA*	*Singapore FTA*
If a party may grant a patent based on an examination of the invention conducted in another country, it may extend the term of a patent for up to 5 years to compensate for the unreasonable delay in the issuance of the patent granted by such other country where that country has extended the term of the patent based on such delay			X
Patent applicants may at least once make amendments, corrections, and observations in connection with their applications	X	X	
Measures Related to Agricultural Chemical Products of Granting Marketing Approval: the submission of information concerning safety or efficacy of the product is protected for 10 years and protection of proof data of pharmaceutical products for 5 years	X	X	X[d]
A party can protect public health following: (i) the Declaration on the TRIPS Agreement and Public Health (ii) any waiver of any provision of the TRIPS Agreement (or its amendments to implement the Declaration) granted by WTO Members in accordance with the WTO Agreement	X	x	
Enforcement of IPR			
General obligations 1. These rules should respect principles of due process and the foundations of its legal system 2. Final judicial decisions and administrative rulings of general applicability shall be in writing[d] 3. Each party shall publicize information,[e] including any statistical information 4. The parties are not obliged to put a specific judicial system in place for the enforcement of IPRs	X	X	X
Civil and Administrative Procedures and Remedies	X	X	X[f]
Provisional measures		X	X
Special Requirements Related to Border Measures for Counterfeit Trademark Goods or Pirated Copyright Goods		X	X
Criminal Procedures and Remedies			
Remedies that include judgments of imprisonment and deterrent monetary fines to future infringements, consistent with a policy of removing the monetary incentive of the infringer. Judicial authorities shall order the seizure of suspected counterfeited or pirated goods	X	X	X
Limitations on Liability for Service Providers regarding copyrights			X

(*Continued*)

Table 9.1 (Continued)

Provision	*Colombia PTA*	*Peru PTA*	*Singapore FTA*
Promotion of Innovation and Technological Development	X	X	
Understandings on biodiversity and traditional knowledge			
(1) Previous informed consent to accessing genetic resources under the control of such authority	X	X	
(2) Equitably sharing the benefits arising from the use of traditional knowledge and genetic resources			
(3) Patent examination should ensure that the conditions of patentability are satisfied. Each party shall seek ways to share information by providing: (i) publicly accessible databases with relevant information; and (ii) an opportunity to cite, in writing, to the appropriate examining authority prior art that may have a bearing on patentability			

a Singapore is not obligated to give effect to Articles 6 and 7 of the Trademark Law Treaty
b No reference to the Paris Agreement
c The deadline is 4 years from the date of filing of the application with the party, or 2 years after the submission of the request for examination of the application
d The Singapore agreement regulates it more in detail and includes the marketing of products patented in other countries
e For Singapore where such publication is not practicable, made publicly available, in a national language, to enable the other party and right holders to become acquainted with them
f It does not refer to administrative procedures

FTA = free trade agreement, IP = intellectual property, IPR = intellectual property rights, WIPO = World Intellectual Property Organization, WTO = World Trade Organization

Sources: Colombia-US PTA https://ustr.gov/trade-agreements/free-trade-agreements/colombia-fta/final-text
Peru-US PTA https://ustr.gov/sites/default/files/uploads/agreements/fta/peru/asset_upload_file78_9547.pdf

application was first filed. This program also sought to implement a technological platform for information dissemination and technology transfer. Each PA patent office has complemented the PA PPH guidelines to facilitate access to the program (Callo and Pérez Restrepo 2016).

The PA IPR promotion contrasts with the institutional and hard law system implemented by CAN. However, in both cases, the result does not necessarily correspond to the objectives of these hard and soft law measures. An empirical study on the impact of these programs among PA member states found that patent-intensive exports are a significant share of PA exports to the world. However, the study found that most regional patent-intensive exports are concentrated in Mexico because of its patent-intensive exports to the North American Free Trade Agreement (Callo and Pérez Restrepo 2016). The study also found that the main beneficiaries of the PA PPH system have been multinationals that show important cross-border patenting and licensing activities in the sectors of motor vehicles, industrial machinery, electrical equipment, and ICT-related industries. This means that the small and medium-sized enterprises of the subregion would have limited access to the PA PPH and cross-border patenting (Callo and Pérez Restrepo 2016). Another study also found that one barrier to implementing innovative policies within the PA is the structural deficiencies in the member states, such as low educational quality, lack of university–industry linkages, and meagre investment in research (Arredondo-Trapero et al. 2016). However, soft law policies adopted by PA member states may have more potential to foster patents than many other regional organisations (Arredondo-Trapero et al. 2016). This is only sustainable if public policies are oriented towards improving education and research. In addition, the PA IP protection system has also been criticised because it is not aligned with the current GVC and digital economy trends, which is also the problem of the TRIPS framework (Corredor 2019).

ASEAN, similar to the PA, lacks a binding legal IPR framework. In 1995, a framework agreement sought cooperation to enhance IP institutional development in the region. This was followed by the creation of a Working Group on Intellectual Property Cooperation in 1996, and later in 2009 to the launch of the ASEAN Patent Examination Co-operation, a de facto harmonised system (Degelsegger et al. 2016). However, ASEAN has not adopted a supranational patent protection regime, contrary to some scholars' recommendations on creating a unitary ASEAN patent system to increase competitiveness (Nguyen 1999). ASEAN has also relied on the universities to promote innovation in partnership with the industry, guided by Singapore's leading role in protecting IPRs (Degelsegger et al. 2016).[20] ASEAN's soft law approach to regional IPR regulation has been justified by the need to balance and coordinate the promotion of mutual regional interests with respect for diverse national interests (Ng 2013, Yu 2018).

9.4 Patents and new generation FTAs

Regional organisations with supranational institutions, such as CAN, the EU, and the European Free Trade Area (EFTA), have created their IPR system. EU law (regulations, directives, and decisions) and treaties such as the European Patent Convention (EPC) regulate EU patent regimes, and the EU FTAs reflect this regulatory framework. EFTA FTAs apply IP provisions of the EFTA Convention, its protocols, the European Economic Area Agreement, and, in some cases, the EPC (Valdés and McCann 2014). In contrast, CAN member states have weakened the CAN IPR regime to conclude FTAs with the EU and EFTA that are clearly TRIPS-plus models. Regional integration groups with IPR systems tend to create subsystems around them, particularly developed countries such as the EU and the US. Other countries such as Chile, Japan, and Mexico also have subsystems of IPR regulation, which is explained by the generalised use of templates during the negotiations (Valdés and McCann 2014). In Asia, with the spaghetti bowl created by the multiple trade agreements signed, the relevance of the ones signed with the US and the EU is not as clear as in South America.

FTAs' IPR protection is crucial because multilateral negotiations are not at the centre of IPR regulation anymore. The WIPO abandoned the Substantive Patent Law Treaty in 2006, and the Doha Round excluded IPR strengthening (Morin and Surbeck 2019). FTAs systematically adopt TRIPS-plus clauses, and about 50% of those that include IPR provisions refer to IPR WIPO treaties but without a clear pattern (Valdés and McCann 2014). Partisans of strengthening IPR protection systematically adopt bilateral or regional negotiations instead of multilateral negotiations. They mainly belong to developed countries because they want to protect their innovations and IPR royalties that represent an important revenue source. In contrast, net knowledge importers resist the strengthening of IPR to avoid higher prices when acquiring foreign technologies (Morin and Surbeck 2019). TRIPS-plus clauses also have a multiplication effect because many FTAs can affect third countries because of the most-favoured-nation clause (Morin and Surbeck 2019).

IPR clauses in regional trade agreements (RTAs) have systematically increased from 2000 onwards. In particular, the RTAs combining developing and developed countries have the 'highest proportion of high or moderate IP content' (Valdés and McCann 2014, pp. 34–6). TRIPS-plus clauses in FTAs are a concern because states may be prevented from using TRIPS flexibilities (Grosse Ruse-Khan 2018, Valdés and McCann 2014). TRIPS-plus clauses result from asymmetrical negotiations as joint positions of net importers in multilateral WIPO and WTO negotiations that reject a reinforced IPR protection are broken by negotiating bilateral or regional FTAs adopting TRIPS-plus clauses. These clauses may transplant detailed national IPR regulations of developed countries, which do not necessarily consider the context of developing member states (Morin and Surbeck 2019, Grosse Ruse-Khan 2018). Some FTAs also seek the accession of non-WTO members to the TRIPS Agreement (Valdés and McCann 2014).

Valdés and McCann (2014) found that 174 of the 245 RTAs they analysed contain diverse types of IPR provisions, such as general statements, TRIPS-plus regulations, cooperation, technical and legal assistance and training, ITT facilitation, or IPR conditionality (e.g. the accession to other IP treaties such as the Convention Establishing the International Union for the Protection of New Plant Varieties or the Budapest Treaty on the International Recognition of the Deposit of Microorganisms for the Purposes of Patent Procedure [The Budapest Patent Treaty of 1980]). Moreover, 58% of all RTAs containing IPR clauses include diverse IPR enforcement procedures, mainly when developed states are parties. The enforcement procedures are varied, from just reiterating TRIPS' enforcement to more detailed civil, administrative, or criminal procedures. After 2009, the RTAs increasingly include border measures in all RTAs concluded exclusively among developed countries and in 62% of RTAs between developed and developing or transition countries (Valdés and McCann 2014). In contrast, exhaustion clauses basically follow the TRIPS regime even if the EU has a regional regulation of exhaustion (Valdés and McCann 2014). Some RTAs include IPR as a form of investment or part of the definition of investment, particularly after 2000, in the Americas or Asia (Valdés and McCann 2014).

TRIPS-plus clauses are controversial because they can obstruct access to medicines, copyrighted educational materials, seeds from the previous seasons, or new green technologies at affordable prices. However, up to now, the concrete effects on these sectors have not been proven as the empirical literature on the economic consequences of IP law are not conclusive (Morin and Surbeck 2019). From a legal and political perspective, the increasing fragmentation of the IPR international regime and the undermining of the national policy space provided under TRIPS represent a challenge (Grosse Ruse-Khan 2018). In Asia, the spaghetti bowl created by the conclusion of multiple FTAs makes for an even more complex IP protection governance as many of these FTAs have reinforced IPR protection. However, as the development level among Asian countries is diverse, the reasons Asian countries accept TRIPS-plus clauses is not necessarily to foster innovation and ITT; at least it is not the only reason to accept them (Antons and Hilty 2015).

FTAs' TRIPS-plus clauses are also relevant for patents on new plant varieties, which is crucial for countries with high biodiversity, such as many South American and ASEAN countries. Many FTAs require member states to adhere to the reinforced patent protection for new plant varieties regulated by the Protection of New Plant Varieties (UPOV) and the Budapest Patent Treaty. The empirical study shows that almost 40% of RTAs with IPR clauses include references to UPOV, particularly when the RTAs are concluded by the US, European, or other developed countries (Valdés and McCann 2014). Although TRIPS does not regulate access to traditional knowledge or genetic resources, since 2010, almost 25% of the RTAs refer to these issues, particularly when developing countries are member states. This is related to the reinforced protection to pharmaceutical and agricultural products included in the US and European FTAs (Valdés and McCann 2014). The CPTPP chapter on IP for the Asia-Pacific region builds on the multilateral treaties, mainly TRIPS, although it also incorporates TRIPS-plus clauses, such as more stringent enforcement rules and the requirement of signing the UPOV (Table 9.2).

9.5 IPR Clauses in FTAs of CAN and ASEAN with the US and the EU

The EU and the US promote new generation FTA TRIPS-plus clauses that have changed the WTO system. This section reviews the IPR clauses of FTAs concluded by the US and the EU with CAN, PA, and ASEAN member states (i.e. FTAs concluded with Colombia, Peru, Singapore, and Viet Nam). The figures of the RTA notifications to the WTO show that ASEAN countries conclude more FTAs with countries in the region whereas South American countries conclude FTAs among them and with the US and the EU. As a

Table 9.2 Selected IP-related Indicators for ASEAN and South American Countries, 2013–2018

	Royalties and Licences Fees Payment (% Import Service) 2013	*IP Payment 2018*	*Royalties and Licence Fees (% Export Service) 2013*	*IP Receipts 2018*	*National Resident Office Patent Application 2013*	*Patent Application by Origin 2018*	*PCT Resident Applications 2013*	*PCT International Applications, by Origin 2018*	*Patent Families Filed in at Least Three Offices 2013*	*Patent Families Filed in at Least Two Countries 2018*
Singapore	1	1	27	17	40	32	19	20	18	18
Argentina	7	7	34	34	60	62			45	69
Thailand	22	19	57	79	58	65	68	60	66	64
Indonesia	24	31	61	78	80	85	90	107	69	113
Colombia	31	41	25	52	87	72	62	49	56	72
Brazil	33	10	29	32	62	52	56	51	42	61
Malaysia	35	50	38	65	50	59	35	57	44	40
Chile	39	11	49	49	66	68	44	39	58	46
Philippines	40	56	96	90	81	84	82	97	65	91
Peru	47	51	76	67	101	99	85	87	63	89
Venezuela	50				108					
Ecuador	62	81			113	92	46	95	69	106
Bolivia	73	32	39	35		104				100
Uruguay	78	70	107	100	86	86			36	59
Cambodia	81	105	88			120				88
Paraguay	110	89	6		82	83			69	81
Viet Nam					70	67	79	88	69	98

Source: www.globalinnovationindex.org/analysis-indicator.

result, WTO TRIPS+ clauses may have a stronger impact in South American, than in ASEAN, countries.

9.5.1 Structure and clauses

FTAs concluded by the US and the EU generally have similar structures and clauses. In the government procurement clauses, the US explicitly preserves the policy space of member states to protect IPR. The EU–Colombia–Peru FTA explicitly stipulates that IPR protection should converge with international rules but be balanced with the public interest. Also, the EU created a specialised body to oversee IP compliance.

Regarding investment, the US model includes IPR as a form of investment that allows the use of investor–state dispute settlement mechanisms. The Viet Nam–EU FTA contains an investment treaty that stipulates the same, but the Colombia–Peru FTA does not refer to IPR as an investment.

The IPR chapters are similar in the US and EU FTAs signed with ASEAN, CAN, and PA member states. The general provisions require or encourage member states to adopt some multilateral IP treaties if they have not ratified them. US FTAs required Andean countries to adhere to the Budapest Patent Treaty (1980) and the Patent Law Treaty (2000). The same is true for EU FTAs that stipulate that Andean countries should make 'all reasonable efforts' to accede to the Patent Law Treaty (2000). According to this treaty, the EU–Viet Nam FTA requires accession to the PCT and the simplification of patent registration procedures.

On the coordination with TRIPS and other WIPO agreements, only the US preferential trade agreement with Peru reaffirms their existing rights and obligations under the TRIPS and WIPO IPR agreements. The EU FTAs, in contrast, define IPR according to the TRIPS Agreement (that covers patents, plant varieties, undisclosed information, and protection against unfair competition, also based on the Paris Convention [10 bis]). EU FTAs also reaffirm the rights and obligations under the TRIPS and WIPO agreements, stipulate that no provision (including IPR enforcement) will contradict or be detrimental to these multilateral agreements, and recognise the freedom of member states to establish their regime for the exhaustion of IPR according to the TRIPS Agreement.

With respect to IPR (patent) holders' rights, the US–Singapore FTA explicitly authorises patent owners to transfer or transmit their rights even through licence contracts. The US FTAs exceptionally authorise the revocation or nullification of a patent following the Paris Convention. However, this convention is not mentioned for Singapore, which authorises exceptions to the patent monopoly according to TRIPS [31]. The three US FTAs authorise exceptions to patent holders' exclusive rights while respecting the legitimate interests of holders and third parties. The EU FTAs also authorise measures to prevent abuse by IPR holders or restrictive practices that restrain trade or affect the ITT.

9.5.2 Sectors related to public health, the right to food and genetic resources

The US FTA with Colombia and Peru authorises measures to protect public health following the Doha Declaration on the TRIPS Agreement and Public Health (2001) or any waiver of a provision of the TRIPS Agreement. The EU FTAs also recognise exceptions and flexibilities permitted by the Doha Declaration and by multilateral IPR agreements. Also, the EU–Colombia–Peru FTA recognises the flexibilities mentioned in the Resolution on the Global Strategy and Plan of Action on Public Health, Innovation, and Intellectual Property (WHA/2008).

However, all US and EU FTAs include specific regulations for the pharmaceutical and agricultural sectors. They all allow claiming compensation for unreasonable delays in the issuance of a patent, including delays in the authorisation for the marketing of the patented products. Holders of patents granted in another country where claiming compensation is possible can also claim it. EU and US FTAs also protect pharmaceutical and agricultural proof data and information related to these chemical components' security and include the bolar clause. The EU–Colombia–Peru FTA added that data protection should follow the TRIPS Agreement [39] and domestic legislation. This FTA excludes Peru from data protection of biological and biotechnology products. It also recognises the policy space of member states to regulate exceptions based on public interest, cases of national emergency, or extreme urgency that would allow third persons to access those data. This agreement also authorises abbreviated marketing approval procedures in their territory, based on another member state's marketing approval. The CPTPP, applicable in Viet Nam and Singapore and in Peru upon its ratification, also foresees a ten-year obligation on data protection for agricultural chemical products and pharmaceutical obligations relating to patent linkages and regulatory review exceptions.

Regarding the exclusive use of genetic resources, the US FTAs with Colombia and Peru protect plant patents following TRIPS clauses but require these countries to implement a patent system by the preferential tariff agreements' entry into force. These FTAs also include an understanding of biodiversity and traditional knowledge. The EU FTAs recognise the Convention on Biodiversity. Still, only the EU–Colombia–Peru explicitly refers to protecting biodiversity and traditional knowledge according to the convention. Therefore, they listed ways to enforce this provision, such as databases or digital libraries that would facilitate patentability examination of inventions related to genetic resources and associated traditional knowledge. None of the EU or US FTAs with ASEAN countries refers to plant protection, although all require adherence to the UPOV. The following countries have used this mechanism: Australia, Canada, Chile, China, 14 EU countries (Belgium, Bulgaria, Czech Republic, Finland, France, Germany, Italy, Hungary, Latvia, The Netherlands, Poland, Slovakia, Spain, the United Kingdom), India, Japan, Mexico, Korea, Russia, and the US. China has the largest number of microorganism deposits, followed by the US and Korea. The EU countries' figures together are inferior to those of the US and almost 50% of China. These figures show the most biodiverse countries do not have a deposit of microorganisms; only a minority of developing countries do. No ASEAN country has used this patent mechanism, and only two PA members have registered microorganisms so far.

Regarding the Budapest Patent Treaty,[21] only Chile has an international depositary authority (Budapest Patent Treaty [7]). All the FTAs concluded by the US and the EU with ASEAN or CAN and the PA require member states to adhere to the Budapest Treaty as a condition to sign or implement these agreements. This clearly benefits home countries of patent applicants and not the countries with genetic resources.

Why ASEAN countries are not active in protecting genetic resources and traditional knowledge remains unclear. Although all ASEAN countries had signed the Convention on Biological Diversity (1992), they do not appear as active in protecting genetic resources and traditional knowledge as South America. However, the CPTPP regulates access to genetic resources, informed consent, and benefit-sharing in various chapters related to IPR, the environment, and development and biodiversity (Rimmer 2018). The CPTPP is the first agreement in the Asia-Pacific that regulates cooperation on traditional knowledge protection by developing the possibility of patenting traditional knowledge on genetic resources. It is possible that ASEAN follows this international trend and adopts a regional patent system with explicit references to IPRs on genetic resources and traditional knowledge.

9.5.3 Civil and administrative measures

Regarding civil and administrative measures, the US FTAs follow the general rules of national systems. Still, they require these rules to be in writing and made public (with the particularities for Singapore). All US FTAs, except for the one concluded with Colombia, authorise border measures. The three US FTAs analysed include criminal sanctions and seizure of products. The EU FTAs emphasise the role of judicial authorities when imposing restrictive measures to protect IPR. The EU–Viet Nam FTA is the only one that mentions civil provisional and precautionary measures. However, both FTAs foresee corrective measures (withdrawal, removal, or destruction, including materials and implements used to manufacture those goods). The EU FTAs also stipulate judicial injunctions in line with the TRIPS Agreement [44.2] to prevent or cease current IPR infringement. These FTAs also authorise alternative measures to compensate monetarily when the person acted unintentionally and without negligence.

All EU and US FTAs analysed define the scope of the damages. Some particularities for ASEAN member states are that the EU–Viet Nam FTA stipulates that when the IPR is infringed on a commercial scale, the judiciary may order the recovery of damages and the precautionary seizure or blocking of the property of the alleged infringer.

9.6 Self-regulatory mechanisms

As in other areas of business law, some corporate social responsibility mechanisms also refer to compliance with IPR regulations, although the subject is not completely developed up to now. The EU–Viet Nam FTA encourages the development of codes of conduct that would promote the transfer of technology and the enforcement of IPR. This contrasts with the UN Special Rapporteur's soft law regulations on everyone's right to enjoy the highest attainable standard of physical and mental health. The UN Special Rapporteur also released the Guidelines for Pharmaceutical Industry (2008) and a special report (2013) to encourage pharmaceutical industries to facilitate access to essential medicines in line with development goals. The Global Strategy and Plan of Action on Public Health, Innovation, and Intellectual Property (WHA/2008) of the World Health Organization, included in the EU–Colombia–Peru FTA, also encourages fair IPR protection, compatible with respect, protection, and fulfilment of the right to access essential medicines, and the right to benefit from R&D results. Along the same line, the UN Global Compact released a practical note on 'Human Rights, Access to Medicines, and the Pharmaceutical Industry (2011)' to promote responsible business in line with the UN goals.

Another ongoing trend is compliance with international standards that protect IPRs as one of the indicators of good governance, which complements other compliance assessments related to anti-corruption and anti-tax evasion and avoidance. This option has been discussed in the framework of establishing public procurement standards or due diligence requirements to assess risks in value chains. Although compliance with IPR protection is indeed a good indicator, it is important to consider the context of the countries involved as stringent IPR protection does not always translate into welfare benefits for developing countries.

9.7 Conclusions

In the literature, no overall consensus exists on how patent regulation is linked to innovation levels and technology transfer. However, most analysts agree that country development levels correlate with levels of innovation and technology transfer. Developed countries systematically promote stronger IPR protection than developing countries. From the empirical evaluation of a series of indicators related to IPR at the country level, generally speaking (i.e. across regions), higher levels of innovation seem to be associated with being more active in negotiating and signing FTAs. This observation is independent of the observation that ASEAN countries score – on average – higher on innovation output (including patents) than South American countries, even if this result cannot be matched easily with differences on the innovation input side (i.e. determinants of innovation). The latter show a mixed picture, with great intra-regional diversity, with Latin America – on average – scoring better on institutional quality and FDI liberalisation policies.

Regarding the role of regional IPR protection, CAN developed a supranational institutional framework bearing similarities with that in the EU. CAN has also pioneered in regionally regulating IPR since the 1970s. However, this has not translated into the member states' clear progress in innovation, technology transfer, and the corresponding upgrade of their GVC participation. The relative institutional homogeneity of CAN member states, which contrasts with ASEAN's diversity, did not foster an effective regional technology transfer or innovation policy. In contrast, PA IPR protection is less institutionalised and corresponds more to a regional model of coordination of policies and implementation of soft law mechanisms to facilitate IPR development and enforcement. Although no concrete results of these soft law measures are visible yet, this is a complementary policy to the free trade orientation of the member states that is considered positive.

The TRIPS-plus clauses of the new generation FTAs are important because they have modified the legal framework of the WTO and the WIPO on IPR protection and enforcement. This chapter focused on patent regulations of the FTAs-plus clauses in the framework of FTAs concluded by the member states of ASEAN, CAN, and the PA with the US and the EU. These include the US–Singapore, US–Colombia, US–Peru, EU–Colombia–Peru (to which Ecuador recently joined), and the EU–Viet Nam FTAs. The main findings coincide with the literature: these FTAs have similar structures without clear regional particularities. In general, they aim at promoting innovation and technology transfer. They also adopt IPR clauses with stronger patent protection and enforcement than the TRIPS and WIPO multilateral legal framework. Another important finding is that regional blocks in general and the EU and the CPTPP seek to strengthen their IPR regime through the FTAs. In contrast, CAN partially dismantled its IPR regime to allow its member states to conclude FTAs with TRIPS-plus clauses with the EU and the US.

In turn, ASEAN and the PA, rather than creating binding regulations on IPR at the regional level, promote cooperation and soft law mechanisms to foster innovation and IPR protection. Although their effectiveness have not been tested empirically, the mechanisms are increasingly used to reach more willingness to respect IPR than binding obligations that create resistance.

Regarding possible policy recommendations, some aspects seem relevant. First, it is not clear whether strong institutional patent protection brings concrete results in terms of innovation and technology transfer, particularly in developing countries. Therefore, governments need to adopt a context-sensitive approach and balance stringent IPR protection and the host country's economic and institutional level. The previous assessment seems clear that stringent IPR policies do not automatically foster innovation and ITT. Governments need to adopt policies that strengthen education, research, and infrastructure as necessary conditions to foster innovation and ITT.

Second, concluding FTAs can be part of an appropriate strategic policy mix for governments. Those that have concluded most FTAs (such as Singapore and Chile) show better economic and institutional results. In contrast, those that reject them (such as Argentina, Brazil, Indonesia, and Venezuela) seem to find themselves in more complicated economic and institutional situations. However, (sub)regional integration groups of developing countries can increase their bargaining power when negotiating FTAs with developed blocs such as the EU or the CPTPP. This way, they can claim to review the current TRIPS-plus clauses adopted by many FTAs that have not been the most convenient for developing countries.

Third, compared to the solid supranational framework adopted by CAN, soft law and coordination mechanisms adopted by either ASEAN or the PA seem to result in more effective innovation and ITT. Regional blocs, such as the EU, have increasingly promoted corporate social responsibility mechanisms that increasingly involve good governance standards to assess compliance with IPR protection rules. These soft law approaches can also positively affect innovation and technology transfer and do not require complex treaty negotiations and legislative approvals.

Fourth, from a regional perspective, ASEAN and Latin America enjoy high levels of biodiversity and traditional knowledge that represent a potential for sustainable development of these regions. These topics are also crucial in patent protection, as biodiversity is becoming a valuable and scarce asset being appropriated by governments and companies that do not have it, and not always in fair terms. CAN and PA member states are leading developing states in protecting traditional knowledge and genetic resources. However, these issues have apparently not been crucial for ASEAN countries so far. Since Singapore and Viet Nam became member states of the CPTPP, this topic will probably be part of the IPR agenda and could influence other countries in the region.

Notes

1 Technology transfer differs from technology spillovers. The latter refer to market externalities by which developers, as third persons (including competitors), may benefit from information beyond the technology owners (Maskus, 2004, quoted by Kowalski et al. 2017, p.9).

2 Patent protection beyond the national borders is based on the Paris Convention and the Patent Cooperation Treaty (PCT). The first agreement requires the patent claimant to file patent applications in each country or region where he or she seeks to protect the invention. The PCT, in contrast, allows patent applicants, who are nationals or residents of a PCT state party, to file an 'international' patent application to protect an invention simultaneously in various states parties.

3 Patent holders may conclude a licence contract with a third party to exploit their IPR rights during a limited term and territory. As licensing is a sensitive topic for host countries, many countries regulate it in detail. Sometimes they require a registration of licence contracts to oversee the convergence between international technology transfer (ITT) and national policy objectives and between foreign exchange regulations and royalties (Kowalski et al. 2017).

4 Innovation and ITT also relate to imitation in developing countries. The relevance of IPR protection only increases when countries develop local R&D. Patent registration does not necessarily reflect local R&D because it depends on

legislation, commercial and societal practices, enforcement, and entrepreneurship. For instance, in Colombia, since 1980 non-residents highly participate in patent applications compared to the level of applications of resident patent applications. In addition, patent claims are concentrated in few sectors and few patent holders (Campi et al. 2018).

5 The WIPO (2010) included additional variables, such as the ownership of the technology, the life-cycle stage of technology, the availability of alternative technologies, their costs, and the type of actors involved (Kowalski et al. 2017).

6 Measurement of the economic climate are based on indicators such as the World Bank's Doing Business rankings, the World Economic Forum Competitiveness Index country rankings, or indicators from private organisations such as the Heritage Foundation's Economic Freedom, and are possibly influenced by developed country investment strategies.

7 In general, WTO+ and WTOx provisions are becoming common features of FTAs. The former clauses deepen existing multilateral commitments in areas such as liberalisation of trade in services, anti-dumping, or government subsidies. The latter clauses include regulatory domains that go beyond the current scope and mandate of the WTO such as human rights, labour or environmental clauses (Horn et al. 2010). TRIPS+ clauses have a similar scope as they enlarge TRIPS protection.

8 WIPO Statistics Database, November 2018.

9 Southern Common Market. Its official members are Argentina, Brazil, Paraguay, and Uruguay.

10 CAN member-states had rules on industrial property since the 19th century. For example, Colombian Law 35/1869 or Law 31/1925 regulated invention patents and their enforcement.

11 The North American Free Trade Agreement (1994) represents a milestone because next to the usual provisions of FTAs (on tariffs, rules of origin, exclusions), it included regulatory issues such as IPR protection.

12 Other decisions on the same topic were Decisions 84-85/1974 and 344/93.

13 Regarding patents and traditional knowledge, Decision 182/1983 created the Andean System 'José Celestino Mutis' on Agriculture, Food Security, and Environmental Conservation. Decision 445/1993 established the Common Regime for the Protection of the Rights of Breeders of Plant Varieties and Decision 391/1996 established the Common Regime on Access to Genetic Resources and Related Contracts that Must Include the Fair and Equitable Distribution of Benefits. Decision 486/2000 (26) stipulates the procedure for patent applications on traditional knowledge and/or genetic resources.

14 The International Classification of Patents is open to member-states of the Paris Convention for the Protection of Industrial Property (1883). Only 62 states have adopted this agreement so far, but it is being used by many national and regional patent offices and by the WIPO Secretariat in administering the Patent Cooperation Treaty (1970). See https://www.wipo.int/treaties/en/classification/strasbourg/.

15 This decision extended the deadline to vindicate the right to priority, requested additional specifications in the description of the invention, allowed compensation to patent holders for unreasonable delays in the patent registration, except for pharmaceutical products, allowed the application of the bolar clause (the use of protected materials by a patent to generate the needed information to support the application to commercialise a product), and authorised a multiclass register of trademarks and border measures for trademarks of products in transit.

16 In 2013, the ATJ upheld Decision 689, as it became a 'Decision 486+' scheme that reflects the minimum criteria that member-states can complement (ref 01-AN-2010).

17 National tribunals frequently use preliminary rulings, and the decisions of the ATJ are part of the legal system. Case law of the ATJ is relevant in IPR national regimes (Helfer and Alter 2014, pp. 247–8).
18 Seehttp://www.gob.mx/cms/uploads/attachment/file/100549/13_-_2015-10-08_AP.pdf
19 PPH is a work-sharing mechanism without harmonising national legal systems on patent claims. Worldwide, countries may choose among diverse models: bilateral agreements among patent offices (the traditional PPH model); the PCT – PPH model or the Mottainai model. The latter was adopted by PA because it is considered the most advanced and expeditious (Callo and Pérez Restrepo 2016, pp. 14–6). See http://www.sic.gov.co/procedimiento-acelerador-de-patentes-regionales.
20 Endeshaw (2016) further analyses IPR in Asia in the post-TRIPS period from a law and politics perspective.
21 Cf. status on 23 July 2018.

Bibliography

Alter, K.J. and L.R. Helfer (2017), *The Law and Politics of the Andean Tribunal of Justice*. New York: Oxford University Press.

Antons, C. and R.M. Hilty (2015), 'Introduction: IP and the Asia-Pacific "Spaghetti Bowl" of Free Trade Agreements', in C. Antons and R. M. Hilty (eds.). *Intellectual Property and Free Trade Agreements in the Asia-Pacific Region*. Berlin, Heidelberg: Springer, pp. 1–23.

Arredondo-Trapero, F., J.C. Vázquez-Parra and J. de la Garza (2016), 'Factores de Innovación para la Competitividad en la Alianza del Pacífico. Una Aproximación desde el Foro Económico Mundial', *Estudios Gerenciales*, 32(141), pp. 299–308.

Asheim, B.T. and M.S. Gertler (2005), 'The Geography of Innovation: Regional Innovation Systems', in J. Fagerberg and D.C. Mowery (eds.), *The Oxford Handbook of Innovation*. Oxford: Oxford University Press, pp. 291–317.

Blyde, J.S. and C. Acea (2002), *The Effects of Intellectual Property Rights on Trade and FDI in Latin America*. Washington: Inter-American Development Bank.

Callo, M. and C. Pérez Restrepo (2016), 'Patent Cooperation Mechanisms in the Pacific Alliance: An Initial Assessment of the Effectiveness of the Patent Prosecution Highway for Intra-regional Trade Integration', *World Trade Institute Working Paper* No. 16/2016, https://www.wti.org/media/filer_public/18/ca/18cab13c-a98f-44f1-8361-23c249d12e59/working_paper_no_16_2016_vasquez_and_perez.pdf (accessed 15 February 2021).

Campi, M., M. Dueñas, and J. Zuluaga (2018), *Evolución del Patentamiento en Colombia en un Contexto de Reformas*. https://ssrn.com/abstract=3160242 (accessed 15 February 2021).

Chaves García, C.A. (2018), 'Aproximación Teórica y Conceptual para el Análisis de la Alianza del Pacífico', *Desafíos*, 30(1), pp. 21–45.

Corredor, R. (2019), 'The Pacific Alliance: Adding Value to the Global Intellectual Property Rights Regime?', in P. Sauvé, R. Polanco Lazo, and J. Álvarez Zárate (eds.), *The Pacific Alliance in a World of Preferential Trade Agreements. United Nations University Series on Regionalism*, vol 16. New York: Springer, pp. 203–214.

Degelsegger, A., S.O. Remoe and R. Trianes (2016), *ASEAN Economic Community and Intellectual Property Rights: An Assessment of Framework Condition for Innovation*. Vienna/Bonn: SEA-EU-NET.

Dhar, B. and R.K. Joseph (2016), 'Foreign Direct Investment, Intellectual Property Rights, and Technology Transfer', in *Economic Challenges for the Contemporary World: Essays in Honour of Prabhat Patnaik*, New Delhi: Sage.

Endeshaw, A. (2016), *Intellectual Property in Asian Emerging Economies: Law and Policy in the Post-TRIPS Era*. London: Routledge.

Falvey, R.E., N. Foster and O. Memedovic (2006), *The Role of Intellectual Property Rights in Technology Transfer and Economic Growth: Theory and Evidence*. Vienna: UNIDO.

Gardini, G.L. (2013), 'The Added Value of the Pacific Alliance and "Modular Regionalism" in Latin America', *International Affairs at LSE*, 25 June.

Gehl Sampath, P. and P. Roffe (2012), 'Unpacking the International Technology Transfer Debate: Fifty Years and Beyond', *Issue Paper* 36, Geneva: ICTSD. https://www.files.ethz.ch/isn/152815/unpacking-the-international-technology-transfer-debate-fifty-years-and-beyond.pdf (accessed 15 February 2021).

Grosse Ruse-Khan, H. (2018), 'From TRIPS to FTAs and Back: Re-conceptualising the Role', in *Netherlands Yearbook of International Law 2017: Shifting Forms and Levels of Cooperation in International Economic Law: Structural Developments in Trade, Investment and Financial Regulation*, The Hague: TMC Asser Press, pp. 57–107.

Helfer, L.R. and K.J. Alter (2014), 'The Influence of the Andean Intellectual Property Regime on Access to Medicines in Latin America', in R. Dreyfuss and C. Rodriguez-Garavito (eds.), *Balancing Wealth and Health: The Battle over Intellectual Property and Access to Medicines in Latin America*. Oxford Scholarship Online, pp. 247–262.

Herreros, S. (2016), 'The Pacific Alliance: A Bridge between Latin America and the Asia Pacific?' in S.B. Das and M. Kawai (eds.), *Trade Regionalism in the Asia-Pacific: Developments and Future Challenges*. Singapore: ISEAS–Yusof Ishak Institute, pp. 273–294.

Hofmann, C., A. Osnago and M. Ruta (2017), *Horizontal Depth: A New Database on the Content of Preferential Trade Agreements*. Washington, DC: The World Bank.

Horn, H., P.C. Mavroidis, and A. Sapir (2010), 'Beyond the WTO? An Anatomy of EU and US Preferential Trade Agreements', *The World Economy*, 33(11), pp. 1565–1588.

Hudson, J. and A. Minea (2013), 'Innovation, Intellectual Property Rights, and Economic Development: A Unified Empirical Investigation', *World Development*, 46, pp. 66–78.

Kalinova, B., A. Palerm, and S. Thomsen (2010), 'OECD's FDI Restrictiveness Index: 2010 Update', in *OECD Working Papers on International Investment* No. 2010/03, Paris: OECD Publishing, https://doi.org/10.1787/5km91p02zj7g-en.

Kowalski, P. and D. Rabaioli, and S. Vallejo (2017), 'International Technology Transfer Measures in an Interconnected World', *OECD Trade Policy Papers* No. 206, Paris: OECD Publishing. http://dx.doi.org/10.1787/ada51ec0-en.

Lizarazo-Rodríguez, L. and P. De Lombaerde (2015), 'Regional and Inter-regional Economic Rules and the Enforcement of the Right to Health: The Case of Colombia', *Global Social Policy*, 15(3), pp. 296–312.

Lizarazo-Rodriguez, L., L. Chen and P. De Lombaerde (2015), 'Health-Related IPR Provisions in FTAs in the Atlantic Community', in J. Roy (ed.), *A New Atlantic Community: The European Union, the US, and Latin America*. Miami: Miami–Florida European Union Center, University of Miami, pp. 145–157.

Mamani, W. (2013), 'Los Cambios de Política en Materia de Propiedad Intelectual en la CAN: De un "Régimen Común" a un "Régimen sui Géneris"'. Sede Ecuador: Universidad Andina Simón Bolívar, Corporación Editora Nacional.

Maskus, K.E. (2004), 'Encouraging International Technology Transfer', *UNCTAD-ICTSD Project on IPRs and Sustainable Development, Issue Paper* No. 7, Geneva: UNCTAD-ICTSD.

Maskus, K.E. (2015), 'Intellectual Property in a Globalizing World: Issues for Economic Research', *Asia-Pacific Journal of Accounting & Economics*, 22(3), pp. 231–250.

Morin, J.F. and J. Surbeck (2019), 'Mapping the New Frontier of International IP Law: Introducing a TRIPS-plus Dataset', *World Trade Review*, 19(1), pp. 109–122.

Ng, S-K.E. (2013), 'ASEAN IP Harmonization: Striking the Delicate Balance', *Pace International Law Review*, 25, p. 129.

Nguyen, C.H. (1999), 'A Unitary ASEAN Patent Law in the Aftermath of TRIPS', *Pacific Rim Law & Policy Journal*, 8, p. 453.

Peng, S.Y., H.W. Liu and C.F. Lin (eds.) (2018), 'Introduction', in S.Y. Peng, H.W. Liu and C.F. Lin (eds.), *Governing Science and Technology Under the International Economi `c Order: Regulatory Divergence and Convergence in the Age of Megaregionals*. Cheltenham: Edward Elgar Publishing, pp. 3–12.

PRA (2018), 'Executive Summary', *2018 International Property Rights Index*. Washington, DC: Property Rights Alliance.

Rimmer, M. (2018), 'The Trans-Pacific Partnership and Sustainable Development: Access to Genetic Resources, Informed Consent, and Benefit Sharing', in K. Adhikari and C. Lawson (eds.), *Biodiversity, Genetic Resources, and Intellectual Property*. Routledge, pp.169–202.

Sweet, C.M. and D.S.E. Maggio (2015), 'Do Stronger Intellectual Property Rights Increase Innovation?', *World Development*, 66, pp. 665–677.

Valdés, R. and M. McCann (2014), 'Intellectual Property Provisions in Regional Trade Agreements: Revision and Update', *WTO Staff Working Paper* No. ERSD-2014-14.

Watson, F., N. Johnstone and I. Haščič (2009), 'Using Patent Data as an Indicator of International Technology Transfer', *World Bank Research Observer*, 17, pp. 191–235, https://www.oecd.org/env/consumption-innovation/44384969.pdf (accessed 18 February 2021).

Yang, L. and K.E. Maskus (2009), 'Intellectual Property Rights, Technology Transfer and Exports in Developing Countries', *Journal of Development Economics*, 90(2), pp. 231–236.

Yu, P.K. (2018), 'TPP, RCEP, and the Crossvergence of Asian Intellectual Property Standards', in S-Y. Peng, H-W. Liu, and C-F. Lin (eds.), *Governing Science and Technology under the International Economic Order: Regulatory Divergence and Convergence in the Age of Megaregionals*. Cheltenham, UK: Edward Elgar Publishing, pp. 277–297.

Index

Note: Page numbers in **bold** indicate tables, page numbers in *italic* indicate figures and page numbers followed by n indicate notes.